The Sci-Fi Siren

Who Dared Love Elvis

and Other Stars*

John L. Flynn, Ph.D.

This special, fully-illustrated edition is limited to 1,000 copies worldwide.

Galactic Books
Greenacres, Florida

Galactic Books
4300 South Jog Road, #540861
Greenacres, Florida 33454

The Sci-Fi Siren Who Dared Love Elvis
and Other Stars

PRINTING HISTORY
First Edition / August 2020

Acknowledgments: Most photographs used in this book were given to me by Angelique Pettyjohn who, in turn, acquired them from studio publicists anxious to promote her work in television and movies. Prior to her death in 1992, she made me promise to use them to illustrate her story. I make no claim to ownership or copyright. They are used to showcase her work in Hollywood. Other photos are owned by individual rights holders, and are reproduced in this academic study as part of the fair use doctrine. While the words "star" and "trek" are trademarked by CBS, historical record shows Ms. Pettyjohn worked on *Star Trek* in 1967. Mr. Hooper's cover photo was shot at his Las Vegas studio in 1980, long after Angelique had worked on *Star Trek*. She made her own costume and props for the shoot, and also wore them to promote the TV series in the 1980s, without any renumeration from CBS. I purchased the rights from Mr. Hooper to use the photograph on my cover.

Editor: Jeanie Loiacono Cover Photo: Robert Scott Hooper
Book Design & Layout: John L. Flynn

Library of Congress Cataloging in Publication Data
Flynn, John L. Sci-Fi Siren

1. Angelique Pettyjohn. I. Performing Arts. II. Biography.
III. Television Series, Motion Pictures History.

ISBN: 978-164871021-6

PRINTED IN THE UNITED STATES OF AMERICA

10 9 8 7 6 5

Table of Contents

Dedication Page

To my friend, Angelique Pettyjohn,
With Love. Always.

Siren

si·ren
/ˈsīrən/

noun

1. In Greek mythology, the sirens lured unwary sailors with their enchanting music and singing voices onto the destructive rocks protecting their fantastical island.

2. A seductively beautiful woman, especially one who beguiles men to act against their better nature.

3. In Science Fiction, a female denizen of a faraway planet who seduces the captain or a member of the crew with her beauty and charms to risk danger and/or some deadly situation.

Foreword

Angelique Pettyjohn was an amazing woman. Groomed by Hollywood's old studio system to be the next Marilyn Monroe, she defied all the odds to become the iconic "Girl in the Silver Bikini." During her lifetime, she was adored by millions of fans worldwide, and since her death in 1992, that number has continued to increase every year.

I am both thrilled and honored to write the foreword for this wonderful new book that has taken author John L. Flynn twenty-eight years to research and write. He was by Angelique Pettyjohn's side for the last ten years of her life, and loved her as the one true friend she had in the world.

Today, critics and historians regard her as one of the last, great Hollywood icons of the Golden Age of Television and Silver Screen. She was an actress, comedian, and entertainer. Also, as a performer in the old Las Vegas, she headlined many marquees as a showgirl and exotic dancer. Although I never got to know her the way my friend John did, Angelique Pettyjohn was very important to me as well. She was my birth mother…

I am the son of the late Elvis Presley, born out-of-wedlock, unbeknownst to Elvis, on December 24, 1961, in Gary, Indiana, the result of a liaison between Elvis Presley and Dorothy Lee

Perrins (aka Angelique Pettyjohn), a young actress and dancer who went on to become a cultural icon in her own right. At the time, Angelique worked as a showgirl in Las Vegas and caught the eye of my father. Elvis was at the height of his fame and was known worldwide as the King of Rock-n-Roll. Women loved him and men wanted to be just like him. Elvis' manager, Colonel Tom Parker, feared that a marriage to Angelique, as well as his impending fatherhood, would seriously damage the King's reputation thereby destroying his wealth and fame. Great pressure was exerted upon the young actress to have an abortion. While Angelique refused to abort the baby because she believed so solemnly in the sanctity of human life, she did agree to deliver the baby in secret in order to spare Elvis the shame and negative publicity of a Hollywood scandal. She also agreed to allow the baby to be adopted immediately following the birth. Colonel Parker, an orphan adopted by a circus couple, drew upon his own experience, and arranged to have a young, Yugoslavian couple, known as "The Vargas" performers, who were traveling with the Ringling Brothers Circus throughout North America, adopt the child. Arrangements were made, and immediately following the birth, when Pettyjohn gave up her son, her words to the couple were, "Take special care of this boy. He belongs to Elvis."

I grew up with the name "Philip Stanic" under the dazzling lights of the circus, completely unaware of the tremendous sacrifice my birth mother Angelique had made and ignorant of the knowledge Elvis Presley was my father. When I reached the age of five years-old, I stepped into the spotlight as a circus clown. Then later, I shared that spotlight with exotic cats I trained as the youngest wild animal trainer in the world (at age fifteen). My lovely cats were featured in many commercials, including those for Kit Kat chocolate bars and Cougar Lincoln Mercury, and also played in several movies, including *Sahara* featuring Brooke Shields and the remake of *Cat People* with Natasha Kinski.

At sixteen, I discovered I could sing, and I began performing in clubs and showcases at night, while I continued to work with my cats during the day. When I reached my 21st birthday, my parents confessed to me I was adopted. They said my real father was Elvis Presley and my biological mother was Angelique Pettyjohn. After much inner struggle, I realized I wanted my true identity acknowledged. I applied for and was granted the legal right to be known as Elvis Aaron Presley, Jr. Regrettably, I never got to know my birth parents. Elvis Presley died in 1977, and Angelique Pettyjohn died in 1992.

Several years ago, my manager told me he had received a letter from a man who was writing a biography about my birth mother. Apparently, John Flynn, a psychologist and former college teacher, was a friend and confidant of Angelique Pettyjohn for the last ten years of her life. They had met at a *Star Trek* convention in 1982 where Pettyjohn was greeting fans and signing autographs, and instantly developed a relationship that blossomed into true friendship. I wanted to speak with him, and after a beautiful two-hour phone call, I felt I had met someone who could have easily been my brother. He talked lovingly about their relationship, and told me how much my mother regretted her decision to give me up for adoption. "It was the only choice that Angelique Pettyjohn could have made," he said, "but it weighed heavily on her right up until her death."

Flynn's words rang true. In 1999, I spoke with John Harris, a renowned Hollywood producer and talent agent who had represented Angelique Pettyjohn (among others), and he had said the same thing. "During many conversations I had with Angelique," Harris wrote me in a notarized letter, "she told me about her son who was the son of Elvis Presley. And, she wanted to meet you but was terrified of Colonel Parker for some reason." I only wish I had known that when she was still alive.

Earlier this year, when John told me that he had submitted the manuscript to his agent for publication, I asked if I could write the foreword. He was genuinely moved by my offer, and worked with me to make it happen.

There have been countless books written about actors and actresses who were a part of old Hollywood and old Vegas; many, perhaps too many, by those seeking to profit from their experiences. But until now, I would wager that not one has been written as personal, or as moving, or as powerful as the one John has written about my mother, Angelique Pettyjohn. He truly loved her, and his powerful words give real insight into the life of an amazing yet troubled woman who sacrificed all for her art.

My thanks to John for breathing real life into the woman who gave me birth, then gave me up so that I would live such a truly extraordinary life.

— Elvis Aaron Presley, Jr.
August 4, 2019

Figure 1. Elvis Aaron Presley Junior.

Prologue

District Court, January 21, 1986

At 8:55 on that particular Tuesday morning, I scrambled down the third-floor corridor of the United States Federal Court Building, which was home for the Eighth Judicial District Court in Las Vegas, and stopped outside Courtroom #3 fleetingly to adjust my tie and to button the top button of my three-piece, gray flannel suit in the reflection of the door's glass window.

She had called me twice already at my hotel room to remind me where to meet her. The third call I'd taken in the lobby of the Hilton; the anxiety in her voice told me that she was moments away from breaking down into a full-blown panic attack. I recognized the symptoms from all the times I'd picked up the phone to listen to her crying or drunk on the other end. I raced down the linoleum floor in my penny-loafers to lend my support. It really didn't matter what this was all about. I had given her my word that I would always be there for her. Just a phone call away. And while I had celebrated many of her greatest successes with her and her fans, I was really the only person in her life who knew just how fragile her world was, and just how easily it could be ripped away from her by cheating husbands, unscrupulous agents, predatory casting directors, over-sexed managers, back-stabbing costars, drug-addicted pushers, and a Janus-faced paparazzi that had made her career with one glamorous photo of her in the iconic silver bikini, and then torn it asunder with yet another of her, drunk, puking her guts out.

By age forty-three, she had already lived such a full life. She had experienced great triumphs, and endured so much personal tragedy I just did not think she could manage one more disappointment. I cared for her deeply, not as a lover or a spouse or a shrink, but as the one true friend in her life.

Rounding the final corner, I felt relieved to see her still in one piece. She was standing there, waiting for me, outside Courtroom #2, her hands trembling at her side, ready to fall apart. At that moment I was also grateful few people recognized her or would have known who she was, dressed elegantly in a black Marc Jacobs business suit, a charcoal trench coat, a bright yellow Hermes scarf, a large-brimmed hat, and Ray-Ban sunglasses. Just like the ones popularized by Audrey Hepburn in *Breakfast at Tiffany's*, she had chosen to hide her identity from the public by disguising her familiar features beneath a floppy hat and sunglasses. A celebrity, best known as "the Girl in the Silver Bikini," she had made a real effort to hide the fact her heart was about to explode out of her chest, like one of those creatures in *Alien.* But then I could always tell when she was acting and when she was being real.

As she tucked a stray strand of her gorgeous blonde hair behind her right ear, in an attempt to mask her deepening anxiety, I realized that while she may have wanted to pose as one of the nameless, unwashed masses of people who passed daily through the building, she was still the delicate flower whose grace and easy composure belied a person of manner and breeding. No one would have mistaken her for an attorney or someone with business before the court. She was a woman unlike any other woman. To me, she was more than just a Hollywood star; she was a cultural icon who had come to represent a time that had long since passed away.

"Oh, John, thank you for coming," she said, with a husky, deep sigh of relief. "I don't know what I would have done without you."

She then smiled at me with those bright, beautiful green eyes of hers and took my right hand in hers. She was still trembling, as we briefly scanned through the docket, but I could sense a real effort on her part to keep it altogether. We then entered the courtroom through the rear door, and looked around for a couple of seats. I hadn't been in Courtroom #2 since workers had completed the renovations to the south end of the building earlier in the year, but the room didn't look all that different from my recollection of the place.

At the back, where we stood, the gallery was one-quarter filled, mostly with the usual reporters, curious spectators, attorneys, their clients, and other interested parties. They all sat on pew-style benches made out of a dark mahogany wood that looked like it belonged in the old Episcopal church downtown rather than in a modern courtroom. With all of the advances in modern technology and ergonomic furniture design of the eighties, I was quite surprised the District Court was still using benches made over a century-and-a-half ago. At the very least, I thought officials could have provided bench cushions to ease the discomfort of those solid, wooden pews on my lower backside. I'll be the first to admit I am a sensualist. I do like my creature comforts. But for her, I was willing to do most anything, even sitting on petrified wood for several hours of courtroom testimony if necessary.

Soon after she had completed her scan of the gallery, she pointed to two seats in the next to the last row, and we sat down, still holding hands, next to all the other visitors of the court. Her palm was moist against mine. I could tell she was still very anxious as her hand never stopped shaking. Not once. I wanted to ask her what was wrong, but she made me promise not to ask her any questions. She had her own reasons for being there, and I was confident she would eventually tell me what they were. Over the ten years we had known each other, we had spent long hours on the phone and together in person, talking about every aspect of her life. I probably knew more about her life than her four husbands, lovers, two stepsisters who called her family, her agent, her shrink, and all the men and women whose lives had intersected hers. I was her friend. She trusted me like no one else in her life. That was a huge honor and a great responsibility. I was not about to let her down by demanding answers now while we sat solemnly in court. The only thing I knew was that we were there for a pending case on the docket, involving a man named Phillip Stanic, a name not familiar to me and, to the best of my recollection, had never come up once in the thousands of conversations we had had over the years.

Shortly after nine, an official entered the courtroom through the front door. I followed him with my eyes, noting he must be the bailiff or someone acting in an official role for the court. He crossed in front of the judge's bench and the witness stand, then stood next to the desks where the court clerk and court reporter sat.

Some spectators, knowing the routine, started to climb to their feet before he said loudly and formally, "All rise."

The rest of us gathered in the courtroom slowly got to our feet as District Court Judge Carl J. Christensen, dressed in a plain, black robe, entered through the front door, and sat down behind the desk. He waited patiently for the bailiff to say a few additional words, then looked at us from the bench. "Good morning, everyone. Please be seated," he said, all business. He waited until everyone was seated, then added, "We have a full docket today, and I'd like to press right through those cases as quickly as we can, unless there are any objections. We'll start with the petition of Phillip Stanic for a name change."

I had just sat down and eased back in my seat with the intention of taking a short cat-nap between cases when suddenly I heard Stanic's name called by the bailiff. I sat bolt upright, fully alert. She glanced my way and reminded me, by gently squeezing my hand, he was the reason why we were there. I nodded, then leaned slightly forward as Phillip Stanic and his attorney approached the bench. Stanic was a young Caucasian man, roughly twenty-five years-old, strong, muscular with a medium-sized build. His hair was long and black, and his sun-tanned features looked strangely familiar even though I could not place him. This wasn't unusual. She was always introducing me to people in the entertainment industry. He may well have been a stunt man or animal wrangler who had worked on a recent show with her. Again, Stanic looked familiar, but I didn't really know who he was nor why it was so important to her to be there. So, with my own curiosity heightened, I leaned forward and listened.

"I have reviewed the documents you have submitted," Christensen said, his booming voice filled the courtroom. "Federal investigators of the government of the United States of America have also conducted a thorough investigation, including an examination of lie detector tests, blood tests, and other evidence. After sufficient documents, sworn testimonies, and additional evidence provided by independent third parties were presented to this judge and after proof having been made to the satisfaction of the Court, that notice of hearing thereon was given in the manner and form required by law and no objections having been filed by any person, Phillip Stanic, it is the decision of this court that you will be henceforth known as and recognized as Elvis Aaron Presley, Jr." The judge punctuated his last statement, by striking his gavel against the surface of the sound block. With one strike, it was made official: Phillip Stanic was Elvis Aaron Presley, Jr.

Elvis Aaron Presley, Jr., I repeated the name to myself several times, then looked again at Phillip Stanic. I studied his face for a long moment, then nodded my head in recognition. The reason why Stanic's features had looked so strangely familiar to me was that he resembled a younger version of Elvis Presley, the King. *The* Elvis Presley I had grown up listening to.

I was just about to turn to my right, when I noticed she was no longer at my side. In those precious few seconds, she had gotten up from her seat and exited the courtroom. By the time I had managed to get out of Courtroom #2, she was already down the hall, her body flattened against one of the elevator doors, the index finger of her left hand pushing the down button repeatedly. She looked like she was going to explode right then and there.

Slowly, with no desire to upset her further, I approached, and stood at her side. Looking deeply into her green eyes, I placed my left hand gently over hers and placed my finger over her finger. She stopped pressing the down button.

"Are you okay?" I asked, concerned the anxiety that had built up in her heart would explode out of her chest into a full-blown panic attack.

She had stopped moving, faced me square-on, and whispered, "I don't want him to see me like this."

"Well, who is he?" I pushed her for an answer.

"He was ... my son…" she replied, breathlessly, weeping to herself.

I didn't fully understand her reply, but I felt the answer was sufficient for right then. I reached for my friend, gathering her up in my arms. She melted into them, burying her tear-stained face in my chest.

When the elevator door finally opened, I held onto her, pulling her literally up by the belt in her trench coat, and escorted her to the first floor of the Federal Court Building. She was moving under her own power by the time we stepped off the curb and had walked a few steps onto the parking lot.

Suddenly she stopped and turned to me. "John, I've got to go, and try to sort this all out."

"Call me, later?"

She nodded, then reached up and kissed me gently on the cheek. By the time I had the chance to touch my cheek, the elegant blonde in the wide-brimmed hat and sunglasses was gone. She had totally disappeared from sight. I suppose I could have gone after her, but there was really nothing I could do for her as long as she didn't want to be found. An alcoholic and a sex addict, she had her own method of self-medicating. Sure, I could have searched for her in every bar serving hard liquor or in every flop house in the city renting rooms by the hour, but I decided to go back to the Hilton and wait for her call.

That night, like a thousand nights before it, she called me at 10:30. I could tell she had been drinking because of the way she slurred her words, but I had already made up my mind not to say anything about her alcohol abuse. I just let her talk, while I listened patiently to yet another one of her heart-breaking stories. Perhaps, the most heart-breaking story I had ever heard!

She cried for hours that night on the phone. I just tried to comfort her in the only way that I knew how. By listening. During the last ten years of her life, as her friend and confidant, I spent thousands of nights just listening to her talk about her life and career. I knew her story better than most. Her story was not only a tale of personal and professional triumph and tragedy but also a reflection of the way Hollywood and Las Vegas used to be before the post-modern era.

Showgirl. Stripper. Scream Queen. *Star Trek* Siren. Actress. Dancer. Model. Porn Star. *Femme Fatales*. Comedian. *Playboy Pin-up*. Wife. Mother. Friend. During her thirty-year career on stage and screen, the late Angelique Pettyjohn was versatile enough to have played each of these roles at least once in pursuit of an ideal of perfection that always remained elusive to her. As one of the last great starlets, she was primped and pampered to be the next Marilyn Monroe in order to sell the fantasy of glamour and glitz, beauty and sex, fame and fortune that millions of people around the globe believed still existed in California's dream factories. As "the Girl in the Silver Bikini," she became a cultural icon who epitomized the "era" of old Hollywood and old Vegas that had long since passed into legend and obscurity. While she readily embraced the image that was propagated by the great publicity departments of the crumbling studio system, Pettyjohn also sought simply to act in front of an audience. More than anything else, she wanted to be known as an entertainer, like the great entertainers that she had loved while growing up in the late forties and early fifties. Jack Benny, Bing Crosby, Danny Kay, Fred Astaire, Bob Hope, Frank Sinatra, and even Elvis Presley had all left an indelible impression upon her. In fact, when she first started out in show business, she patterned herself after the daffy character Gracie Allen had played opposite George Burns.

Figure 2. Angelique Pettyjohn at age 43 in 1986.

Highly intelligent in real life, Pettyjohn embodied the vaudeville archetype of the beautiful blonde woman who was forever misunderstanding what was said to her. If a word had multiple meanings, she'd choose the wrong one every time. She became so good at playing the "dumb blonde" persona that most casting agents did not know it was all an act. They'd just take one good look at her perfect 38C bust measurements, her long dancer's legs, her beautiful blonde hair, and face, and cast her as the voluptuous blonde bimbo nearly every time. Angelique worked very hard to shake that stereotype, and even though it dogged her for most of her career, she also produced some truly outstanding work as well. She took direction from great directors like Otto Preminger, John Derek, and Gene Kelly as well as infamous filmmakers like Doris Wishman, Paul Rapp, and Fred Olen Ray who were probing the boundaries of decency and exploitation with their independent movies. She acted alongside some of the finest actors of her day — Jack Lemmon, Walter Matthau, James Colburn, Dean Martin, Liza Minnelli, Glenn Ford, Art Carney, Barbara Hershey, among others — in order to learn and improve her craft as an actress. And even when facing demons (often of her own making, like alcoholism, drug abuse, and sex addiction) she was determined to overcome them and succeed at all costs. Of course, it helped that Angelique's model good looks, high energy, and splashy personality opened a lot of doors for her in Hollywood and Vegas that might have ordinarily remained shut.

I met Angelique Pettyjohn in 1982 at one of the *Star Trek* conventions she attended as a guest, while I was studying to become a psychologist and working very hard to establish myself as a professional writer. We became very close friends, and during the final decade of her life, we spoke nearly every day on the phone when she was not working or otherwise engaged in some project. We commiserated with each other over births and deaths, divorces, graduations, christenings, engagements and weddings, and other events that held special importance in our lives. She clung to me like a real lifeline, heaping more and more responsibility for her happiness on my shoulders the closer we got to each other. I cared for her deeply, and the love that developed between the two of us was more profound than anything I had experienced in my life before and since that time.

During our last conversation, Angelique told me she wanted her story told by someone who would not sensationalize it, but tell it accurately, warts and all. I promised her that one day I would. She died shortly after that final call. The book you hold in your hands is the result of our undying friendship, which lasts beyond the grave, and twenty-eight years of intensive research and interviews with people who knew her well so that I could tell her story accurately, and with love. The italicized text throughout the book and the quotations from Angelique Pettyjohn represent her actual words. She and I spoke often, and I am happy at long last to share the incredible story of her life and loves with those of you. May her indomitable spirit reach out and touch your lives just as she has touched mine.

— John L. Flynn, Ph.D.
September 21, 2019

Figure 3: Angelique Pettyjohn & John Flynn in 1984.

1
Humble Beginnings

I have to warn you, I'm a very crazy lady.
But I'm honest.

On March 11, 1943, Angelique Pettyjohn was born Dorothy Lee Perrins in a small, middle-class suburb of Los Angeles, California, not far from the tinsel and glitter of the Hollywood dream factories that turned fantasies into reality. Those of us who befriended the beautiful, vivacious, and talented "Girl in the Silver Bikini" in later years never once doubted Angelique was born to be a star. But it may have been very hard for her neighbors, schoolteachers, and local shopkeepers to imagine how a little, buck-toothed girl, who would dance and sing and tell everyone she was going to be a movie star someday could possibly have made her dream a reality, having been born to dirt-poor, working-class parents who labored in obscurity in the San Fernando Valley.

Angelique Pettyjohn had actually lived the kind of rags-to-riches story Hollywood legends were often made from. If it hadn't been such a familiar tale, one could just imagine how some big-time studio mogul, or some clever, young studio publicist might very well have dictated it that way for her. Smart, sexy, and stunningly beautiful, she was the classic small-town girl with the big Hollywood dream. Dorothy Lee Perrins was determined to become a star, and as Angelique Pettyjohn, she had the energy, drive, and unyielding ambition to make it happen.

The “girl” may have appeared to simply burst out on the scene in the mid-sixties, wearing her iconic “silver bikini,” but her life growing up was far less spectacular.

Figure 4. Dorothy Lee Perrins, the "girl next door."

The Young and Enke Families

Born under the twelfth sign of the zodiac, Pisces, Dorothy Lee Perrins was the only child of Richard Lee Perrins (1909-1983) and Maia Irene "Micky" Enke (1922-1972). Her German-born mother named her Dorothy, which meant "gift of God," after Dorothy Gale, the heroine of L. Frank Baum's *The Wonderful World of Oz* (1900), and Lee, which meant meadow or pasture, after her late father.

Apparently, Dorothy was a very popular female name, ranking 6 out of 4275 names for females of all ages in the 1950 U.S. Census. Many parents named their daughters Dorothy in the 1940's, and the name came to characterize a woman with a compassionate and charitable soul. Had she chosen a completely different path for her life, the name Dorothy Lee Perrins would have suited her well. However, for someone craving the limelight and had spent her youth telling everyone she would one day be a star, Dorothy was far too common a name for her ambitions. And yet, even after she had discarded her birth name in favor of the more glamorous stage name, Angelique, (then later, Angelique Pettyjohn) she came to rely on Dorothy and Dorothy Lee for those times when she wanted to live quietly in the suburbs out of the limelight. She never once regretted discarding the name Perrins because to her, the name recalled painful memories of an absentee father and a stern, humorless mother.

While Angelique's mother was born in Germany in 1922 and had immigrated to the United States in 1923 with her parents Karl and Maria Moll-Enke, her father Richard Lee Young had been a third- or fourth-generation immigrant who could trace his heritage proudly back to Europe and great families in France and England. Her father's family name, Young, was established in France, with branches in Normandy and the Norman Conquest stretching back hundreds of years to the Middle Ages, to Duke William of Normandy and the Battle of Hastings in 1066 A.D. Young suggested youth and vigor, strength and stamina; popular among knights because it referred to the finest qualities of a knight of the realm.

The name Enke was first found in Bavaria, meaning "servant" or "worker," and made a considerable contribution to feudal society, which shaped modern Europe, as craft makers and storekeepers. Later, they packaged cigars, and were among the first cigar manufacturers. Some of the first Enkes to settle in the United States came on cattle boats during the great immigration of the 1860's and 70's. They moved to Illinois and Kansas, then later put down roots in Nevada and California. They came to America seeking a better life, free from religious and social persecution, and found the true riches of the "American Dream" as the result of their hard work. Her parents lived for a brief time in Bunkerville, Nevada, with other German immigrants, before settling in the sprawling area known as Los Angeles.

His family had moved to California more than two decades before the Dust Bowl migration of the 1930's to work as laborers in the oil fields. They also saw emerging opportunities for entrepreneurs who were determined to put their nose to the grindstone and work hard. Oil had been discovered near the sleepy seaside village of Los Angeles in 1892 by Edward L. Doheny and Charles A. Canfield, two old prospectors. According to legend, they used the sharpened end of a eucalyptus tree to dig in a tar deposit near the present-day location of Dodger Stadium and found oil. Within two years of their find, eighty wells were producing crude oil. By 1897, the number of wells had increased to 500. California soon took the lead as the nation's number-one oil producing state, and by 1923, California produced one-quarter of the world's entire output of oil.

Members of the Young family accustomed to hard work, took various jobs supporting the burgeoning oil economy. Some of the heartier ones became riggers and drillers, others built the homes, drove the trucks, or tended the shops that supported other families. Still others continued on to Alaska and Hawaii looking for other opportunities. Those who stayed in the San Fernando Valley helped to turn the small seaside village of Los Angeles into a boomtown. In less than eighteen months, the three hundred wooden houses outlining a web of dirt roads that etched their way alongside the coast of Southern California were transformed into a community of thousands of people, doubling the population between 1895 and 1905, then tripling it between 1905 and 1915, and finally quadrupling it between the years 1915 and 1925.

Richard Lee Young

Angelique's father, Richard Lee Young, was born on May 9, 1909, in the Territory of Hawaii, during the population explosion of the 1900's, and was raised on the Schofield Barracks Military Reservation in Honolulu where his father, Ross George Young (1885-1919), was a career soldier, and his mother, Rosa Christina Dodson (1890-1979), was an Army wife who worked numerous part-time jobs; one as a dressmaker to supplement the family income. Much like their namesake, the Youngs were very hard-working people, and Richard never had pretenses about who he was. Reared with three younger brothers — William Henry, Patrick Allen, and George Ross — he quickly learned that every member of the family worked, and often worked hard at heavy, labor-intensive jobs. The Young family had little time or patience for formal education as his parents taught him the value of working for the common good of the family. He never questioned what he had been taught by his parents, and it served him well throughout his life.

After a very short-lived childhood, in which Richard lived with his family in a one-room house nestled at the foot of the Waianae Mountain range on the island of Oahu, he and the rest of the Young family moved to Phoenix, Arizona. They rented a single-family home in Maricopa County, first on Third Avenue, then later on West Polk. Rosa took in laundry from neighbors to make ends meet; Ross found part-time work as a day laborer, a structural iron worker, and other odd jobs after his stint in the Army. The labor was often bone-crushing for a man in his mid-thirties, and ultimately contributed to his death in 1919. Richard was only ten years old when his father died, an incident which left an indelible impression on his life. Less than two years after his father's death, he quit school with what amounted to an eighth-grade, grammar-school education, and started driving a truck, delivering goods to local area businesses. Because he was tall and lanky, no one ever questioned his age.

In 1922, three short years after her husband's death, Rosa Young married Walter Edward Perrins (1886-1952), who subsequently adopted her four sons, and proudly gave them his last name Perrins. They rented a home for thirty dollars a month in East Garfield, and lived on the east side of Phoenix, not far from the Red Mountain Freeway. Richard continued driving a truck and soon found himself partnering with his younger brother, William, delivering goods on a well-established route. He also picked up the occasional odd job, such as operating a tractor at construction sites, and would have been quite content to drive a truck or operate some other form of heavy equipment the rest of his adult life simply because it was expected of him. In his late twenties, and still considered a young man, Richard Perrins moved to Bakersfield, in central California, to take a full-time job at a factory, driving a tractor. There, in Kern County, he would eventually meet and marry his first wife, Addie Mildred Blumenauer, and make plans for an uncertain future together.

When he was not working, Richard would gather with the other men — some not much older than himself — at the general store and swap tales. At the time, the general store and the church were the hubs of activity, just as they had been in Kansas, Illinois and throughout small town America. And while his future wife, Addie, and the other townswomen preferred meeting in small groups at the church, the men gathered at the storefront. It was like a village green except the front of the store was a slab of concrete. From there, they could watch the wells pumping oil in the distance, and not one of them took rumors of an oil shortage seriously. The Stock Market Crash was something that happened a million miles away. They all felt insulated from it and everything else happening in their small, close-knit community.

In the thirties, thousands of other families poured into California from Texas, Oklahoma, Missouri, Arkansas, and other states affected by the drought creating the great Dust Bowl. Some members of the Young family, including two uncles who had remained in Phoenix, were caught up in the panic and frenzy of the mass migration west. Many of them were not farm workers. At least half of the Youngs had been living in some small town or city, laboring at blue-collar jobs, when unemployment or stories about the rich opportunities in California caused them to pack up their families and hit the road. Most of these migrants headed for Los Angeles. However, California's Indigent Act, passed in 1933, made it a crime to offer sanctuary or help indigent persons entering the state. This act, which was the first of many tough vagrancy laws, was meant to discourage migrant families from crossing the state line, and hopefully stem the tide of those seeking public assistance. More than two dozen people were tried and convicted for the crime of helping relatives move to California from the Dust Bowl states. When these laws failed, other harsher methods were employed. In 1936, for instance, the Los Angeles police department established a border patrol at most major road and rail crossings. This "Bum Blockade," as it was called, used force to turn back

Figure 5. The Dust Bowl Migration.

Figure 6. The Dust Bowl Migration.

migrants who lacked obvious means of support. Some were beaten and killed; others were stripped of all of their belongings and forced to head back. Eventually, the American Civil Liberties Union challenged the legality of such actions and forced the U.S. Supreme Court to consider the issue of restricting interstate migration.

But long before the highest court handed down its landmark decision (Edwards Vs. the State of California, 1941), the Young family took matters into their own hands. They broke the law by smuggling relatives through the border patrol crossings and helped them find jobs and a decent standard of living in some of the neighboring cities and towns not far from Bakersfield, California. In a truck, Richard Perrins would often deliver much-needed supplies to migrant families trying to scratch out a living beyond the borders, unafraid of what the local law enforcement would do to him if he was caught. And then on his return trip to Los Angeles, he'd hide two or three family members under the refuge he was taking to the dump. The police and their deputized militia never suspected him, so he was able to save dozens of family members and friends with his daring exploits. In time, the laws changed and Americans had more to worry about than illegal immigration.

The Advent of the Second World War

The winds of fortune were also changing for Richard Perrins as the rise of Fascism in Europe and the rise of Nationalism in Asia gave way to World War II.

On September 1, 1939, Germany, led by Adolf Hitler and the National Socialist German Workers' Party, invaded Poland. Great Britain and France responded by declaring war on Germany two days later, and the Second World War began. The German *blitzkrieg* rapidly overwhelmed Poland, then Norway, the Netherlands, and Belgium, and finally set its sights on France, with Greece and Yugoslavia soon to follow.

Figure 7. New Laws put an end to the Dust Bowl Migration.

Some years prior to the outbreak of the Second World War, Angelique's mother, Maia Enke, and her family (Karl and Maria Enke) had been fortunate enough to escape from Germany in the twenties, and immigrated to the United States with many other German nationals. They followed the same path west many members of their extended family had, finding homes for themselves in Los Angeles with others of their kind, after a brief stay in Nevada.

By the summer of 1940, Germany had conquered most of Western Europe, but had failed to gain a foothold in England. Hitler then turned his armies on a former ally, the Soviet Union, with a surprise attack. The United States remained neutral, which pleased many members of the Young family. But unfortunately, at this time, Richard's marriage to Addie Blumenauer was starting to unravel. Married for less than a year, Richard Perrins could no longer keep his wife happy and they agreed to a divorce before the end of the year. He left Addie and their daughter Joann Fisher behind in Bakersfield, California.

Maia Irene "Micky" Enke

Late one afternoon in 1940, following a routine delivery, Richard Perrins caught his first site of a beautiful, young woman named Maia, who had just moved with her parents to the San Fernando Valley. They were stocking up on goods at the general store for their new home, which was little more than a wooden shack on the west side of town. She barely noticed him, the young truck driver whose face was smeared with grease, but several of his fellow men, gathered out front, saw the twinkle in his eyes and teased him about her. He took the teasing in stride, boasting he was going to marry her someday.

Later, when Angelique's parents were formally introduced at a Lutheran Church social a month or so later, it was love at first sight. She said she saw it in his big brown eyes, and it was sealed forever when he took her petite, gentle hand in his big, coarse one and escorted her to the church garden for their first kiss. Not long after, he took a job as a truck driver with a local trucking company, earning $1700 a year, and rented a home on North Figueroa Street in Los Angeles for twenty-three dollars a month. Richard and Maia were married a few months later. They were both hard workers who lived and worked alongside other like-minded newlyweds for the next couple of years, building a nest egg of their own. The Great Depression had made communal living for most families a necessity, but as more and more Americans went back to work, the hope of purchasing a home of their own one day was what fueled most American dreams.

Richard and Maia shared that dream.

But when Japan launched a sneak attack against the American fleet stationed at Pearl Harbor, Hawaii, on December 7, 1941, the United States was drawn into the global conflict. Several Youngs responded to the call for volunteers to join the Army and served valiantly when the western Allies invaded North Africa (1942) and Sicily (1943).

By the summer of 1942, Maia was pregnant with their first child, and he was determined their baby would be raised in a house of their own. With money they had saved, Richard purchased a small home in a middle-class neighborhood of Los Angeles County. He had achieved his American dream, and yet he could not enjoy the riches of his new life when he was confronted with the war news.

Richard, who had been born in Hawaii and was personally touched by the Pearl Harbor attack, followed the other men in his community to the Enlistment Office in Santa Ana, California, officially joining the U.S. Army Air Corps on June 4, 1942. Perrins was thirty-three years old when he enlisted, at least eight to ten years older than most of the young enlistees. His fellow soldiers called him "Pappy," an affectionate term that reminded Richard he was nearly old enough to be their father.

Germany and Japan were winning the war. It was only a matter of time before the Axis forces crushed the Allies and sent our heroic soldiers back in body bags. He refused to face that nightmare. Richard Perrins joined the Blackjacks as a flight officer in the Quartermaster Corps and served as a member of the 53rd Troop Carrier Squadron. Maia understood his reasons for going but never truly forgave him for joining the service. At his age, Richard Perrins could have received a deferment or served in a supply unit running supplies between the different military bases in the United States. But Richard felt it was his duty to serve overseas, particularly when his father had been a career soldier.

During the war, the 53rd Troop Carrier Squadron played an integral role in the success of the Allies Forces in World War II. Their remarkable accomplishments are reflected in the award of six campaign streamers for Sicily, Naples-Foggia, Normandy, Northern France, Rhineland, and Central Europe. Activated in June 1942, the 53rd Troop Carrier Squadron was first assigned to the 12th Air Force and deployed in North Africa during May 1943. The squadron's aircraft flew men and supplies to front-line units in Algeria and Tunisia during the North African Campaign, which supported Patton and Montgomery and broke the string of Rommel's victories.

Figure 8. The Unsung Heroes of World War II.

In Italy, the squadron was engaged in several combat operations, dropping airborne units into Sicily during the Operation Husky invasion and later into areas around Anzio and the Balkans. As a flight officer, Perrins flew many missions behind enemy lines to haul guns, ammunition, food, clothing, medical supplies, and other materials to the partisans and to drop propaganda leaflets. Later, the 53rd Troop Carrier Squadron dropped paratroops and needed supplies into Normandy, then later the Netherlands as part of Operation Market Garden. They also supported the 101st Airborne Division in the Battle of the Bulge by towing gliders full of supplies and dropping them near the besieged city of Bastogne on December 27, 1944. They were also among the first air assault teams across the Rhine River near the end of the war.

Not long after the U.S. Army linked up with the Soviets at the Elbe River in Central Germany, Richard Perrins collapsed from fatigue and exhaustion at an Army hospital not far from his wife's ancestral home. He had neglected his health, having lost more than thirty pounds, and was suffering from a form of battle fatigue, which most psychologists would describe today as post-traumatic stress syndrome. He was not unlike the many soldiers who had broken down after the extended exposure to combat, and could no longer cope with the unremitting and horrendous stresses of war. Within weeks, Perrins returned to the United States, and was discharged from the Army Air Corps. The person who returned to Maia and his two-year-old daughter, Dorothy Lee, was a mere shell of a man. Even though he had often dreamt of embracing his daughter for the first time, he found it very difficult to muster any enthusiasm for little Dorothy, his wife Maia, or his life in general. He remained cold and indifferent, until the day he asked his wife for a divorce, living another thirty years until his death at age seventy-three in Long Beach, California, on February 1, 1983.

Life in Salt Lake City

Four-year-old Dorothy Lee Perrins and her mother Maia moved to Salt Lake City, Utah to be near her friends and relatives soon after the divorce. The "Crossroads of the West" had been founded one hundred years earlier, in 1847, by a group of Mormon Pioneers led by Brigham Young who had had a vision of a sanctuary free from the hostility of the East. In many ways the bustling metropolis of Salt Lake City provided a safe haven for the two of them as well. They lived on the west side of town, not far from the railroad station. Maia Perrins worked in a large Victorian home, renting rooms to travelers. The boardinghouse became an important stopover for first-time visitors to the city, and so she made the best of her life. She also took in laundry, which she washed and folded for the locals, and canned goods that sold at the general store. Most days, she worked seventeen hours to earn a living for them.

Mrs. Perrins had long since resigned herself to the nature of her situation in life. She was a poor, uneducated woman with few, if any, skills. As a divorcee with a young daughter, the prospects of finding an eligible man to marry were very slim. The War had produced far too many widows and divorcees, with the prettier ones outnumbering plain ones, like her, ten to one. Content to raise Dorothy on her own as a single mother, faith, fortune, and fate had its way in changing her expectations, and so miraculously intervened in her life.

Figure 9. Salt Lake City, Utah.

Dorothy's mother caught first sight of Claude Herbert, Jr. at the railroad depot during the first few months of 1947. She had gone to meet a friend and Mr. Herbert had just returned from a funeral back east. He was the son of German-born parents, Claude and Christine Herbert. Later, Maia Perrins was invited to a game of pinochle, a popular card game at the time sponsored by their local schoolteacher Judith Appleby. Claude Herbert was invited to attend as Judith's partner, who had already set her sights on him, one of the few eligible bachelors in town. But that was not to be, as Maia had already seen and laid claim to him herself.

Claude Herbert and Maia Irene "Micky" Enke-Perrins were married a few months later in the Lutheran Church, and together with Dorothy, they moved into a house on American Beauty Drive in the Rose Park community of Salt Lake City. Claude and Maia welcomed their first son, Jerald Claude Herbert (1948-1993), on February 1, 1948. Subsequently, Maia gave birth to two additional daughters, Janice Marie Herbert (1950-2007) and Diana Kay Herbert (1952-2013). Maia and Claude Herbert were married for 25 happy, long years. Their middle-class life was the envy of all their friends and neighbors. Maia died at home of natural causes on July 29, 1972. She was buried at Wasatch Lawn Memorial Park in Salt Lake City. Her funeral was attended by hundreds of locals who had gotten to know her through her involvement in the community.

A Thespian is Born

As a child, I hungered for attention and approval of an audience. Even if it was an audience of one. I just needed to hear applause, for that meant acceptance. Love. In school, I was always performing, singing and dancing in the auditorium, or playing the lead in school plays. That is what I lived for. I used to love putting on the make-up and dressing up in costume. But when the curtain went up and all eyes were on me, there was no greater feeling in the world. The voices in my head that told me I was no good were suddenly silent, and the only sound that really mattered was the sound of applause. The sound of acceptance. Love.

In 1948, Dorothy Lee Perrins was enrolled in Kindergarten at Onequa Elementary School, located at 5th Street North and 11th, just a couple of blocks away from the State Fairgrounds. She continued to sing and dance and tell everyone she was going to be a movie star someday, yet her youthful declarations of success were often met with a fair amount of skepticism by her peers and hardworking adults in the Salt Lake City community. Just after her mother married Claude Herbert, she was moved to Rose Park Elementary School at 1105 West 1000 North, a short walk from her home on American Beauty Drive. The community was a middle-class one, bordering the Union Pacific Railroad on the east side of town and the airport on the west side. She could see the snow-covered mountain peaks off in the distance and often played in Highland Park and Pioneer Park, swam in the Jourdan River, and acted like a tomboy, playing chicken on the nearby railroad tracks, much to the disapproval of her mother and the authoritarian hand of her stepfather. There were many instances when she was sent to bed without her dinner or given a good spanking just for acting out like a normal child with a great deal of energy.

Dorothy, faced with the prospect of growing up without a loving father, had always sought out her mother's approval, but Maia was a stern woman with little humor or warmth. Mrs. Herbert worked very hard to provide a roof over her daughter's head and to pay for the singing and ballet lessons Dorothy desired so much. "I had ballet training from the time I was six years old and was a professional dancer before I became an actress," Angelique once told me. She sought out acting, particularly the approval of the masses, as a way to fill what was missing.

Throughout most of her mother's life, she tried very hard to obtain her elusive love, always just too busy for her daughter.

Dorothy hungered for a strong parental figure in her life, particularly since her biological father had abandoned her at such a young age and her mother had started a new life and family with a man who was little more than a stranger to her.

Not surprisingly, Dorothy Lee Perrins had very little in common with her stepbrother, Jerald, or her two half-sisters, Janice and Diana. Roughly five years older than Jerald, she was much more refined than he, and certainly more cultured. Nearly everywhere Jerald went, he wore a coon-skin hat and carried a BB rifle, like the pioneer figures Davy Crockett or Daniel Boone he idolized. Later in the fifties, as he matured, Jerald became obsessed with *Tom Corbett*, *Space Patrol*, and *Science Fiction Theatre*. He read comic books and collected bubble-gum cards of his favorite Major League ballplayers. Dorothy preferred to read *Modern Screen*, *Photoplay*, and *Silver Screen Romances* in order to keep up on the latest news and gossip from the world of Hollywood. Seven to nine years older than the girls, Dorothy had long since traded in her dolls for making Hollywood-inspired costumes at her mother's manual sewing machine. She would often daydream about wearing one of the costumes she had made to her very own Hollywood premiere, perhaps on the arm of a handsome singer like Elvis Aaron Presley. About the only thing the three girls could agree on was their undying love for the King of Rock-n-Roll, Elvis.

> *I had had a difficult time adjusting to my life in the Herbert household. I had almost nothing in common with my two half-sisters, and I was a bit jealous of the affection they received from their father that I never got. But we all have our special memories. I suppose the one memory that stands out most in my mind of Diana and Janice is the first time the three of us saw Elvis live on television. We all loved his music, but when we saw his face, the three of us started screaming. He was just so dreamy. Those deep-set eyes, the full, pouting lips... There was something magical about*

him. I'll never forget the first time I saw his face, the face of Elvis Presley.

Elvis Aaron Presley first appeared on national television in the United States on January 28, 1956, on *The Dorsey Brothers Stage Show*, telecast live from CBS Studio 50 in New York. Most people in America had heard his music on the radio or on records, but few had actually seen him perform live. His famous performance on the *Ed Sullivan Show* was still a year away. On Saturday night, Dorothy and her two half-sisters waited in front of the television in their parent's living room to see Elvis perform on *Stage Show*, which aired at 8:00 p.m. and was produced by Jackie Gleason largely as a cheap warm-up act for his own 8:30 p.m. program.

Elvis Presley's appearance wasn't a blockbuster, not like the first time he would perform for Ed Sullivan, but it got respectable ratings. Presley performed two songs, "Shake, Rattle, & Roll / Flip, Flop, & Fly" and "I Got a Woman." When he first appeared on stage, hundreds of girls in Studio 50 began screaming. Two thousand miles away, in Salt Lake City, Dorothy

Figure 10. Elvis Presley on Television.

and her two half-sisters added their own screams, and for one instance in time, they were joined together as a family.

Two years later, on March 24, 1958, the three of them shared another poignant moment (along with millions of other fans) when they watched tearfully as Elvis Presley was inducted into the Army. He started the day as the King of Rock-n-Roll, but ended it as a lowly buck private, fulfilling his patriotic duty and obligation. Elvis served in the United States Army between March 1958 and March 1960. At the time of his draft he was the most well-known name in the world of entertainment. In the Spring of 1960, the King reclaimed his rightful throne.

At age fourteen, Dorothy Lee Perrins entered high school as a Freshman at West High School, 241 North 300 West Street, just outside of downtown Salt Lake City. West High School had a student population of 2,494 students and served a diverse socio-economic and ethnic community with the affluent Capitol Hill and middle-class Rose Park neighborhoods. During the fifties, West High had earned a poor reputation for the way it treated and served the poorer minority students. Under the strong leadership of several progressive-thinking principals, the school added more remedial courses to its vocational and college-level academics, such as the prestigious Advanced Placement and International Baccalaureate programs, designed for serious academic students. In addition, West was committed to a strong program of character education. The teaching staff was committed to excellence, motivation, and challenging students in the classroom as well as encouraging participation and involvement in athletics, clubs, artistic activities, and community service. Dorothy soon joined the school's drama and speech clubs in an effort to garner attention.

Dorothy earned her first role in *Berkeley Square* at West High School, in 1959. She played the part of Kate Pettigrew in the John L. Balderston play. First produced in 1926 at St. Martin's in London, then in New York in 1929, the successful stage fantasy was about a modern-day London scientist romantically fascinated by the 18th Century. A freak accident propels him back to 1784, where he

Figure 11. West High School in Salt Lake City.

assumes the identity of one of his own ancestors. He falls in love with his distant cousin, Helen Pettigrew, but his other relatives, including her sister Kate, regard the time-traveler as a "sorcerer" due to his disturbing knowledge of future events. Gradually, he becomes disillusioned by the squalor and bigotry of the 18th Century and bids farewell to Helen, explaining he will actually be born years after her death, but they will be reunited "in God's time."

Returning to the present, he discovers Helen died young without ever marrying. He renounces his own fiancée and determines to live out his life as a bachelor, to be united with his true love in death. The high school production ran for six performances, giving sixteen-year-old Dorothy her first real exposure to live theater. She was hooked, and couldn't wait for the next role.

During her tenure at West High School, the young thespian auditioned for and won the lead in *Time Out for Given*, an original scripted play, and one of the female leads in *Arsenic & Old Lace.* Both productions were mounted by drama club in 1960, further solidifying Dorothy's desire to work as a stage actress since reviews from her teachers and peers were generally good. In particular, the review in her school newspaper for *Arsenic & Old Lace* singled Dorothy Perrins out for her "great sense of comic timing" and the way in which she "filled" the stage with her presence. It truly looked like she was bound for Hollywood or Broadway. Unfortunately, neither her mother nor her stepfather understood Dorothy's obsession with acting; never even really tried to understand her. They considered all the time she prepared for each production a waste. Both her parents were hard-working individuals who had survived the Great Depression by elbow grease. They wanted to see Dorothy learn from their example. Claude Herbert tried several times, unsuccessfully, to find his step-daughter a part-time job she could work after school.

The voices in her head always seemed to agree with her parents, constantly reminding her she was "no good." They also reinforced her parent's notions that the entertainment business was not the right place for her, saying, "You'll never make it in life as a dancer or entertainer." "You don't have what it takes." "You're not pretty enough." "You're not talented enough." To get rid of the voices in her head, Dorothy took her first drink at age fourteen. By the time she was seventeen, three years later, she was drinking her stepfather's Southern Comfort nearly every day. Dorothy was also sneaking his cigarettes, a habit she started when she was twelve. She refused to listen to the negative thoughts and dug deeper into her studies with a plan of finishing school early, so she could find a job acting or dancing right after graduation.

> *I exhibited all the signs of an addictive personality at a very young age. At first, I was a compulsive overeater, and very chubby as a child. Then I started smoking at twelve, and drinking when I was fourteen. Once I started drinking, I couldn't really stop. I drank Southern Comfort and whatever else was in the liquor cabinet to silent*

the voices in my head. The ones that told me I was worthless.

Sexy, smart and stunningly beautiful, Dorothy Lee Perrins had matured into a young woman who was very determined to become a star, possessing the energy and unyielding ambition to make it happen, yet she still fought a daily battle with personal demons. Those qualities were reflected in her 1961 West High School yearbook when she was recognized by the student body for all of her achievements in the drama, speech, dance, and booster clubs.

Dorothy, the classic small-town girl with the big Hollywood dream, was also very popular on campus; characterized by a warmth and charisma that just drew people to her on a regular basis. While she had many friends of both sexes, she had no real boyfriends or sweethearts. Dorothy would have been the first one to say she didn't have time for boys, but in truth she was always looking for love. She thought the love of being in front of a live audience was what drove her ambition, but it was really a hunger buried deep inside her to be loved, cherished, and accepted unconditionally for who she was. She projected power and strength, but also vulnerability, a very complicated and beautiful human being.

Figure 12. Ed Sullivan Ticket.

On January 20, 1961, a few days after her early graduation from West High School, Dorothy and her family gathered around the television for yet another seminal moment in time, the inauguration of President John

F. Kennedy. They watched as a clerk of the U.S. Supreme Court held the large Fitzgerald family Bible as John F. Kennedy took the oath of office to become the nation's 35th president. Against a backdrop of deep snow and sunshine, more than twenty thousand people huddled in twenty-degree temperatures on the east front of the Capitol to witness the event. John Kennedy, having removed his topcoat, projecting both youth and vigor, delivered what has become a landmark inaugural address. His audience reached far beyond those gathered before him, to people all around the world. In preparing for this moment, he sought both to inspire the nation and to send a message abroad signaling the challenges of the Cold War and his hope for peace in the nuclear age. He also wanted it to be brief.

What many consider to be the most memorable and enduring section of the speech came towards the end when Kennedy called on all Americans to commit themselves to service and sacrifice: "And so, my fellow Americans, ask not what your country can do for you, but ask what you can do for your country." Kennedy then continued by addressing his international audience: "My fellow citizens of the world, ask not what America will do for you, but what together we can do for the freedom of man."

Having won the election by one of the smallest popular vote margins in history, Kennedy had known the great importance of this speech. People who witnessed the speech or heard it broadcast over television and radio lauded the new President with his vision for the future. Even school children, like Dorothy's two half-sisters, wrote to him with their reactions to his ideas. Following his inaugural address, nearly 75% of Americans expressed approval of President Kennedy.

Kennedy's inaugural address inspired millions of young people with its optimistic view of the world. The American Dream was within reach if only people were to reach out and grab it. The optimism of the early sixties inspired many people to grab for their dreams, and Dorothy Lee Perrins was like most young people her age, swept up in the optimism of the period. She decided she was going to study theatre arts at Salt Lake

Community College and earn a degree in acting as a stepping-stone to stardom. So, on the day after Kennedy's historic speech, Dorothy submitted her application to attend college in the Fall of 1961. The only thing standing in her way was tuition. And for that, she clearly needed a job; a job paying well enough to allow her to use her talents as a dancer and an actress.

Figure 13. Photos featuring Dorothy Lee Perrins from The Panther High School Yearbook.

2
Love Me Tender

I think he [Elvis] singled me out from all the other girls because I was so young — I had just turned 18 only a few days before — when most of the other showgirls were in their twenties and thirties.

A couple of weeks after her graduation from high school, Dorothy Lee Perrins left her home in Salt Lake City, and headed to Las Vegas to work as a dancer. She had heard the money was very good and jobs for attractive, young girls, like her, were plentiful in a town known synonymously with sex and sin. She also figured whatever work she found would still allow her time to pursue her dreams of becoming an actress.

"Moving away from home was the best thing I ever did," she later explained to me. "Throughout my childhood and adolescence, I was always being told I didn't have what it took to be successful. 'You're no good!' 'You'll never make it!' 'You're not pretty enough!' 'No one is going to want you!' The best thing I ever heard was the door to my house slamming behind me. I thought, *I'll show them! I'll be rich and famous! I'll be a somebody!*"

The moment she stepped off the bus in Vegas, Dorothy got a room in back of the Thunderbird Hotel with a couple of other girls. She walked out to the bright neon lights of the Strip, closed her eyes, and spun around. When she opened them again, she shouted, "I'm finally ready to begin my life!"

At age seventeen, she felt emancipated, totally free to reinvent herself, to create a whole new identity and reality for her life. She discarded her last name, and adopted the stage name Dorothy "Harmonie," to protect her identity and family name. (As a newbie, she was completely unaware another Dorothy had already claimed "Harmony" as her last name and was a regular girlfriend of the King.) Still very naïve about the way things worked in Vegas, she also got a crash course about performing and the stark differences between jobs for dancers, showgirls, and strippers.

Not long after she cleared the hurtle of changing her name, Dorothy landed her first Las Vegas review and discovered what it was like to perform topless before a large audience of men. “Nudity didn’t offend me, although the first time I walked on stage I felt as if everyone was staring at my nipples,” she recalled. She was also soon to learn about the late-night party scene *and* have a relationship with the most popular entertainer in the world; a relationship that would change her life in ways she could not possibly imagine.

Figure 14. Downtown Las Vegas (circa 1961).

Figure 15. Thunderbird Hotel (circa 1961).

Showgirls, Dancers and Strippers

In the late fifties and early sixties, the image of the Las Vegas showgirl came to represent the unofficial icon of the resort town in the Nevada desert. As the Las Vegas Strip developed and grew, the competition between the various casinos to produce the biggest and the brightest shows became fierce as each resort competed for every dollar coming into town.

Every resort on the Strip had its own line of beautiful girls wearing very skimpy costumes, known as showgirls, who traditionally opened and closed for headlining celebrities. Soon, very elaborate stage productions by Harold Minsky, Donn Arden, or Jack Entratter, which came to be known as the "Las Vegas-style Review," were developed, featuring chorus girls with outrageously large headdresses. Big resort casinos, like the Sands, Flamingo, or Tropicana, began offering twice-nightly shows, each competing to be more spectacular than the other.

Minsky's *Follies* was the first to feature showgirls appearing on stage at the Desert Inn topless. Donn Arden followed with *The Lido de Paris*, which took the topless showgirls of Minsky's *Follies* and incorporated them into a large stage production at the Stardust. *The Lido* was so wildly successful it ran for thirty-one years. Other shows, such as *Vive Paris Vive* at the Aladdin, the *Folies Bergère* at the Tropicana, and *Cleopatra's Nymphs of the Nile* at the Flamingo were among the top attractions in Las Vegas for many years. Yet, just off the Strip were clubs featuring entertainment of a different kind, entertainment that appealed to a thriving sex industry.

Not surprisingly, a hierarchy developed among the girls performing in the casino shows; not only to established rank and years of service but also what the girls would and would not do on stage. A showgirl, on the one hand, was a female performer who would parade around the stage topless in the big headdresses, all decked out in feathers and jewels. They often had the minimum height requirement of being at least 5'9½", but they didn't need to have any skills as dancers. They were considered living mannequins, dressed to adorn the stage with beautiful large costumes. A dancer, by way of contrast, was a woman who had trained professionally as a dancer and would dance around the stage topless. They had the minimum height requirement of 5'5". The third kind of girl was the stripper, and she would often act alone, removing or stripping her clothes off in tune to a selection of musical favorites. Strippers rarely worked the big reviews, like the showgirl or dancer, but they could make a lot more money by hustling drinks or doing lap dances in between their sessions on stage. Being a showgirl or a dancer was considered more respectable than being a stripper. Strippers were a dime-a-dozen, showgirls were simply mannequins modeling glitzy clothes, but dancers were the real professionals.

"It's really hard to be a showgirl," Angelique Pettyjohn told me. Throughout her long career in the Las Vegas clubs and casinos, she had been a showgirl, a dancer, and a stripper, and had actually spent more time on stage than in the movies.

Figure 16. Showgirls and Dancers from the 1960s.

Showgirls follow a very regimented schedule, have a special diet, and they must stay out of the sun as much as possible because the showgirl herself is considered a piece of art. Strippers have much more fun. But let's be clear, there's not much gray area here. The only way you'd wind up working in a strip club was if you'd set out to work in a strip club. The work was long and hard, and the customers very demanding, expecting a lot for their twenty bucks. But a really gifted stripper could make a thousand bucks a night, while a showgirl really worked for little more than minimum wage. The truly talented performers in Vegas were always the professional dancers.

When she first came to Las Vegas in 1961, Dorothy Perrins sought work as a showgirl, yet dreamt of being a dancer. But it didn't start out that way. For her first couple of auditions, she responded to advertisements in the local tabloid promising big money in exchange for short working hours. Naively, Dorothy Harmonie walked into several seedy bars just off the Las Vegas Strip and found herself taking her clothes completely off as the part of the audition. The old, disgusting men that watched and slobbered over her seventeen-year-old body gave her the creeps; almost sent her packing for home. She remembered running out of several of the joints in terror; throwing her lunch up in the first alley she could find.

Eventually, the auditions got easier, and she landed her first job in Vegas, stripping at a small club about a block away from the Thunderbird Hotel. The hours were longer than she expected, especially after she learned the only way to make the big money was to put in double shifts for the lunch and dinner crowds. Dorothy relied on her training as a dancer to get her through most of the sets, but she often felt humiliated and degraded whenever the bouncers would turn a blind's eye for their

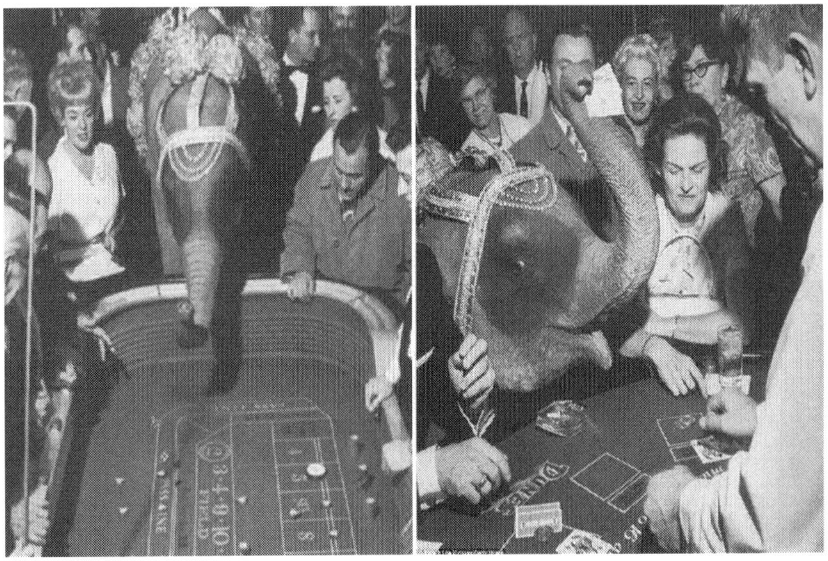

Figures 17 and 18. Tanya the Baby Elephant at the Dunes.

high rollers with their filthy hands, as they pretended to stuff dollar bills in her G-string, while they grabbed her ass. Despite her earning good tips, Dorothy had to pay a fee to the house to work every night, so she couldn't afford to be choosy about the clientele. She needed them in order to earn her keep. The work was inherently degrading and exploitative, a mere cut above legalized prostitution. And contrary to popular opinion, prostitution was, and still is, illegal within city limits.

Five or ten years earlier, Dorothy Lee Perrins might have worked in burlesque, where stripping was considered a fine art and women like Blaze Starr, Dixie Evans, Sally Rand, Cindy Barr, Lili St. Cyr, Tempest Storm, and others demonstrated there was so much more to stripping than a G-string and tassels.

After World War II, Las Vegas became the striptease capital of the world and paved the way with pasties. These women set the Strip aflame with a form of striptease that relied on storytelling far more intimate than naked bodies writhing on a stage. Rarely did audience members holler "take it off" as they were so mesmerized by the show. Tempest Storm earned as much as $10,000 a night. The best of the acts made the easy jump to the showrooms, as early casinos, like the El Rancho and the Silver Slipper, began hosting headline strippers like Sally Rand and Tere Sheehan, the "girl in the champagne glass." St. Cyr's bath-and-towel act at the El Rancho was so sizzling District Attorney Roger Foley charged her with lewdness in 1951, but she paid the fine of $250 and all was forgiven. Las Vegas worked very hard to keep burlesque's rich history alive.

Unfortunately, the number of women stripping in the burlesque tradition declined as did the whole notion of burlesque across America. Few strip clubs could sustain anything near the Las Vegas glamour of the large-scale reviews. Girlie magazines and sexploitation films forced nightclub striptease to become more and more sexually explicit. More strippers were forced to incorporate "floor work," such as shimmying while lying supine on the floor, into their acts. Stripping lost its sense of artistry, an integral part of the world of burlesque, and devolved it into something grotesque and degrading for its performers. For

Figure 19. When she first arrived in Las Vegas, Dorothy Lee Perrins didn't have a clue what actual stripping was.

Dorothy Lee and the other girls who worked as strippers in the sixties, stripping had turned into a cynical mechanism to separate the girls from their clothes as quickly as possible. It was fortunate the great Marliza Pons (1936-2011), world-renowned for her belly-dancing and as a choreographer of Middle Eastern dance, happened upon Dorothy's striptease act one night and set her straight about the hierarchy of performers in Vegas. She may well have saved the young innocent's life.

Cleopatra's Nymphs of the Nile

The next day, Dorothy Harmonie started her job search anew. Working from the same tabloids that had led her to the strip joints, she concentrated on legitimate work as a showgirl and dancer, which meant showing up for cattle-call auditions with hundreds of girls just like her and going through the same humiliating dance routines she already knew by heart, day after day.

Finally, after having done more than a dozen cattle calls, she happened upon an audition for a show playing at the Flamingo

Hotel, *Cleopatra's Nymphs of the Nile.* The creative director and choreographer for the show was none other than Marliza Pons. She remembered Dorothy from the striptease act and asked her to demonstrate her dancing skills. Dorothy Harmonie showed off her classical training as a ballet dancer. While not exactly what Marliza was looking for, she saw potential in her. Pons hired her as a showgirl for *Cleopatra's Nymphs of the Nile*, but insisted Dorothy learn Middle Eastern Dance during the day as part of a work regimen.

Figure 20. Choreographer Marliza Pons (1936-2011).

> *I was drawn into nudity slowly because the first job I had was as a topless showgirl in a huge Las Vegas show where there were fifty other girls without tops on. All of us wore beautiful costumes and big headpieces. Once I got used to the initial idea, I was very proud of my body, which everybody told me was beautiful.*

Dorothy Perrins soon discovered that the life of a Las Vegas showgirl was definitely not always a glamorous one, even though showgirls were (and still are) known worldwide for their glamour. The working hours were long and hard. Most showgirls, like Dorothy, were up by 11:00 a.m., and were expected to follow a schedule of exercise to keep their bodies fit and in shape for the stage performances. In the afternoon, some would take two hours of dance class, with the hope of one day transitioning from showgirl to dancer. They'd go home for dinner and rest, and arrive back at the theatre by 7:00 P.M. for an 8 o'clock performance time. Then sometimes they'd perform another show at 10 or 11:00 P.M., finish by 1:00 A.M., and arrive home around 2 in the morning. Dorothy would repeat this same schedule seven days a week for two weeks straight, and then have a single day off before repeating the cycle.

She made friends, and was actually paired with two other girls in the show to share a small room in back of the Flamingo. Of course, the room was not free, and the daily room-rate was deducted from her weekly salary. But she looked upon the room at the Flamingo as a huge cost-savings because she couldn't afford the cost of a vehicle and didn't like taking public transportation.

Figure 21. Flamingo Hotel (circa 1961).

As a showgirl, Dorothy Harmonie's weight was strictly monitored; she was not allowed to fluctuate more than a pound or two either way, without facing stiff fines from the show runner. She was urged to follow a special diet to maintain muscle but not gain body fat. Since most show costumes could weigh as much as fifty pounds or more, she was drilled constantly in how to move with a twenty-five-pound, five-foot headdress on the top of her head or how to walk down a four-story staircase of about hundred steps, wearing three-inch high heels, without falling. As a beginner, it was "sheer terror, especially when you realize there's no one nor nothing to catch you," she said. "You're just worried that you've got five minutes to get from one side of the stage to the other, and hit your mark, or you're going to incur the wrath of the director."

Because of her unusual hours, Perrins said it was often difficult to have much of a social life, or even to meet people not in the business. She'd spend whatever time she'd have free in the day, running errands with friends, doing laundry, or just sleeping. Many girls in the show liked to party after hours, but since they were not allowed to drink alcohol or take drugs, and gambling was simply forbidden, there was little to do to have fun. Of course, for the few risk-takers, sex was always a reasonable alternative to fun, and was often encouraged by the casino owners who wanted their special patrons with money to stay put in their hotels. Prostitution was illegal within the city limits, though not within the suburbs of Clark County, and the girls were strictly forbidden from discussing any kind of transaction involving sex. But if the wealthy clients felt like tipping them for a good time, then no one's feelings were hurt.

During her first six weeks or so, working at the Flamingo Hotel, Dorothy Harmonie managed to keep herself busy, while still avoiding the late-night party scene. She hadn't had any serious boyfriends or sweethearts in high school, and didn't see the need to find a man for the few hours she had left over in her day. Dorothy claimed she never missed love, but in reality, she was starving for the affection of an older, more experienced man to literally sweep her off her feet with his charm and charisma. Just after her eighteenth birthday in March 1961, she would meet such a man.

Figure 22. Publicity Photo of Elvis from *Blue Hawaii* (1961).

Elvis in Las Vegas

Much has been written about the career of Elvis Aaron Presley, and while it is not the objective of this writer to rehash most of that information again, it is important to set the stage for this next part of the story.

Elvis first performed in Las Vegas in 1956 at the New Frontier Hotel and Casino, then called the New Frontier Hotel. He was paid a thousand dollars a week and the casino owner comped him all the liquor he could drink, as well as chips every day to play in the casino. Because Elvis Presley was a religious man, he declined to gamble at any of the tables or machines, but he did keep the barmaids busy supplying him and his buddies with all the alcohol they could handle.

At first, the whole notion of Elvis performing in Vegas would appear to be a match made in heaven. Songwriter Mike

Stoller said there "was a coolness factor, a hip factor. [Elvis] brought something to Vegas it [sorely] needed." But honestly, of the twenty-nine shows he did in 1956, every single one of his performances were poorly received by the older, more sedate crowd staying at the New Frontier Hotel.

His drummer, D.J. Fontana recalled, "They were fifty and sixty-year-old people. They were eating their hundred-dollar steaks and drinking their fifty-dollar drinks in the main room, and they didn't want to hear the racket we were making. They weren't ready for rock 'n' roll. Liberace was playing there. He was the big Vegas star of the time."

Tom Jones knew Presley well and said it best, "Vegas simply wasn't prepared for him the first time around."

Due to this bad experience, Elvis Presley did not perform in Las Vegas again until 1969, and when he did return as a performer, the King played 645 shows there, during a six-and-a-half-year period, between July 31, 1969 and December 12, 1976, at the Hilton (formerly the International Hotel). Each night he'd perform two shows, sometimes three. Even though he had had a poor experience his first time around performing in Vegas, he still loved the city and enjoyed all of the night life, especially all of the dazzling showgirls.

One might say Elvis had a thing for showgirls. Whenever he and his boys — the original members of the Memphis Mafia: Lamar Fike, Red West, Joe Esposito, Jerry Schilling, and Charlie Hodge — needed to blow off some steam, they'd all pile into a car or board a jet, and head to Las Vegas. Their late-night parties at the Sahara hotel were infamous; more like Roman bacchanals with plenty of liquor flowing and dozens of naked girls jumping from bed to bed.

During the month of January 1961, preview audiences had reacted poorly to Hope Lange's character's suicide in *Wild in the Country*, a dramatic film featuring Elvis Presley in a non-singing role. Executives at 20th Century-Fox were all very worried the motion picture, budgeted at $2,975,000, would be a big flop. The last two Elvis films, *GI Blues* and *Flaming Star* (both released in 1960), had underperformed at the box office, and it appeared his film career had fizzled before it had ever really gotten rolling. So, Fox executives ordered Director Philip Dunne to fix it. Since Dunne had shot most of the film on location in Napa Valley, near the Silverado Trail, he was forced to recall some of the principles, including Elvis and Hope Lange.

Presley, known for his low tolerance for boredom, spent much of the time during the re-shoots waiting impatiently for Dunne to get something right that he felt should have been done right the first time around. In the end, Dunne shot a completely new scene in which Irene Sperry (Lange) survives and sees Glenn Tyler (Elvis) off to college. The re-shoots pushed the film over budget and cost the production another three weeks (plus time to rewrite and re-edit the sequence). The tinkering on *Wild in the Country* cost Elvis a great deal of time from his schedule; primarily some much-needed, personal downtime before the start of production on *Blue Hawaii*.

On February 25, 1961, Elvis Presley appeared in Memphis at a luncheon in his honor, then headlined two shows at the Ellis Auditorium to benefit thirty-eight Memphis-area charities. "Elvis Presley Day," as proclaimed by Tennessee Governor Buford Ellington, was a huge success, raising over $50,000 for charity. By the time he had finished promoting his latest hit "Surrender," which later would climb to number one on the Billboard chart for the last week of March 1961, and had completed several other promised obligations, Presley was feeling very tired. He needed to take a break, to blow off some steam before heading to Hawaii.

Elvis and his entourage headed to Las Vegas to have some fun. Shortly after they arrived at the Sahara Hotel, Fike, West, and Hodge put out a call to a number of the showgirls they knew, letting them know Elvis was back in town. They ordered booze and stocked the suite with plenty of food for a week-long orgy. Several girls in Dorothy Harmonie's show at the Flamingo went the first couple of nights and couldn't stop talking about all the fun they had. So then, one of Dorothy's roommates, who knew Presley's money manager, got the three of them invited to

Figure 23. Publicity Photo of Elvis with a few of the girls from *Blue Hawaii* (1961).

the next party in Presley's suite at the Sahara. That was where Dorothy Harmonie met Elvis for the first time.

> *I think he [Elvis] singled me out from all the other girls because I was so young — I had just turned eighteen only a few days before — when most of the other showgirls were in their twenties and thirties. We sat together at the piano and he played songs for me. I remember specifically asking him to sing "Love Me Tender," and the way he looked at me as he sang it, took my breath away. He urged me to get out of Vegas, to find some other line of work, or otherwise I would end up becoming like the other, older showgirls — worn out and washed up well before my prime. We talked about a lot of other things that night, too.*

> *[Presley] told me he was a very spiritual man, and we discussed his thoughts about God and the mysteries of the Universe. Later, when I told him Iwas still a virgin, which most people find pretty hard to believe when you're a showgirl, it just blew his mind. I thought it would be great to have him as my first lover. It's got to be somebody. It might as well be Elvis. And so, I set my sights on him.*

In the early morning hours, after they had partied throughout most of the night, Elvis Presley offered to walk Dorothy Harmonie back to her room she shared with two other showgirls at the Flamingo Hotel. Outside the room, he pulled her close and "took my face in his hands. He kissed my forehead, each eye, my nose, and finally my mouth. It was the gentlest and yet the most passionate kiss I had ever experienced in all my life," Pettyjohn recalled many years later. They then spent the next few hours kissing and talking, and kissing some more, as they watched the moon move across the night sky.

When Elvis Presley finally got up the courage to ask her back to his private room in the suite, Dorothy thought "it was funny he had waited so long to ask me." She always felt it was the sign of a real gentleman, and she agreed to go to his bed without a second thought. Dorothy Harmonie later confessed to several of her fellow showgirls that sex with the King was somewhat of a letdown, but she couldn't seem to get enough of his kisses.

Sometime before dawn, he escorted her discreetly back to her room and asked very politely to see her again without agreeing to a specific time or date. She said "yes," and then gave him one last kiss before he left.

Blue Hawaii (1961)

Elvis Presley and his entourage left Las Vegas on Saturday, March 18, 1961 for Hawaii to prepare for a charity concert he would be performing a week later. His manager, Colonel Tom

Parker, had read a newspaper article revealing attempts to raise funds for the Arizona memorial had floundered, so he and Elvis cooked up the plan to do a benefit concert as a way to kick off their four-week location shoot on *Hawaiian Beach Boy*, which would later be changed to *Blue Hawaii*.

When hundreds of fans mobbed Elvis Presley at the airport upon his arrival, Red West, Lamar Fike, and the other guys in the Memphis Mafia managed to break Elvis and the Colonel free and get them safely to the Coco Palms Hotel on Kauai, Hawaii.

On Monday, March 20, 1961, Elvis Presley began work on *Blue Hawaii*, splitting his time between the location filming and at the recording studio, doing the film's soundtrack. He called Dorothy Harmonie several times from the set at the Coco Palms Resort to talk to her about their amazing evening together, but their calls were always brief ones. With the three-hour time distance between Las Vegas and Hawaii, he was performing when she was free or she was performing when he was available to talk.

Then, on Saturday, March 25, 1961, while Elvis waited backstage at the Bloch Arena at Pearl Harbor to perform his benefit concert, he called and invited Dorothy to join him on the set for a couple of days. She was flabbergasted by the invitation, agreeing without a second thought. He promised to wire her the plane ticket, but soon after the concert he learned Producer Hal Wallis had put his foot down about all the fraternizing going on between Presley and the female stars of the film. Wallis ordered all parties hosted by Presley were off-limits because the girls kept turning up late or looking too tired for shooting. He also insisted Presley, twenty-six at the time, take the production more seriously. Elvis Presley's benefit concert, which turned out to be his last live performance until his 1968 television special, had raised a whopping $65,000 for the memorial, and also helped re-energize the project with much-needed press attention. (Within the year, the rest of the funds were raised, and the U.S.S. Arizona Memorial was completed and opened in 1962 to thankful veterans and the public at large.)

But even though he had had a successful show, Elvis continued to be watched closely by Wallis, so closely he was forced to keep Dorothy Harmonie under cover during the production. She was shuttled between hotels by his buddies and actually spent very little time with him during her short trip to Hawaii. On a visit to the set one day, Wallis caught sight of her in a silver bikini, sunning herself. Elvis quickly invented the story that Dorothy was an extra they'd brought in for the afternoon's shoot. Later, his friends packed her up and sent her back on a commercial flight to the mainland.

Roughly two weeks later, the location filming wrapped — scenes at Waikiki Beach, Diamond Head, Mount Tantalus, and Hanauma Bay, a volcanic crater open to the sea, near the bedroom community of Hawaii-Kai, a few miles away from Waikiki. The Coco Palms Resort, located on the east coast of Kauai, served as the backdrop for most of the resort scenes, especially the beautifully elaborate wedding scene where Elvis croons "The Hawaiian Wedding Song" to Joan Blackman as they ride their flower-bedecked double-hull canoe through the lagoon. Virtually, the last twenty minutes of the movie were shot on and near the grounds of the Coco Palms.

Following location filming, the crew returned to the Paramount lot to finish most of the interior scenes for the film. With late-night parties out, Presley would relax during filming by giving karate demonstrations with his friend and employee, Red West, which resulted in Presley's fingers becoming bruised and swollen. He called Dorothy Lee a couple more times, once from the Paramount Lot in Hollywood, but by then, the romance had started to cool down. Dorothy was overjoyed to receive his calls, but the loving words and overall tenderness she had experienced that first night with him was missing. Elvis Presley was overly polite, almost business-like with her. Clearly, he had done the best work of his career working on *Blue Hawaii*, but the bloom was off the rose, and it would cost him dearly.

Figure 24. Poster from *Blue Hawaii* (1961).

An Unwanted Pregnancy

Back in Las Vegas, Dorothy Harmonie continued to work at the Flamingo Hotel, but as time passed, she gradually started noticing changes to her body, not all at once but evolving over the span of several weeks' time. Her breasts felt swollen and tender, and she made frequent bathroom trips throughout the day and night. Sick and nauseous most of the time, she couldn't seem to stop vomiting first thing in the morning. She also felt very tired, drained as if she had the flu or some horrible disease. When she missed her first monthly cycle, Dorothy thought she had contracted cancer, and scheduled a physical with the doctor most of the other showgirls saw. He examined her and said she was fine physically, relieving her anxiety about cancer, but then explained she was pregnant and could expect the child sometime in late December. Dorothy was shocked by the news and started weeping uncontrollably, mumbling to the doctor that she didn't think it was possible for a virgin to get pregnant. She was so naïve.

Back in 1961, Dorothy Lee, like so many other, young women her age, didn't know a great deal about sex; most of what she did know she learned from other girls. For someone working in the entertainment industry, selling sexual fantasy to its clients on a daily or nightly basis, she was ignorant about sex, which wasn't taught in schools, nor did parents talk with their children openly about it. Most states prohibited the distribution of contraceptives to unmarried people and abortions were something done in back alleys with coat hangers. Better family planning education, birth control advice, and requirements which forced fathers to pay child support were concepts years away. The stigma of unwed motherhood was so great few women were willing to have sex outside of marriage, and those who did get "knocked up" faced social ostracism. Single, unwed mothers were considered pariahs, banished from schools and churches, ostracized by their peers, and sent out of town to give birth in secret. They were considered whores or women of ill-repute. Even women willing to have sex outside the sanctity of marriage could demand a promise of marriage in the event of pregnancy, but Dorothy Harmonie knew full well she couldn't — no, wouldn't make such a demand of Elvis. She wasn't about to trap the King into marriage if he didn't love her.

Dorothy faced a real dilemma, at merely eighteen. She felt like she carried the weight of the entire world upon her shoulders. As a Protestant raised in the Lutheran Church, abortion was absolutely out of the question. She wasn't going to take a life in order to protect her future. She also refused to consider the possibility of making Elvis Presley marry her, simply because she carried his child.

Dorothy kept abreast of the entertainment news of the day and knew Priscilla Beaulieu had promised to spend the summer visiting Elvis in Los Angeles. With Priscilla back in his life, the first time since he had been released from the Army, Elvis would have very little time for a pregnant girl. Besides, what would the world think if the man they loved and admired suddenly turned up with an unwed mother as his bride. She would be vilified for tarnishing his great image.

Having thought briefly about keeping the child, raising him/her as a single parent, she wondered how she would support the two of them within the limitations of her contract with the Flamingo. Perhaps the best thing she could possibly do for the child was to find a couple willing to adopt him or her. But was that the right thing to do with the King's baby?

Colonel Tom Parker

She wrestled with her dilemma for several months. A couple of her closest friends, fellow showgirls, knew she was pregnant, but did not know the identity of the father, even though they might have guessed. Each recommended she have a quick and simple abortion, supplying the names of several doctors prolific in similar procedures. At the time, abortion was strictly illegal, but that didn't stop abortions from happening. Dorothy listened to them, but held steadfast in her beliefs not to seek one. She talked with others about what she should do, but at the end of the day, she realized there was only one other person's whose opinion really mattered to her. What would Elvis do??

Dorothy Harmonie was smart enough to know she couldn't approach him directly at a party or event, without tipping her hand. She'd have to talk to the one man who knew him better than anyone else, Colonel Tom Parker.

"The Colonel," as he liked people to refer to him, displayed a "ruthless devotion" to Elvis Presley and his interests, and turned a simple country boy and ex-truck driver into one of the greatest performers of his generation. In the beginning, Colonel Tom Parker had been like a second father to Elvis, and used his business acumen to manage nearly every facet of his life. He often selected the songs, the venues, the clothes, everything.

In 1955, Elvis signed with RCA Records, in a lucrative deal masterminded by Parker. Subsequent deals, worked out by the Colonel, found Presley scoring his first #1 single with "Heartbreak Hotel," as well as his first #1 album, *Elvis Presley*, and signing a movie contract with Paramount Pictures ultimately worth millions of dollars. Presley once said (of Parker), "I don't think I'd have ever been very big if it wasn't for him. He's a very smart man." And under his brilliant, skillful, and cunning guidance, his one and only client, Elvis, reached unimaginable heights. Few ever suspected Colonel Thomas Andrew Parker of Huntington, West Virginia, wasn't who or what he claimed to be, but in 1981, a few years after Elvis' death, the Colonel was discovered to be a fraud. He always said he was an American, but was born Andreas Cornelis Van Kujik in Breda, Holland. He was actually an illegal immigrant, who at the age of twenty arrived on a freighter in Tampa Bay, Florida, from the Netherlands. He never applied for a green card and had no formal experience as a manager or "king"-maker.

With extreme caution and a great deal of personal trepidation, Dorothy Harmonie managed to contact the Colonel

Figure 25. Elvis and Colonel Tom Parker..

and set up a meeting through a series of backdoor maneuvers worthy of a top spy. Her number one concern was she didn't want Elvis to know of her pregnancy, until Parker agreed. At first, when she told the Colonel of her condition, he did not seem overly surprised. Women of all ages had been coming to him for the last seven years with similar stories, and he was able to dismiss most of them with a few hundred dollars and an autographed picture. Dorothy's story was different somehow; her sincerity warranted some investigation. Once he was able to verify what she had told him as fact, Colonel Parker looked at the big picture, and did not like what he saw.

In 1961, Elvis Presley was at the height of his fame, known worldwide as the King of Rock-n-Roll; a man of virtue and high moral character bobbysoxers adored and young men wanted to emulate. Record sales were at an all-time high and his movies were box office bonanzas garnering millions of dollars in ticket sales. The executives at Paramount Pictures were banking on *Blue Hawaii* topping $4.5 million in overall revenue, more than double his last movie outing.

The Colonel, seeing into the future, feared if news of Dorothy's pregnancy got out, it would seriously damage the King's reputation, thereby destroying his wealth and fame. He never considered whether Elvis would marry her as part of some shotgun wedding or what the potential of impending fatherhood might do to his career in the long run. The bottom line for Parker was protecting the revenue stream. He didn't give a damn whether the two young people were in love or not.

At their next meeting, Colonel Parker exerted great pressure on the eighteen-year-old showgirl to have an abortion. He offered her money, parts in future movies, help with her own career, and then even more money. Dorothy Lee stood her ground. Although she was unwilling to abort the baby, she did eventually agree to deliver the baby in secret, thereby sparing Elvis the shame and public humiliation of a Hollywood scandal. Dorothy still loved him, even if her love was unrequited.

In the end, she also agreed to allow the baby to be adopted immediately following the birth. Colonel Parker claimed to have been an orphan adopted by a circus couple and therefore drew on his own experience and began combing the circus troupes for a suitable couple.

As the U.S. release date of *Blue Hawaii* (November 22, 1961) drew near, Colonel Parker was anxious and determined to have Dorothy Hamonie sequestered from the public. His biggest fear was she would have a change of heart and come forward with her secret, and thus ruin what had been planned to be Elvis' biggest payday yet.

He had arranged for her to take a small flat on Chicago's far south side, which had been modestly furnished and stocked with everything the expectant mother could ever need. He had also secretly bribed several officials at a nearby hospital in Gary, Indiana to keep the news of an unwed mother's birth out of the papers, which was a tradition at the time. The Colonel also found a young Yugoslavian couple, known as "The Vargas" performers, traveling with the Ringling Brothers Circus throughout North America. He arranged a hush-hush adoption involving two married circus performers, Anna and Jacob Stanic. The young couple very much wanted a child of their own and, at the time, was unable to conceive. Arrangements were made and the plan was set into motion.

Dorothy Perrins got an extended leave from work and took up residence at the apartment the Colonel had arranged a few weeks before *Blue Hawaii* was released (the Wednesday before Thanksgiving). She spent the Thanksgiving holiday alone in her apartment, watching the Macy's Day parade on a little black-and-white television and eating her own turkey and fixings. She kept up with the entertainment news by reading the Chicago Sun-Times the next morning.

By Friday, November 24, 1961, *Blue Hawaii* was declared a hit, with box office receipts totaling more than double its closest competitor. By the end of the year, it had finished as the 10th top-grossing movie of 1961, and 14th for 1962 on the Variety national box office survey, earning five million dollars. Not only was the film a popular success, but it was also a critical one as well. Critics liked the image Elvis projected as the more mature leading man with sacred family and marriage values. And, of course, it didn't hurt to have the fantasy of King Elvis ruling over a magical warm land, like Hawaii (a newborn state), especially during the cold desolate months of winter the rest of the country was experiencing. The song ballad "Can't Help Falling in Love" also became an instant hit, and to this day is performed at weddings around the world.

Blue Hawaii established the pattern for the dozen or so Elvis movies that followed. The screenplay by Hal Kanter was later nominated by the Writers Guild of America in 1962 in the category of Best Written American Musical. Dorothy Perrins was happy to read about Elvis Presley's success in the morning newspaper, and kept clippings from *Blue Hawaii* as a way to pass the time during the last few weeks of her pregnancy.

Colonel Parker dropped in several times to make sure she was still there and to see if there was anything he could get for her. As the Christmas holiday approached, he brought her a small fake tree. He showed her every courtesy, and at times when Dorothy had doubts about her decision, he was there to both console and bully her to keep to their plan. The Colonel knew everything depended on Dorothy keeping her word; giving the baby to the circus couple he had found to adopt him or her.

Elvis Aaron Presley, Jr. is Born

On a snowy, Christmas Eve morning, December 24, 1961, Dorothy Lee Perrins gave birth to a beautiful little boy at an undisclosed hospital in Gary, Indiana, not far from the great metropolis of Chicago. Immediately following the birth, when Dorothy gave up her son to the couple, her words to Anna and Jacob were simply, "Take special care of this boy. He belongs to Elvis." But would he resemble his father's likeness? Only time would tell, but Dorothy Harmonie really felt it was important she said something.

Colonel Parker did everything in his power to keep the secret; going so far as to bribe the local official at the hospital to have the names of the adoptive parents placed on the child's birth certificate and any information about Dorothy Lee Perrins or Dorothy Harmonie stricken from the hospital records. For all intents and purposes, Anna Stanic was the mother of record, with her husband Jacob as the child's father.

The conditions of the adoption were simple, and the young couple adhered to them. First, they were not to reveal, under any circumstances, the child's biological parents until the infant reached his 21st birthday. Second, they were to never seek any monetary compensation from the Presley family on behalf of the child. Parker paid them off and settled the hospital bill in cash, with a generous donation to all who had participated in the birth. He also offered Dorothy Perrins a huge sum of money to keep quiet, but she took only enough to replace her lost wages from the Flamingo and to catch a bus home.

With the adoption complete, the infant began life as Phillip Stanic surrounded by the glittering circus world. At the tender age of five, Elvis, Jr. first entered the spotlight as a circus clown being mentored by the likes of Blinko and Gene Randall. He later trained exotic cats, and by the age of fifteen was known as the youngest wild animal trainer in the world. Thanks to his unique skills, several of his cats were featured in television commercials and bit parts in movies, notably *The Cat People* (1982), opposite Natasha Kinski, and *Sahara* (1983), opposite Brooke Shields.

During this same time, he discovered he had a natural talent for singing and performing before a crowd. When Phillip reached the age of twenty-one, his parents told him the truth about his birth mother and father. On January 21, 1986, he applied for and was granted the legal right to bear the name Elvis Aaron Presley, Jr. by the Eighth Judicial Court of the State of Nevada. After sufficient documents, sworn testimonies, and additional evidence presented by independent third parties were presented to the Honorable Carl J. Christensen, a District

Court judge, Phillip Stanic was recognized as Elvis Aaron Presley, Jr. under the federal law of the United States. To this day, however, the Presley family has yet to embrace him as one of their own, and his story remains a a sad and controversial one.

The Love-Children of Elvis Presley

Dorothy Lee Perrins was true to her word. She never told anyone about her son until well after Elvis' death in 1977; she also never sought to profit from the brief affair she had with him. She truly loved Elvis Presley and made a huge sacrifice to protect his career from scandal and public humiliation. Over the years, many other women have come forward with their own claims about a love-child, each with hidden agendas involving fame and fortune. It's a story as old as Rock-n-Roll itself: Rock star has sex with groupie and blows town the next day, leaving her "knocked up." Actually, it's very likely the world has many people claiming to be the offspring of Elvis Presley, given his reputation for having been "nothin' but a hound-dog."

Over the years, like most Americans, I have watched the seemingly endless parade of impostors and fakes who have felt entitled to the Presley legacy with a great deal of skepticism. At the time of this writing, no fewer than four new women or their offspring had come forward with stories about being the son of Elvis Aaron Presley. Whether for riches or fame, a number of people have claimed to be the "love-child" or to have had the "love-child" of Elvis Presley. Some have claimed to be the King's son or daughter as the result of a one-night stand their mother had with Elvis. Some of these individuals seemed sincere in their beliefs, while others appeared to be simply seeking fortune and fame.

"Elvis was the most famous entertainer in the world. He loved women and wasn't faithful in his marriage or to his girlfriends," according to Presley historian Cory Cooper, who points out that people have been claiming to be Elvis Presley's love-child since before the King died. "But I don't think Elvis has three-dozen offspring scattered around the world." Possible, but not very likely.

In 2014, no fewer than four new women came forward with claims. Zona Marie Roach claimed her son, John Dennis Roach (aka John Smith), was born in July 1961, nine months after she had had a one-night stand with Elvis. They cited a Texas Department of Health birth certificate showing the birth father's name as Elvis A. Presley. Fifty-four-year-old Desiree Presley, a former Los Angeles model, claimed she had a twenty-four-year-long secret romance with the King, which her mother chronicled in the infamous Elvis tome *Are You Lonesome Tonight.* Deborah Presley Brando, a Hollywood extra who was married to Marlon Brando's late son, Christian, was back in the news, hoping to reverse a 1988 appeals court ruling. She claimed to be Elvis Presley's daughter and was entitled to half of the family estate. And Lisa Johansen, a forty-four-year-old Swedish woman, filed a $130-million lawsuit against the Presley estate for defamation and emotional distress, claiming she was "the real Lisa Marie Presley." Apparently, she had been forcibly exiled to Sweden after Elvis' death, and replaced by an impostor; a fake Lisa Marie who went on to marry Michael Jackson, among other things. Johansen's memoir, *I, Lisa Marie,* was scrapped after her publisher sued her for refusing to take a DNA test that would have proven the truth about her lineage.

"Why is everyone in such a rush to be Elvis' kid?" critic Serene Dominic, contributor to Creem and the New York Times, posed the question in a 2013 Internet article about Presley's love children. "It's not like millions of Elvis impersonators don't have that area well-covered. And it's not like Lisa Marie's career was helped any--and she's a legitimate heir!"

Elvis and the Women of Star Trek

Even before Angelique Pettyjohn beamed aboard the *Enterprise* in its second season as Shahna, the Drill

Thrall from the planet Triskelion, Elvis Presley had become a big fan of *Star Trek*. Though Elvis would never have been mistaken as a Trekkie, the show was more like his latest obsession in a long line of obsessions. According to a 2017 documentary for Sky Arts, titled "The Seven Ages of Elvis," the narrative revealed that Elvis would arrange his breaks and time-off to coincide with his watching the Thursday (and then later Friday) night airings of the series. In fact, he loved the show so much he named his horse "Star Trek." Later, while prepping for one of his tune-filled comedies, he made a big deal about welcoming Celeste Yarnell, who had been featured on a memorable *Star Trek*, to the set of *Live a Little, Love a Little* (1968) with a big hug, confessing, "I just couldn't wait to meet you. I knew you were coming. And I know you from *Star Trek*." Yarnell wasn't the first co-star to get such a warm welcome from the King of Rock-n-Roll. Elvis Presley especially liked all the beautiful women who appeared on the NBC television show, and found it easy to imagine himself in the role as Captain James T. Kirk, making love to one or more of them in the course of a 53-minute dramatic episode. Like Pettyjohn and Yarnell, nearly a dozen other actresses had appeared in key roles on *Star Trek* before making an appearance in an Elvis movie. Not surprisingly, they represented a who's who of up-and-coming, young starlets in Hollywood.

Laurel Goodwin (1942-), the child model-turned actress, made her film debut as Presley's leading lady Laurel Dodge in *Girls, Girls, Girls* (1962), but is best remembered as Yeoman Colt opposite Jeffrey Hunter's Christopher Pike in *Star Trek's* first pilot, "The Cage" which was incorporated into the two-part episode "The Menagerie." She was to have portrayed the Captain's Yeoman in the Pike-centric *Star Trek*, but when the pilot was not picked up, her character was dropped from the series. Like Goodwin, Julie Parrish (1940-2003) also played in *Star Trek's* only two-parter as Miss Piper. She didn't fare as well with Elvis as a love interest in *Paradise, Hawaiian Style* (1966). Nor did Mariana

Hill (1942-), a familiar character actress, who as Lani Kaimana chased the King all throughout *Paradise, Hawaiian Style* in a sexy-white negligee and heels. As Captain Kirk's former flame, Doctor Helen Noel in "Dagger of the Mind," their past romantic history may be the only thing that keeps her from ending up in a psycho ward. Of course, I'm sure it also helped that she was one of the 19 women Shatner kissed on the original *Star Trek.*

In addition to personally welcoming Celeste Yarnall to the set of *Live a Little, Love a Little* (1968), Elvis Presley was "giddy as a school boy" the day Emily Banks reported for rehearsal, too. Banks was born in Norfolk, Virginia, in 1933, and made the rounds to many of the most popular shows of the 1960s. On *Star Trek's* "Shore Leave," Banks as Yeoman Tonia Barrows traded her mini-skirted, Starfleet uniform for that of a Fairy Princess who is first threatened by Don Juan, then later romanced by Dr. McCoy (DeForest Kelley). Yarnall acted in another *Trek* favorite, titled "The Apple." As Yeoman Martha Landon, she is romanced by an overly-amorous Ensign Chekov (Walter Koenig). In the same episode, Shari Nims from *Easy Come, Easy Go* (1967) is scantily-clad as a primitive girl who worships the pagan god Vol with her people. Nancy Kovak played yet another primitive, Nona, in "A Private Little War," enslaving Kirk with her witchcraft, while she was featured player in "Frankie and Johnny" (1966).

Tanya Lemani (1945-), an Iranian-born Russian dancer, belly-dances in both *Trek's* "Wolf in the Fold" (as Kara) and Elvis's 1968 Comeback Special. Plucked from her ballet class at age 16, Tanya worked alongside Angelique Pettyjohn at the Flamingo. Yvonne Craig (1937-2015), the original Batgirl, performed in the ballet in Monte Carlo before appearing on television and movies. Her training as a dancer pays off as Marta, the green Orion slave girl, in *Trek's* "Whom Gods Destroy," while she takes a vacation day with Elvis in *It Happened at the World's Fair.* (1963).

Both Terri Garr and Angelique Pettyjohn appeared in *Clambake* after their individual turns on *Star Trek*. Garr who was featured in six Elvis movies, including *Viva Las Vegas* and *Kissin' Cousins* (1968), was a favorite of the King. He tried to fit her in whenever he could. On *Star Trek*, Garr played the adorable but ditsy Roberta Lincoln who goes to work for Gary-7 (Robert Lansing) in the proposed *Trek* spin-off "Assignment Earth." She later surfaced in Mel Brooks' *Young Frankenstein* (1974) and Steven Spielberg's *Close Encounters of the Third Kind* (1977). As for Angelique, well...

***Clambake* (1967)**

She met Elvis as Dorothy Harmonie (aka Dorothy Lee Perrins), and her connection to Elvis simply would not have been complete without revealing what happened after she gave birth to his son. Unlike so many of the other women in Elvis' life, she never sought to profit from her situation. She gave the Colonel back nearly everything he wanted her to take, except for a few dollars for a bus ticket and money to cover her lost wages at the Flamingo. But it actually cost her a great deal more than lost time.

When she left the hospital in Gary, Indiana, in 1961, Dorothy soon discovered she was incapable of having any more children. The doctors had performed a procedure on her, without her knowledge, rendering her sterile. Now, whether it happened under direct orders from the Colonel or was part of a deliberate plan to target unwed mothers and curb the epidemic of teenage pregnancies, we'll never know. Dorothy returned to her life as a showgirl, and when she had earned enough money to attend college, she returned to Salt Lake City and enrolled in the theatre arts program at the local community college to earn an Associate of Arts degree.

Ironically, six years later, she appeared in the movie *Clambake* (1967), Elvis Presley's twenty-fifth movie, in her biggest role thus far as Bill

Bixby's girlfriend Gloria. She was supposed to have played Presley's love interest, Dianne Carter, and Shelley Fabares was hired to play Gloria. But when Colonel Tom Parker learned that Pettyjohn had been hired for the production, he feared that she might say something about the child to Elvis. Parker met with Lynn Stalmaster, the casting director, and producers Arthur Gardner, Arnold Laven, and Jules Levy, and convinced them all to switch the two girls around. He said he thought Elvis had better chemistry with Fabares. Whenever the Colonel interceded in a production, everyone listened and agreed with his decisions. Fabares got the showier role, and even though she was disappointed, Angelique played the role of Gloria.

Billed as Angelique Pettyjohn, Elvis didn't remember the eighteen-year-old showgirl that he met so many years earlier when they were re-introduced. Dorothy Lee Perrins would have been devastated, but as Angelique Pettyjohn, she was not the least bit surprised. The much worldlier actress

Figure 26. Poster for *Clambake* (1967).

had already learned to stay clear of parties during production, and subsequently earned high praise from Director Arthur Nadel for her professionalism during filming. She also kept her word to Colonel Parker and never said a word to Elvis Presley about the child she had birthed and given up for adoption. She considered the matter closed, part of a completely different life.

Clambake (1967) was a tuneful, light-hearted romp that resembled one of American International Pictures' lightweight beach party movies, like *Beach Party* (1963), *Muscle Beach Party* (1964), or *Beach Blanket Bingo* (1965), but was a far cry from earlier Elvis films, like *Jailhouse Rock* (1957) or *King Creole* (1958), his personal favorite, that had been made a decade earlier. The plot was fairly predictable: Elvis Presley plays Scott Heyward, a millionaire playboy and heir to an oil fortune who's tired of women fawning all over him because of his wealth. When he meets Tom Wilson (Will Hutchins), who's on his way to start a new job as a water-ski instructor at a posh Miami Beach resort, the two agree to swap lives. Tom gets to enjoy all the perks of being wealthy, while the real millionaire Scott works hard as a water-ski instructor, and even finds time to tinker together a speedboat to race in the Orange Bowl Regatta. He's very determined to see if girls will like him for himself, rather than his father's money. One girl in particular, Dianne Carter (Shelley Fabares), is out to marry rich and has her sights on James J. Jamison III (Bill Bixby), a wealthy young playboy who plans to enter his own boat, *The Scarlet Lady*, in the race. She has no real interest in the "poor" Scott, so he sets out to make her fall for him before she finds out the truth. Angelique played "kooky" Gloria, a wannabee singer and one of the denizens at a swanky hotel who, along with the other female guests, flip for rich playboy Tom. Scott's father, Duster (James Gregory), blows a gasket when he finds out what his son is doing, but ultimately, he agrees to keep silent, very proud of his son's actions. With all of the bikini-clad, rock-n-roll cuties on hand, it doesn't take too much of a stretch to figure out that Scott beats Jamison in the race, wins the hand of lovely Dianne, and lives happily ever after.

Figures 27 & 28. Angelique Pettyjohn is featured on two of the lobby cards from *Clambake* (1967) .

Though set in Miami, most of the scenes were shot on the West Coast. It's truly amusing watching for the various goofs in geographical location, such as having the sun set over the beach when clearly it is impossible as the sun rises in the East over Miami Beach. At one point, when Presley drives Diane to the Miami airport and professes his true love for her, audience members can see mountains over his shoulder — mountains, real "Florida mountains." Similarly, the palm-fringed shores and the Biscayne skyline are superimposed over the race scenes, with lots of wide-angle shots of Elvis Presley's double driving the boat. The playground sequence, in which Presley sings "Confidence" to a group of children, was also shot in Los Angeles with child actor Corbin Bernsen in a small walk-on role as one of the kids at the playground. Lee Majors, still years away from playing Colonel Steve Austin on *The Six Million-Dollar Man* (1974), can be seen in the background of the restaurant scene, wearing a fake mustache.

Shortly after the production ended, on May 1, 1967, Elvis Presley married Priscilla Beaulieu in a private ceremony amongst a small group of family and friends at the Aladdin Hotel in Las Vegas, Nevada. The two had met in Germany, when Elvis was still in the Army, and Priscilla was just fourteen-years-old. They had enjoyed a seven-and-a-half-year courtship. The couple honeymooned in Palm Springs, and nine months later (to the day) after her marriage to Elvis, Priscilla gave birth to Lisa Marie Presley, the King's only acknowledged child.

Clambake premiered October 18, 1967 to a lukewarm box office and horrible reviews. One critic called the film a "silly, tired little frolic," remarking "even staunch Presley admirers will have to strain to justify this one." *Clambake* was the last of his four films he did for United Artists.

Elvis Presley had hoped a successful film would help relieve some of his financial problems, but Clambake actually underperformed in its ticket sales. By 1967, he was so much indebt, due to his purchase of a Memphis ranch with all updated sound and recording equipment, that Colonel Parker had been told to sign a contract not only guaranteeing Elvis' one-million-dollar fee but also a percentage of the box office so that he would not default on any of his loans. This was the last time Presley was offered a million dollars for a movie role by any of the major studios. To make matters worse, while shooting *Clambake*, Elvis suffered a serious fall in his bathroom at home, tripping over an electrical cord and striking his head on the porcelain edge of a bathtub. The resultant injury was serious enough that Presley lay unconscious for an unknown length of time and was briefly hospitalized. The pain-killers he was prescribed to relieve the massive headaches and other effects of his injuries began the drug dependency that was partially blamed for his death a decade later.

Elvis Presley died ten years later, at age forty-two.

Tuesday, August 16, 1977, Angelique Pettyjohn learned Elvis had passed away in his Memphis mansion, Graceland, alone, with his fiancee Ginger Alden and family nearby. Like most Americans, she had heard it on a radio news-flash in the afternoon. She was between gigs, and didn't have a lot of time to process the information until later that night when she spoke with Bill Bixby, her co-star from *Clambake*, on the phone. Then, Angelique remembered crying for hours into the night. She still loved him, and wondered how different their lives might have been had she told Elvis, and not his manager, she was pregnant with his son. Would he have married her, instead of Priscilla, and would the public have accepted her? Their child?

A couple of days later, Angelique flew to Memphis, and joined 100,000 other mourners as they passed through the gates of Graceland for a public viewing of "The King's" body. Other than brief clips of him on television, she had not seen him since *Clambake.* She looked down at his gentle face, and cried, remembering the young, innocent girl she once was and the sweet kisses he gave her. Pettyjohn had come a long way since then, and while beautiful memories of Elvis from that night would continue to haunt her dreams, she never stopped looking for him in all the other men...she dared to love.

3
The Casting Couch

The "casting couch" was very real. Unless you had sex with the casting director or producer of the show, you were unlikely to get the part. There were so many beautiful women in Hollywood that it was a foregone conclusion that talent had little to do with casting. You gave into their advances or you didn't work. It was as simple as that.

After having worked in Las Vegas as a showgirl and stripper for a couple of years, Dorothy Perrins returned to Salt Lake City to study theatre arts at the local community college. She found the living arrangements at home with her mother, stepfather, and two half-sisters an intolerable one for many reasons, not the least of which was the way they pried into her private life. Dorothy chose to leave what happened in Las Vegas back in Vegas and vowed never to speak about what she had done to secure a better future for herself. She soon moved out of her parent's home and took a small apartment in the City.

With all the money she needed to pay for her education, she focused on her studies, and the two years she spent at Salt Lake Community College zipped right on by. Not only did she learn acting, but she also developed a knack for stage craft as well, designing and building sets, creating mood with lights, and designing and sewing costumes, which she had actually done growing up. Dorothy had considered staying another year or two to earn her college teaching degree and work as an adjunct in the theatre arts department, but the desire to become an actress overpowered all other avenues to success. She felt confident if she returned to Las Vegas or embarked on a career in Hollywood, she had what it took to make it. Yet as the voices in her head continued to tell her she "was no good," she struggled to keep them silent by drinking, often to excess. She also developed other dependencies as well.

Las Vegas, 1964 - 1965

At age twenty-one, Dorothy Perrins returned to Las Vegas in March 1964 and picked right back up where she had left off, working as a showgirl. Her first gig was Barry Ashton's *Vive Paris Vive* at the Aladdin. Ashton, English by birth, was a legendary dancer who earned the chance to start staging and producing his shows from the owner of the El Rancho Vegas, Beldon Katleman. He went on to produce more than 100 shows and revues across the United States and around the world, emphasizing burlesque and feminine beauty. But his most famous show was *Vive Paris Vive*, featuring the Barry Ashton Dancers. Dorothy Lee wanted to earn a spot among those dancers, practicing her dance steps every afternoon, sometimes two to three hours every day for several weeks at a time. Later, she went to work at Harold Minsky's *The Wonderful World of Burlesque* at the Silver Slipper Gambling Hall and Saloon, but again as a showgirl, not a dancer. The goal of becoming a dancer in a hit Las Vegas revue remained ever elusive to her.

About a year later, Dorothy Perrins auditioned for the role of a showgirl in what was touted to be the biggest and most elaborate show on the Las Vegas strip, *Ziegfeld's Follies*, at the Thunderbird Hotel and Casino. Inspired by the *Folies Bergère* of Paris and the lavish revues staged by Florenz Ziegfeld, Jr. in New York City in the twenties and thirties, the *Ziegfeld Follies* was conceived and mounted by Monte Proser, an up-and-comer who had started with Harold Minsky. The gigantic production boasted the most beautiful chorus girls, in line with what Florenz Ziegfeld, Jr. had offered thirty-five years earlier, and featured some of the most elaborate costumes by designers such as Erte, Lady Duff Gordon, and Ben Ali Haggin. The show was true to its hype. The hottest ticket on the Las Vegas Strip. Nearly everyone in town wanted to see it. With top-flight entertainment, like Frank Sinatra and his Rat Pack, Liberace, George Burns, Jerry Lewis, and Tom Jones, Las Vegas had become the Broadway of the West. Dorothy got picked from among the hundreds of showgirls wanting to be in the show, and she made the most of her good fortune, delivering her best twice nightly and three times on Saturday.

In his April 15, 1965 article "Vegas Is Still a Gamble," newspaper columnist Buck Herzog wrote: "The girls in the chorus of *Ziegfeld's Follies* are the most beautiful in the world, and have the saddest laughing lips. Nudity no longer draws protests in this community of 55,000 citizens and seventy church groups. The girls are so beautiful only a square could complain about their lack of clothing."

Dorothy Perrins started to grow impatient as her nine-month anniversary in the show drew closer. She had made some good money in the production and had managed to put most of it away as a cushion for those lean months when she might not be working as regularly. She was really anxious to head out to California in order to stake out her acting career. Then finally one morning, after wrestling with her decision all night long, she decided to go. She gave her notice at the front office of the *Follies*, packed her bags, and bought a one-way bus ticket for Los Angeles. Several of her fellow showgirls tried to talk her out of going; one friend even arranged for a meeting for Dorothy with Joseph W. Sarno (1921-2010), one of the most prolific and distinctive auteurs of low-budget sexploitation movies. He tried to convince her to stay in Vegas and make a movie with him, but she had her sights set higher on doing real Hollywood films. She declined his offer, but decided to keep his business card, just in case things didn't work out for her. Naïve, little Dorothy Lee Perrins was headed back home to the bright lights of Los Angeles and the dream factory, known as Hollywood.

Hollywood and the Casting Couch

In the sixties, the casting couch was still, regrettably, very much a part of the motion picture industry. A relic of the Golden Age of Hollywood, it had survived the break-down of the studio system in the fifties, the emergence of television as a viable, alternative entertainment medium, the abandonment of the Hayes code, and the dawning of the sexual revolution. The term "casting couch" had originated in the thirties, as a specific reference to the number of couches in Hollywood offices used for sexual activity between casting directors or film producers and aspiring actresses. It was not to be confused with the slowly emerging adult entertainment industry in which such actions were considered a normal prerequisite of work. In a town where most everyone was willing to sell their body and soul for fame and fortune, the casting couch mentality saw actors, especially women, as little more than a market commodity. Such trading of favors was not considered an abuse of power at the time, even though clearly it was a form of sexual harassment and was rarely

Figure 29. "The Road to Hollywood." Erika Rothenberg's satirical take on The Casting Couch at Hollywood & Highland.

Figure 30. Playfully, Angelique makes fun of the Casting Couch in the photo, even though it was a reality to most young starlets.

(if ever) reported by the women manipulated and often humiliated by those in the front offices of the motion picture industry. Most people within Hollywood simply turned a blind eye, chalking the practice up as a normal part of conducting business. Acknowledged publicly, no, and it never became a subject deemed newsworthy by the press.

Long before Harvey Weinstein and the "Me-Too Movement," Louis B. Mayer, co-founder of Metro-Goldwyn-Mayer (MGM) studios in 1924, Harry Cohn at Columbia Pictures, Jack Warner at Warner Brothers, and many others had built their own dream factories brick by brick and believed they deserved certain perks. As the men in charge, they routinely preyed upon their young starlets. If the women refused to comply to their sexual advances, they'd threaten to ruin their careers or the careers of their loved ones. In one memorable instance, Mayer chased Jean Howard around his office for sex. She said, "No way," and went off to marry agent Charles K. Feldman. To get even with Howard, Mayer then refused to hire any of Feldman's clients to work at MGM. He also allegedly groped teenage Judy Garland and made her sit on his lap routinely for meetings during the making of *The Wizard of Oz* (1939). Trading liaisons for opportunities to appear on the silver screen continued into the forties, fifties, and sixties…and even today!

The most famous actress of the day, Marilyn Monroe, had shared more than one casting couch with a director or producer on her way up the ladder to international fame. Dubbed one of the earliest "bimbos" in the fifties — on the production lot, the term "bimbo" stood for "body immaculate, brains optional" — the luscious blonde bombshell submitted to the casting couch as a way to propel her from plain Norma Jean Mortenson to Hollywood icon. She dismissed the trading of sex for stardom pragmatically as "no big tragedy; nobody ever got cancer from sex" and added she had "slept with producers. I'd be a liar if I said I didn't." Monroe was not only passed from man to man, but famously from president to playwright to center fielder. In her memoir, Monroe wrote heartbreakingly, "I met them all. Phoniness and failure were all over them. Some were vicious and crooked, but they were as near to the movies as you could get. So, you sat with them, listening to their lies and schemes. And you saw Hollywood with their eyes — an overcrowded brothel, a merry-go-round with beds for horses." When 20th Century-Fox awarded Monroe the richest contract of any actress in 1955, she triumphantly declared, "It means I'll never have to suck another dick again!"

The freedom of a big Hollywood contract, the carrot on a stick every actress sought, enabled Marilyn Monroe to say "no," even to the heads of Hollywood's biggest studios. She stood up to the likes of Darryl F. Zanuck at Fox and Harry Cohn at Columbia Pictures. Studio chief Zanuck, well known for his exploits, was often famously "in conference" with a number of aspiring actresses between 4:00 p.m. and 4:30 p.m. As the story goes, one would-be starlet, shown innocently into his office, was rather shocked to find him half naked (from the waist down) and ready for action. Cohn, who most likely invented the casting couch during his long tenure at Columbia, had a secret annex to his office built so he could meet privately with actresses he thought about signing. In a conversation she had with Joan Collins, Marilyn Monroe revealed a particularly unpleasant experience she had with the notoriously lecherous Harry Cohn. Apparently, Cohn had invited Monroe on an overnight cruise on his yacht where she was required to strip naked for him. But when she declined his forward advances, Monroe recalled, "I had never seen a man so angry."

Figure 31. Marilyn Monroe's famous pose from *The Seven Year Itch* (1955).

Contemporaries of Marilyn Monroe, like Joan Collins, Jayne Mansfield, Mamie Van Doren, Elizabeth Taylor and Angelique Pettyjohn who was being groomed to be the next Marilyn Monroe, were not as fortunate as Monroe and had to face the lascivious "wolves" of Hollywood nearly every time they sought a part.

*Ffolliott "*Fluff*"* LeCoque (1923-2015), the grand-dame of Las Vegas entertainment and a personal friend of Dorothy Perrins, had also dreamt for many years of going to Hollywood, and finally sought out a post-war career on the silver screen. During her stay there, Fluff planned to use her dancing skills to make a living, while trying to get a job in the movies. However, even though Fluff had movie-star good looks, she was considered a little too short and too muscular to make it as an actress, so her movie career didn't last long.

She was up for the part of Jane in the new *Tarzan* movie series, starring Lex Barker. The casting director, after looking at her photos, told her to stand up and turn around so he could admire her assets. He said, "I see you're a dancer. Well, how would you like to teach me how to dance?" Wink, wink! From which, she replied, "I think you should try out for the part of the gorilla," and then walked out. Needless to say, Fluff didn't get the part and found herself returning to the Las Vegas Strip to work another sixty years in the entertainment business as a dancer in top-flight revues. She warned many of the girls, including Dorothy, about the casting couch.

In her autobiography, Joan Collins revealed she had had her own notorious run-ins with producers and casting directors, but the worst turned out to be her clash with Darryl F. Zanuck when she was up for the lead in *Cleopatra*, the 1963 epic film which eventually went to Elizabeth Taylor. "I just refused to go to bed with the head of the studio. I had tested for *Cleopatra* twice and was the frontrunner. One day, he [Zanuck] took me into his office and said, 'You really want this part?' And I said, 'Yes. I really do.' 'Well,' he said, 'then all you have to do is be nice to me.' It was a wonderful euphemism in the sixties for 'you know what.' But I couldn't do that. I just acted rather wimpish. I burst into tears and rushed out of his office. What I should have done was kick him in the balls." Not surprisingly, when she refused to sleep with Zanuck, he banished her from "A" pictures. Though she remained under contract at 20th Century-Fox, Joan Collins struggled in "B" pictures, making *Seven Thieves* (1960), *The Road to Hong Kong* (1962), and *Hard Time for Princes* (1962). She then languished in television during the sixties and seventies, doing bit roles on *Batman*, *Mission Impossible*, and *Star Trek*. In 1981, Collins landed the plum role of Alexis Carrington Colby on the nighttime soap opera *Dynasty*, winning a Golden Globe Award for Best Actress in 1982. But she was one of the lucky ones. Although there are no recorded statistics, most actresses in the sixties who refused to lay down on the casting couch found themselves packing their bags for home.

As Dorothy Lee Perrins set her sights on Hollywood, seeking fame and fortune, she recalled what Fluff and several other showgirls had told her about the reality of the casting couch as it related to the motion picture industry, and by extension, television. She had also heard rumors about the proverbial girl from the Midwest with the pretty face who, instead of being invited for an audition in the morning, was summoned for a late afternoon tryst on the producer's couch, and she honestly didn't know how she'd handle the situation if it happened to her. Then, on one of her first calls for a small walk-on part in a movie, she was told the audition was being held on a Saturday night at the casting director's home in Los Angeles. Still somewhat naïve, Dorothy thought maybe it was a normal thing, never suspecting a thing. But when the pajama-clad man answered his door and told her to get down on her knees to orally gratify him, she panicked and ran away. She left him standing dumbfounded at the front door of his house with a cocktail in his hand and his pajama pants down around his ankles.

"I was pretty shocked," Pettyjohn recollected, saying she could see how someone who didn't know any better might worry their career would be ruined if they didn't perform a specific sex act. "I was very naïve in those days, and even though I had heard all the stories about other girls, I never thought it would happen to me. I just didn't know what I would do, and worst of all, I worried he'd report me, then I'd never get a chance to do another audition." Thankfully, the casting director never said a word, leaving Dorothy back in the mix looking desperately for work.

Figure 32. The Famous Hollywood Sign..

On her next audition, Dorothy Perrins agreed to a friendly dinner with a famous producer who shall remain unnamed (at her request). "I had no interest in a romantic relationship at all with him," she remembered; had made that clear to him. All the same, she was in awe of the man's talent and happy to discuss possible roles with him. He had won several Academy Awards for producing some highly-regarded films and was considered a legend in the business. He was an older man, happily married with a beautiful wife and family. Of all the men in the business, she felt pretty safe meeting him for dinner at one of the top restaurants in Hollywood. She knew an alliance with him would have been hugely helpful to her career. So, Dorothy Lee was very trusting when he invited her after dinner to stop by his office on the studio lot, where he had a stack of scripts to show her. Once the door to his office shut, he grabbed her breasts, stuck his tongue down her throat, and pulled at her dress, like some kind of "madman," trying to tear it literally off her body. Thinking quickly, she held him off by claiming she needed to use the restroom, and once she had gotten clear of his office, Dorothy ran off the studio lot in her bare feet. "I never told anybody that story," she explained to me, "because he was such an important person in the industry. And also, I was ashamed with myself for falling for his act."

One of the worst of Dorothy Perrins' entire casting couch nightmares happened when she auditioned for a newly-married Hollywood star who was branching out as a producer and director on his next film. She felt she had done a good job with her audition; fit the small role as if it had been written for her. So, when the star's secretary came into his office with a document that appeared to be a contract, Dorothy felt pretty confident she had gotten the part. Then she looked over the document. It wasn't a contract to appear in the movie at all, but rather a bizarre kind of sex contract with him that he encouraged her to sign; one outlining the kind of sexual acts he expected her to perform, and when and where and how often she was to meet him. There was also a confidentiality clause demanding her absolute discretion in all things related to a sexual liaison with him. In exchange for signing the document, she was guaranteed the occasional walk-on role or cameo in the star's next three pictures, and a salary paid for her exclusivity.

"I just thought, 'Oh my God, your poor wife,'" Angelique recalled years after the fact. "Well, I didn't want to be a marriage-wrecker, and there was no way I was going to sign a sex contract with him or any other man for that matter." Dorothy tore the contract into shreds, left them on his desk, and walked out of his office without saying a word. Ironically, she later met the actress who had agreed to his terms and felt bad for her. The roles this fellow actress got were "shitty" and her career never went anywhere. She realized she had made the right choice after all. Thank God.

Her worst experience, however, happened several weeks later. At a night club, after Dorothy Perrins was approached by an award-winning actor she liked and found "devastatingly" handsome, she agreed to go back to his hotel room to "discuss scripts." She knew they were not really going to his place to discuss a movie script, but she had finally made up her mind to do whatever it took to get a job, even if it meant sleeping with him. The problem was the actor was an S&M freak, something she knew absolutely nothing about and could not have imagined in any of her worst nightmares. When they got to his hotel room, things took an ugly turn. He handcuffed her to the bed post, ripped her clothes off, and started beating her with a cat-of-nine-tails whip. Dorothy started crying out for help, but no one heard her cries, and her cries actually incensed him as a sadist to keep it up. He then raped and sodomized her over the next few hours, under the pretense that her cries were part of their mutual sado-masochistic play. When he was finally finished with her, Dorothy Lee crawled out of his hotel room, her clothes literally in tatters, and hailed a cab for home.

She never reported the rape to anyone, for fear of reprisals, but she decided if that was the best she could expect from Hollywood, she might as well get paid for doing sexploitation movies for Joe Sarno. For after all, what was the casting couch? Nothing more than a way to exploit female actresses for sex. She wanted to scream at the top of her lungs, but there was no one there to hear her.

Sexploitation

The adult film industry that came into its own in the seventies with the releases of *Deep Throat* (1972) and *The Devil in Miss Jones* (1973) was preceded in many ways by a series of motion pictures pushing the boundaries of the Hays Code restrictions of the depictions of nudity and sex on film. Cautionary films from the thirties and forties were the first of these featuring lurid subject matter, but evaded the strict censorship and scrutiny of the era by claiming to be educational. They were considered "cautionary" tales because they warned audiences about the alleged dangers of premarital sexual intercourse or the use of recreational drugs. But while they appeared to be on the side of decency and conservative American values, they were actually subversive works celebrating their subject matter. *Reefer Madness* (1938), *Sex Madness* (1938), and *She Shoulda Said No!* (1949) were among the first and most popular of these kinds of films exploiting women and sex.

The next of these pictures were known as "nudies" or nudist films. Nudist films skirted the Hays Code by purportedly depicting the naturalist lifestyle in the form of educational films shot at nudist camps, featuring mostly beautiful female residents free and unencumbered by clothing in a very natural setting. But since nudity in and of itself was not considered obscene, the producers of the films exploited their naked female subjects in a subversive way no one considered obscene. *Garden of Eden* (1950) was typical of these low-budget, black-and-white films, in which viewers were treated to endless scenes of nudists playing volleyball, nudists practicing archery, nudist performing on the accordion, and nudists doing pretty much everything except having sex. In the context of an educational film, it was acceptable to depict beautiful women showing off their floppy, bouncing breasts or wiggling their fleshy behinds on the big screen, but the moment any suggestion of sex entered the picture, it was considered obscene.

Nudies were soon supplanted by "roughies" in the next step of the evolution of adult cinema. The nudies were fairly innocent films, depicting a nudist lifestyle, but roughies were exploitative films commonly featuring extreme violence against women, such as kidnapping, rape, dismemberment, and murder. Sexual content was still pretty tame by today's standards, but there was enough going on in them about good girls, bad girls, and good-girls-gone-bad to sustain the interest of sexually-repressed Middle America, still years away from the sexual revolution.

Scum of the Earth! (1963) by Herschel Gordon Lewis was thought to be the first roughie, although *Lorna* (1964) by Russ Meyer established much of the criteria used today when describing the genre. Typical stories featured wives forced into prostitution or wives forced to kill their rapists. Most "roughies," like the "nudies" preceded by them, were shot with 16mm hand-held cameras that were perpetually moving, and featured low-low production values. Add an element of sex or nudity, combine rudiments from violent action films, and the producers had low budget films that could be pitched directly to the old burlesque houses or drive-in theater market.

And finally, there were the sexploitation movies, considered the earliest attempts at softcore pornography, in which the film served largely as a vehicle for showing scenes involving nude or semi-nude women. Many of the later ones also contained vivid sex scenes, yet the sex was often simulated; still quite graphic with full frontal nudity and overextended sequences containing nothing but elaborate sex scenes that went on a bit longer than they should. Combining elements from the nudies, the cautionary tales, and the "roughies" to create a unique genre of film, sexploitations played strictly to an all-male audience who enjoyed watching naked women, often in perilous situations. Russ Meyer's work was probably the best-known example of sexploitation, with films such as *Faster, Pussycat! Kill! Kill!* (1965) and *Vixen!* (1968). [Recently, Quentin Tarantino and Robert Rodriguez paid tribute to the "roughies" of the past, with their double feature grindhouse movie, *Death Proof* and *Planet Terror* (2007).]

Sexploitation films initially played in the defunct burlesque theaters on 42nd Street in New York, where "bump-n-grind" dancing and striptease had all but disappeared everywhere, except Las Vegas. The first of these theaters were known as grindhouse theaters, and gradually the term grindhouse came to be interchangeable with sexploitation. However, by the end of the decade, these films that had developed an air of respectability were now actually playing in established cinema chains. As the genre continued to develop under creative directors, like Doris Wishman, the sixties films began showing scenes of simulated sex. These became known as the "chesties," and were meant to deliver graphic titillation that the roughies could never really do.

Initially, Dorothy Perrins was to have headlined a few of these new films, but she had turned her sights on more legitimate motion pictures. So, a Polish stripper, Chesty Morgan, known for her very large breasts, became the lead in *Deadly Weapons* (1973) and *Double Agent 73* (1974), the first of the "chesties" no doubt named after her. The films were boycotted by religious groups and slapped with an X-rating by the Motion Picture Association of America, which considered these sexploitation films obscene.

Customers attending the screenings of sexploitation films were likened to deviant "dirty old men" who wore raincoats and flashed women. [Ironically, several high-profile movies made about the same time earned X-ratings and yet still went on to compete for Academy Awards and the Best Films of the Year — notably *Midnight Cowboy* (1969), which won Best Picture, *A Clockwork Orange* (1971), and *Last Tango in Paris* (1972)].

One of the most prolific producer-directors of the sexploitation films was Joseph W. Sarno. He was one of the few directors who truly believed in the redemptive power of both the cinema and of sex. A man of the Greatest Generation, he took his camera with him during the Second World War and filmed bombing raids over the South Pacific. Upon his return, he blasted away the post-war mores and set the stage for the sexual revolution starting to rear its head with the publication of *Playboy* and the films of Marilyn Monroe. Between 1961 and 1983, he wrote and directed approximately seventy-five feature films that were released theatrically in small art-houses, grindhouse theatres, or drive-ins across the United States. Most were very crude, shot on black-and-white film or video, and had distinctly low production values. They all delved deeply into the dark heart of sexual desire by looking behind the door of Middle America and discovering the secrets of suburbia. All of his movies turned a profit many times over when compared with the cost to produce them. His best-known films in the genre were *Sin in the Suburbs* (1964), *Flesh and Lace*, and *The Swap and How They Make It* (both in 1965), and *Moonlighting Wives* (1966). It was very easy to tell the difference between Sarno's films and those being made by his closest competitor Russ Meyer. Sarno's films were always characterized by their stark lighting, long takes, rigorous staging, and his scenarios always centered around psycho-sexual identity, featuring lots of nudity and sex, predicting the emergence of the softcore pornographic film.

The Love Rebellion (1965)

In 1965, Joe Sarno met with Dorothy Perrins, and convinced her, eventually, to make a sexploitation film, *The Love Rebellion*. During her negotiations with him, she abandoned the name Dorothy Harmony, and adopted the stage name Angelique in an effort to spare her family any embarrassment from the work she had chosen to do. Both her parents were still alive, although she had lost complete touch with her father, two half-sisters, and step-brother. The perfect subject for Joe Sarno's sexual landscape, she represented an innocent from the suburbs that just happened to look like a blonde bombshell, with a 38-24-36 physique. Clothing optional.

> *I was never bothered by doing on-screen nudity at all in the past because I was very proud of my body. I had a beautiful body and I felt that if "the Force" or God — whatever you call the energy that's running the universe — didn't mean for me to share the beauty of my body with the rest of the world, He wouldn't have given it to me. She wouldn't have. It wouldn't have. So, I was always proud of my body and I wasn't ashamed to be nude. When Hustler and some of the other magazines started to go where nudity meant "spread-eagle," to me that lost the beauty or realm of the art. I wouldn't want to pose for that type of picture in magazines or anything of that sort. But I don't mind nudity.*

The Love Rebellion (1965) was produced by Donald Havens, distributed by Cannon Film Distributors, and directed by Joseph W. Sarno. The film starred Angelique, Melissa Ford, Alan

Figure 33. Poster for *The Love Rebellion* (1965).

Hoff, Jeremy Langham, Nick Linkov, and Gretchen Rudolph (using the name Ginger Stevens). The simple plot followed the sexual escapades of a young woman as she gradually came into her own. After she drops out of school, the young Wendy

Fletcher (Stevens) returns to her mother Jo (Melissa Ford) and immediately begins to work in the family business. In order to make new acquaintances, Wendy accepts the invitation to a party from her colleague at work. The timid Wendy knows nothing of the wild sex orgies happening at the party in her colleague's apartment, so is initially appalled by what she sees. One of the girls she meets there, Pam Carpenter (Angelique), takes an interest in her, and helps to show Wendy around and introduce her to some of the men. Eventually, Wendy takes a liking to the extravagant sex lifestyle. Shot in 1965, as the seeds of free love were being sewn by the counterculture movement of the sixties, *The Love Rebellion* anticipates the sexual revolution. Critics regarded the film as a good, sometimes engaging, middle-of-the-road motion picture that, while not great or particularly challenging or inspired, was still satisfying to watch, all the same. Not surprisingly, censors first banned the movie, then passed it in 1967 after it had been heavily edited. The revised film was seventeen minutes shorter than the banned version. The cuts included two scenes involving a striptease and two scenes featuring an orgy.

Dorothy Perrins, now Angelique, earned her first screen credit for the role of Pamela Carpenter in *The Love Rebellion*, while the praise-worthy reviews seemed to single out Gretchen Rudolph (who as Ginger Stevens played the lead, Wendy), most male audiences couldn't take their eyes off the practically-perfect figure (at 38-24-36) of Perrins naked, in all her glory. The exposure was a bit more than what she had anticipated, considering, as a showgirl, Dorothy danced topless every night. But at least in her first role as an actress, she was the center of attention. Joe Sarno had nothing but praise for her first outing on film, complementing her professional, hard-working attitude on the set. He later introduced Angelique to the famous Doris Wishman (1912-2002), the legendary female producer constantly pushing the boundaries of art and decency.

2 Films for Doris Wishman

All of the producers and directors making cheap sexploitation films in the sixties were male — Sarno, Russ Meyer, Don

Edmonds, Herschel Gordon Lewis, and many others. So, when Doris Wishman, the cousin of Max Rosenberg, who founded the British Horror company Amicus Productions, first appeared on the scene, she caused quite a stir. She had studied acting in college and worked as a booking agent for movies, learning the various venues that worked best for the different genres of films. She had a very creative eye and was determined to make sexploitation films that were not just simply grindhouse movies.

For her first feature, *Hideout in the Sun* (1959), Wishman borrowed $10,000 from her sister, Pearl Kushner, and shot a nudist camp documentary a cut above the rest, actually classy. The movie's success allowed Doris to repay her sister the money she borrowed with enough left over to make eight more "nudies." Her next film, *Nude on the Moon* (1960), used science fiction to depict two astronauts landing on a remarkably lush lunar surface only to find a civilization of naked women communicating telepathically with one another through headbands with spring antennae. While banned in New York with no educational value, it showcased Wishman's creative work behind the camera.

Her follow-up film, *Blaze Starr Goes Nudist* (1962), featured the legendary burlesque performer, Blaze Starr, in a funny, poignant, and thoroughly revealing movie. Angelique, actually a fan of Starr, liked how it portrayed the world of burlesque in Las Vegas. Wishman continued to make films featuring nude women, releasing one or two a year, for the next few years. Then as the popularity of the nudie features started to wane, she turned her attention to making sexploitation films far superior to those produced by her male counterparts.

Laboring under the male pseudonym, "Louis Silverman," Doris made the first of her sexploitation films. *Bad Girls Go to Hell* (1965), considered one of the finest early examples of the genre, featured Gigi Darlene, Harold Key, George La Rocque, Standee Norman, Darlene Bennett, Barnard L. Sackett, Marlene Starr, Sam Stewart, and Angelique in an uncredited role. This was her first collaboration (of two) with Angelique who liked Wishman's style. Unfortunately, Angelique's time in front of the camera in both movies amounted to little more than a cameo walk-in at a party and in the second film as a hooker in a dream sequence.

In *Bad Girls Go to Hell*, Ellen Green (Gigi Darlene) is raped by the apartment janitor as she parades around in a sexy nightgown. She kills him out of revenge for what he did to her, then hits the road one step ahead of the police, changing her name to Meg. In the Big Apple, Ellen/Meg encounters a string of nightmare situations where she gets used and abused; first, by a sadistic drunk who lashes her with his best, then a predatory lesbian, and finally, a pleasant landlady with a sex-crazed husband. As the story unravels, Ellen wakes up screaming, relieved what happened to her was only a dream. Or was it?

Figure 34. Poster for *Another Day, Another Man* (1966).

As the credits roll at the end, the viewer watches as the buck-toothed janitor sneaks up on her as she goes to take a shower. Wishman leaves us wondering what was real and what was all a dream. Critics from the sixties hailed *Bad Girls* as Doris Wishman's film noir masterpiece. That may be going a bit too far, but there's definitely a grungy edge to her first "roughie."

Another Day, Another Man (1966) was written, produced, directed and edited by Doris Wishman and photographed by C. Davis Smith. The film featured Gigi Darlene, Rita Bennett, Darlene Bennett, Tony Gregory, Barbara "Barbi" Kemp, Mary O'Hara, Bob Oran, June Roberts, Sam Stewart, and Angelique in an uncredited role. After a montage of still scenes, featuring newly-wed couple Ann (Barbi Kemp) and Steve (Tony Gregory), play-out against a backdrop of jazz music, they move into a furnished apartment. Steve suddenly takes ill with a mysterious ailment and becomes bedridden. Unable to pay the rent on their expensive new apartment, and with bills mounting, Ann turns to her ex-roommate Tess (Mary O'Hara), a call girl, to set up a meeting with her pimp, Bert (Sam Stewart). By day Ann takes care of her husband, by night she's a hooker. Steve makes a miraculous and complete recovery and rushes off to tell his wife the good news, but then makes a shocking discovery about what she has been doing. In between the melodrama of Ann and Steve, Bert the Pimp has a flashback/dream, which recalls how several of his girls met, including Dolly and Daisy (Darlene and Rita Bennett) and Meg (June Roberts). The girls bond by dancing and cavorting in their underwear together. Angelique appears in an uncredited role as a fellow prostitute in the extended dream sequence, and also body-doubled the character of Meg.

During the sixties, films like *Bad Girls Go to Hell* and *Another Day, Another Man* were pumped out very quickly, usually in black-and-white, for the drive-in movie crowd. They were horribly dubbed because Wishman always filmed without sound, and regrettably the dubbing in *Another Day, Another Man* was truly atrocious because everyone sounded muffled like they were in the apartment next store. While the films tended to be a cut above because of the creative force behind the camera,

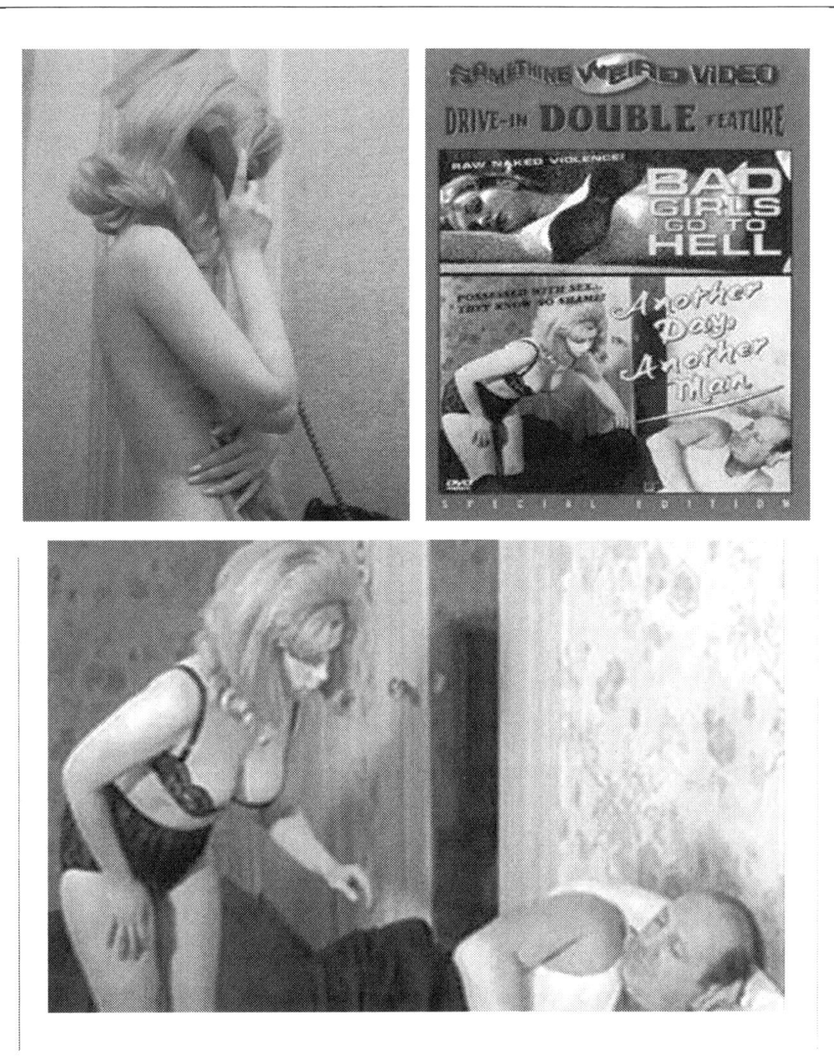

Figure 35. Scenes from *Another Day, Another Man* (1966).

Wishman's obsession with inanimate objects, like potted plants, lamps, and end tables, get more screen-time than totally necessary. The women in Wishman's sexploitation films were almost always pretty, but they played sleazy characters who were always running around nude, or semi-nude, or in skimpy lingerie.

When they change their clothes, the director always seemed to linger as if every woman in America took five minutes to remove a bra as part of a private strip-tease act. The violence was pretty brutal, and inevitably featured women being beaten or raped. Also characteristic of Wishman, from this time period, were the excessively bawdy, lesbian sex scenes — no-doubt added to titillate male viewers — in which clearly heterosexual women succumbed to the joy of lesbian sex with older, more experienced partners.

In addition to a flat fee, Angelique earned a couple of additional screen credits, but little else of value. Both movies were barely a cut above the softcore, pornographic trash being churned out, and only had the briefest hint of legitimacy because they were made by Doris Wishman. Sometime later, when Wishman made the first of her "chesties," she consulted with Angelique about headlining two films featuring the gimmick of a secret agent with two very large breasts, but she declined. She had already started making legitimate motion pictures and was not about to take a step backwards in her career. So, Wishman hired a Polish stripper, Chesty Morgan, known for her very large breasts, to headline *Deadly Weapons* (1973) and *Double Agent 73* (1974). Morgan proved to be such a handful to deal with, the director declined the final option for her three-picture contract. Doris Wishman continued working as a director, well into her eighties when she retired to Florida, and then later died of lymphoma. The two films she made with Angelique were considered quite shocking back when they were first made. Now, they seem ludicrously melodramatic, like items sealed in a time capsule to show us what life was really like back in the swinging sixties.

Before turning to mainstream work, Angelique made several other sexploitation movies: *Professor Lust* (1967) with Director William Rose, in which she played a busty science experiment put through a variety of sexual perversions, and an uncredited walk-on in Anton Holden's *Cargo of Love* (1968). They were not significant motion pictures by any stretch of the imagination. *Professor Lust* and *Cargo of Love* appeared to be produced on an assembly line with a cookie-cutter template. Regrettably, movie-goers had trouble keeping them straight, as they were barely indistinguishable from one another in terms of plot and players. Church groups and the Catholic Church's Legion of Decency had little trouble keeping them straight, however. They were condemned and labeled as softcore trash. The condemnation certainly didn't hurt their box office appeal. They played regularly at the drive-ins as second and third features, garnering a huge following among those who recognized Angelique and her French name in the credits.

She did one last film of this kind, *The Touch of Her Flesh* aka *The Touch of Her Life* (1967), before turning to more legitimate fair.

The Slasher Film

Like the "roughies" and certain sexploitation films, the slasher film came into being in the sixties and thrived in the seventies and eighties as a graphically violent movie typically involving a psychopathic killer stalking and killing a sequence of victims, often women and usually just after they've had sex with one of the potential male victims. The killer's weapon of choice was usually a knife, although axes, machetes, and chainsaws were substituted for effect. These films combined conventional horror or thriller elements with sadomasochistic sex scenes. Critics unfamiliar with the horror film genre have used the term "slasher" in a generic sense to refer to any movie involving graphic acts of murder, but the slasher film really had its own set of characteristics, which set it apart from related genres, like the "splatter" film or the "cannibal" film. *Peeping Tom* (1960), directed by Michael Powell, and Alfred Hitchcock's *Psycho* (1960), released three months later, were considered forerunners of the slasher film. Another early pioneer of the subgenre was *Dementia 13* (1963), Francis Ford Coppola's controversial directing debut which was rushed into production to take advantage of the success at the box office of Hitchcock's black-and-white masterpiece. With the exception of *Psycho*, which played in mainstream theaters, the others were all very popular at the grindhouse theaters and at the drive-ins.

The Touch of Her Flesh (1967) was the one and only slasher film Angelique did in her career, although one could argue she did two because footage shot of the actress for the first film in the *Flesh* trilogy was recycled for its sequel, *The Curse of Her Flesh* (1968). The trilogy was directed by Michael Findlay (1938-1977), who, along with his wife Roberta, produced a number of notorious sexploitation movies that pushed the boundaries of decency right to the very limit. In the mid-to-late sixties, Findlay was prominent among a small group of underground New York filmmakers, like Joseph W. Sarno, producer of some of the earliest slasher films. As the movie unfolds, a cuckolded gun dealer, Richard Jennings (played by Findlay under the pseudonym "Richard Wes") is disfigured in a car accident after finding his wife in bed with her lover. He loses his left eye and the use of his legs. Embittered and full of rage, Richard vows to get revenge on his wife Claudia (Angelique) while recovering in a cheap hotel room. He comes to generalize his hatred for his wife to all promiscuous women, and so goes on a killing spree, murdering prostitutes and strippers with a variety of unique implements, such as poison-tipped rose thorns, a crossbow, and a scimitar. Eventually, he locates Claudia and her lesbian lover, Janet (Suzanne Marre), at a remote cottage. He throws his wife on a workbench, turning on a circular saw, exclaiming, "Those breasts! Let me see them and feel them again before they die." Then he decapitates her before being shot dead by the quick-witted Janet.

Findlay's breakthrough film was surprisingly effective, and though short, at sixty-one minutes, fairly fast-moving for the slasher genre. With its creative murder weapons, *The Touch of Her Flesh* was clearly a cut above many of its contemporary slasher films, and anticipated those to follow, like *The Texas Chainsaw Massacre* (1974), *Halloween* (1978), and *Friday the 13th* (1980). It was also the first slasher series, followed by two sequels, *The Curse of Her Flesh* (1968) and *The Kiss of Her Flesh* (1970), featuring the wheelchair-bound, eye-patch-wearing maniac. Ironically, one of Angelique's closest friends and one of the women who would steer her towards adult films in the late seventies adopted the name "Claudia Jennings" (1949-1979) as her stage name from Angelique's character in the film. Born Mary Eileen Chesterton in St. Paul, Minnesota, she rose to become *Playboy's* Playmate of the Year in 1970 and the star of a number of mainstream and sexploitation films. She died in a car accident in 1979.

Figure 36. Poster for *The Touch of Her Flesh* (1967).

"I did most of those horrid pictures to advance my career," Pettyjohn told me, deflecting criticism of her choices. "Not for the sake of art and certainly not for the money."

Angelique was happy to leave the sexploitation movies behind as she embarked on a new path, but in terms of other actors and actresses, she was not alone in using low-budget exploitation pictures to move their careers forward. Jack Nicholson starred in a number of low-budget horror films in the sixties — *Little Shop of Horrors* (1960) and *The Terror* (1963) — before becoming an Academy Award-winning actor. Clint Eastwood starred in Sergio Leone's Spaghetti Westerns. Caroline Munro screamed her way through several Hammer Horror Films and showed her body off in *A Talent for Loving* (1969). Sylvester Stallone made *The Party at Kitty and Stud's* (1970), a softcore porn film. Marlon Brando and Stephanie Beacham got naked together in *The Nightcomers* (1971). Ursula Andress became a *Sensuous Nurse* (1975), Joan Collins took it all off in *The Stud* (1978) before landing *Dynasty* (1980), and even Bette Davis and Joan Crawford turned to the low-budget horror film *Whatever Happened to Baby Jane?* (1962) when their talents were no longer sought in mainstream pictures. Nearly every actor and actress in Hollywood have done work in their early careers of which they were not necessarily proud, but still took the job to advance their careers. Angelique was simply following the path so many others followed on the way to stardom, and she was very determined to break through.

"I've done a variety of different things, and I've looked different in so many of the different roles that I've had," Angelique explained. "I was sometimes blonde, sometimes brunette, sometimes a redhead, and in *Star Trek*, I had green hair. Some people have seen me in things and couldn't quite put it together because I didn't always play the same person, but I did different types of characters. I played in parts I hated, but I did them because I felt it was necessary to keep working."

In 1966, Angelique played a part she didn't think she would ever play, that of a blushing bride when she married her first husband.

Marriage # 1 — Otho A. Pettyjohn, Jr.

All throughout her time making the sexploitation films with Joseph W. Sarno, Doris Wishman, Michael Findlay, and the others, Angelique continued working as a showgirl on the Las Vegas Strip. Sometimes she worked under contract at the Aladdin Hotel in Barry Ashton's *Vive Paris Vive* or at the Silver Slipper in Harold Minsky's *Burlesque*, then take a leave of absence for a week or more to shoot her scenes. At other times, she would do fill-in work for other girls who needed the time off to get married or have babies, then find herself back at the Thunderbird Hotel in *Ziegfeld's Follies*.

Since she had worked at the shows before, Angelique knew the choreography, and it was just a matter of attending a few rehearsals to get back into the elaborate costumes she wore as a showgirl. Occasionally, between sets, a player at the casino would offer to buy her a drink or take her dinner. As long as Angelique was ready for the next show, the Hotels never discouraged the fraternization between guests and showgirls. In fact, many encouraged it. One such player was Otho A. Pettyjohn, Jr. (1921-1980), a civil servant from Los Angeles.

Otho A. Pettyjohn, Jr. had been born in Oklahoma on December 11, 1921, to Otho and Lucille Pettyjohn. Armenian by nationality, his parents moved to California as part of the Dust Bowl migration in the thirties, traveling along Route 66 with tens of thousands of other families forced to abandon their way of life in Oklahoma due to the severe drought and dust storms. They were known as "Okies."

When they settled in Los Angeles County, his father took a job as a stern high school principal and his mother became a teacher. Otho, Jr. grew up in Glendale, California, a prosperous suburb of LA noted for having one of the largest communities of people of Armenian descent in the United States. He served as a Private in the U.S. Army in a supply unit during World War II and was honorably discharged. He returned home after the war was over. With just a single year of college, Otho got a job working as a civil servant for the city of Glendale. Otho had no real hobbies or interests, didn't follow the horses, and wasn't a fan of professional sports. He rarely dated and had a fairly dull and ordinary life. However, he did like to gamble and so spent much of his free time at the gaming tables in Las Vegas and Reno. And while he was not married, Otho did enjoy the company of pretty showgirls, lots of them.

His favorite showgirl was Angelique. Though twenty-one years older, he was extremely kind to her and treated her like his little princess. He would bring her gifts and treat her to elaborate dinners at some of the finest restaurants on the Strip. He would lavish her with praise, spending his winnings from the gaming tables on buying her whatever she wanted. On Friday, March 11, 1966, her 23rd birthday, he showed up with a birthday cake, which read "Happy Birthday to My Sweet Angel, Love Otho," and the keys to a brand-new Volkswagen Beetle he had bought off the lot that day with cash. She responded to Otho — the missing-from-her-life father figure — by returning his kindness with love. Their relationship was a unique one, transcending age and station in life.

One night, after Angelique had told him about all the trouble she had gone through to get auditions in Hollywood, he offered to quit his job as a civil servant and work as her personal manager. Thrilled, she accepted a subsequent proposal of marriage without a second thought. Dorothy Lee Perrins (aka Angelique) took on the role of blushing bride and married Otho A. Pettyjohn, Jr. at the Clark County Courthouse in Las Vegas, Nevada, (marriage certificate #000227) on Wednesday, May 11, 1966. She became Angelique Pettyjohn. They honeymooned in Vegas the rest of the week at the Sahara Hotel, then he went back home to Glendale, California. On the following Friday, he returned and finalized their plans to live together in the Los Angeles suburb.

Angelique later told me she wasn't really in love with him, the way a woman should love a man, but she was very flattered by Otho's attention and affection. In the kind of show business Dorothy was in, it was rare to meet a man so sincere who treated her with kindness and respect. Most men in show business were either gay or out to get whatever they could from a woman. Otho was completely different. Angelique was also grateful Otho wasn't looking to build a family because she couldn't have any more children. For some men, that would have been a deal-breaker. For Otho, he was simply happy to have his little princess all to himself. Unfortunately, the marriage was far from being storybook, as Otho was soon to learn.

With a renewed determination to make it as an actress in Hollywood, Angelique left the bright lights and glitter of the Strip happily behind and moved to Los Angeles with her brand-new husband. She recalled, "I was very shy and naïve at the time when I got married. That's where I got my name. I was married to a real gentleman with the name Pettyjohn, who unfortunately passed away when he was only fifty-nine years old (in 1980). A super nice guy. They truly broke the mold when they made him. I had been married to him only a few weeks, when we moved to LA. Hollywood beckoned as a very new adventure for me."

Figure 37. Poster for *Cargo of Love* (1968).

4
Bright Lights, Big City

The problem was I wanted to be Jane Fonda, and they wanted me to be Jayne Mansfield. My 38-24-36 figure always got in the way. Most of the casting agents that I met saw me as a sex symbol.

Angelique Pettyjohn packed up her few belongings in Las Vegas and eagerly made the 275-mile trek in her Volkswagen Beetle across the desert to the bright lights of Hollywood. She moved into Otho's modest two-bedroom, two-bath, 1200-square foot split level house in Glendale, California, and spent the next several days turning his bachelor pad into a home for the two of them. Glendale was centrally located for her in Los Angeles County, with Burbank and North Hollywood to the northwest, Studio City to the west, and Beverly Hills and the Sunset Strip to the southwest. Most of the major studios were an easy fifteen-to-twenty-minute drive away on any of the highways in the elaborate freeway system.

As the third largest city in Los Angeles County, Glendale was host to Forest Lawn Memorial Park Cemetery, the final resting place of many noted and infamous celebrities. Angelique once told me she used to like visiting Forest Lawn because the cemetery provided her with a quiet and peaceful backdrop where she could find her own center of balance.

She *truly* needed balance on the first weekend when she met Otho's parents. Even though her new in-laws were very cordial and polite to her, they were disappointed their son had married a woman so much younger. They also disapproved, though never to her face, of the choices she had made in terms of her career. For hard-working folks who had come through the Dust Bowl migration and struggled to make a place for themselves in California, her work as a stripper, showgirl, and some-time actress on films of dubious merit seemed totally foreign to them. Angelique would work very hard to earn their trust, but it was always an uphill battle for her. The same was true for Otho. The moment she started working late, he began to question her sincerity, too.

> *I was faithful to Otho during my first year of marriage. He was a very kind man, and he worked so hard to find me parts. He was better than a manager in that regard. But I began to feel that I was missing out on something, so I started acting out my fantasies. I did many things I'm ashamed of today. But I still did them. God help me, I did them. That's what triggered my sex addiction.*

Membership in the Screen Actors Guild

When Angelique returned to Hollywood, she sought membership in the Screen Actors Guild (SAG), one of the most powerful labor unions in the United States, representing thousands of film and television actors. An actor became eligible to join the Screen Actors Guild by meeting certain criteria, and once met, the SAG card had the potential to open many doors for new actors. Unfortunately, when she first applied in 1966, she was denied membership. After considering the number of movies she had made, the Screen Actors Guild didn't accept the sexploitation movies where she earned billing as the lead in the production as being SAG worthy. The rules were very specific when they came to describing a SAG production, and were enacted in order to protect its large membership from unsafe working conditions, which may have existed on non-union or non-SAG productions. All her past work had amounted to nothing. Angelique was very disappointed, but she studied the criteria clearly with the goal of earning her SAG card just as soon as possible. Interestingly enough, she could still work in the business, but was limited by the number of roles and categories of roles before she had to apply for membership to the Screen Actors Guild.

The principal actor in a SAG production was the goal most new actors in Hollywood sought, a background actor (considered the "three voucher rule") was the next level, and, of course, she could earn a one-year membership if she was affiliated with another union. While Constantine Stanislavski may have famously remarked, "There are no small parts, only small actors," Pettyjohn was very much aware of how the SAG viewed its levels of actors.

Hollywood Beckons

In those first few years, acting as Angelique's personal manager, Otho Pettyjohn arranged for his wife to audition or screen test for several small parts in movies. Now, it's debatable whether Angelique could have landed those roles on her own, or if it took the tireless work of a promoter constantly talking on the phone with the studios, but the fact of the matter is, when Pettyjohn first came to Hollywood at age twenty-one, she failed to land a single, legitimate production. Instead, she was chased around the casting couch by leering old men wanting nothing more than to bed down an innocent starlet or cast her in low budget sexploitation films where she had to give up everything just to be noticed. The second time around seemed to be different. Even though the first few roles were little more than walk-ons, all the parts were in productions being mounted at Paramount, Metro-Goldwyn-Mayer, Universal, Warner Brothers, and 20th Century-Fox. The big studios beckoned for raw talent.

For the most part, however, Angelique's first roles in Hollywood were very small, often just walk-on parts that simply exploited her good looks and didn't tax her limited acting abilities. She was often cast as strippers, go-go dancers, secretaries, or apartment hunters, that is when she was given *any* screen credit. In other instances, she was the "Girl on Wilshire Boulevard," or simply received no credit at all. The road to movie stardom was a long and difficult road; one in which many travel, but few actually find real success. In order to reach stardom, actors and actresses have had to endure numerous auditions, low level jobs, and endless rejections with no real guarantee they'll make it in the end. Sometimes it came down to a combination of talent, drive, and sheer luck. Angelique Pettyjohn had talent and drive; she was just looking for her big break.

She tried to keep a good sense of humor throughout these early first roles, acknowledging that many actors and actresses in Hollywood, like Monroe, Gable, and Dean, started out as extras. Marilyn Monroe was an extra in her first-ever screen appearance, *Scudda Hoo! Scudda Hay!* (1948); glimpsed in a rowboat with another actress. Both Clark Gable and Jean Harlow were extras in several silent films in the late twenties, before they got their breaks in the early "talkies." James Dean was an extra with one line: "The guy's a professional," in the Dean Martin and Jerry Lewis comedy *Sailor Beware* (1951). And in the fifties, Clint Eastwood was an uncredited extra in several films, then worked for Jack Arnold in *Revenge of the Creature* (1955) and *Tarantula* (1955), before breaking into leading man roles. Pettyjohn figured if other actors and actresses had started out that way, and eventually made it big, then she felt she was on the right path for her life. She was just paying her dues.

> *Most of the casting agents that I met saw me as a sex symbol. It didn't seem like anybody cared that I was a good actress. It didn't seem that anybody wanted to see me do Elizabeth the Queen or Anastasia, which I was capable of doing in acting classes. They always saw me as the dumb sexpot, and cast me in roles that fitted their impression of me. For instance, they cast me as a stripper in "Hotel" because I had been a stripper. But I could have played the French lady, if they had given me a chance.*

Hotel (1967)

Based on the best-selling novel by Arthur Hailey, *Hotel* (1967) was a rich, lavish, spectacular motion picture from Warner Brothers, directed by Richard Quine, that depicted the comings and goings of guests as well as rich financers at the fictional St. Gregory Hotel in New Orleans, owned by Warren Trent (Melvyn Douglas). The screen story, as developed by Hailey and written by Producer Wendell Mayes, cleverly weaves together several storylines that intersect and then later converge on the St. Gregory.

With the hotel in financial trouble, Manager Peter McDermott (Rod Taylor) places himself in the overtures of two different buyers. He also takes a romantic interest in Jeanne Rochefort (Catherine Spaak), an upper-class French guest, and deals with a wide range of routine problems, such as a faulty elevator, which provides a nerve-shattering conclusion to the film. Other storylines featured a buyer named Curtis O'Keefe (Kevin McCarthy) who intends to modernize the hotel with conveyer belts carrying luggage automatically around the building, like some sort of modern airport terminal, even sending

Figure 38. Poster for *Hotel* (1967).

the customer's bill on a conveyor belt. Then there's a wealthy couple, the Duke and Duchess of Lambourne (Michael Rennie and Merle Oberon), who are being blackmailed for fleeing a hit-and-run accident, a professional thief (Karl Malden) who is working the hotel with several female accomplices, and a hotel detective Dupere (Richard Conte) who does not appear to be on the level.

Warner Brothers spent $3,651,000 to bring the sudsy Arthur Hailey novel to the screen in 1967 and earned nearly that amount back in ticket sales for the United States and Canada. Supposedly set in New Orleans, only two shots were actually filmed there: the opening shot of the New Orleans International Airport main terminal building, and an open-air shot of Peter McDermott and Jeanne at the French Quarter restaurant, Pat O'Brien's. The other shots are obviously filmed on the Warner back lot, most especially the outside scene between the Duchess and House Detective Dupere (Richard Conte).

Angelique Pettyjohn appears very briefly, in the opening few minutes of the movie, as the First Stripper in a strip-joint in the French Quarter. The role was not much of a stretch for Angelique, considering she'd worked as a stripper in burlesque clubs, but the role did very little to advance her career. Her image appears on the poster.

A Guide for the Married Man (1967)

In *A Guide for the Married Man* (1967), Angelique Pettyjohn played "the Girl on Wilshire Boulevard" in Hollywood who triggers the initial discussion between Paul Manning (Walter Matthew) and his dear friend and neighbor, Ed Stander (Robert Morse), about cheating on his wife. As they drive by the beautiful blonde bombshell, the two men are almost immediately engaged in a conversation about the history and tactics of men who have successfully committed adultery. Each of the stories Ed relates are then dramatized by some of the funniest comedians in the business: Sid Caesar, Phil Silvers, Lucille Ball, Art Carney, Jack Benny, Joey Bishop, Jayne Mansfield, Terry Thomas, and Carl Reiner. And of course Angelique.

Figure 39. Poster for *A Guide for the Married Man* (1967).

With each new story, Paul can't help but notice attractive blondes everywhere, primarily Irma Johnson (Sue Ann Langdon), who lives nearby. He gets close to cheating on his wife, Ruth (Inger Stevens), but he never quite goes through with it. In a scene near the end, when he is in a motel room with another woman, Jocelyn, a wealthy divorcee, Paul hears sirens approaching. He looks out the window to see the police, heading to the room next door where Ed is in bed with Mrs. Johnson. Paul takes this opportunity to flee the scene and run home to his wife, while the ever-careful Ed ends up in divorce court.

Directed by Gene Kelly and adapted by Frank Tarloff, from his book of the same name, the film was a run-away success for 20th Century-Fox, nearly doubling its budget in box office receipts. It was also critically well-received by the Hollywood Foreign Press Association. Most of the New York critics disliked the film, while those outside the Big Apple found it quaintly humorous with its vaudevillian acts that treated extramarital sex with a "wink-wink" sensibility.

For instance, the best guest-star vignette featured Joey Bishop as a man caught in bed with another woman by his wife. When discovered, he calmly puts on his clothes, straightens up the room, and quietly responds to his wife's outrage by saying, "What bed? What girl?"

Many of the other talents seemed to be wasted when their characters were reduced to mere stereotypes they had long since played, such as Jayne Mansfield as a dumb blonde and Jack Benny a tightwad. *A Guide to the Married Man* anticipated the far superior *Love, American Style* produced by Paramount Television and originally aired on ABC television between 1969 and 1974 as a comedic anthology of vignettes about sex and love in Middle America.

Although the production was filmed on the backlot at Fox, or at nearby locations in the Los Angeles area, not all the performers were on the set at the same time. Angelique Pettyjohn worked with the great Gene Kelly, known more for his dancing talents than his directing skills, for several days on the Wilshire Boulevard location, then was released for having completed her work.

She never did run into Linda Harrison, her rival on the film and then later in other productions. Harrison played Miss

Stardust and had a much bigger role, thanks in large part to the fact that Harrison was dating Richard Zanuck, head of the studio.

Completely by chance, Angelique ran into Majel Barrett (1932-2008) several weeks into the shoot. Barrett was playing the role of Mrs. Fred V. and her scenes were scheduled much later in the production schedule. They agreed to meet at the commissary for lunch.

Majel Barrett had a recurring role on *Star Trek* (1966-69) as Nurse Christine Chapel and was also Gene Roddenberry's girlfriend. (They later married in Japan on August 6, 1969, after the network canceled the original series.) She had first appeared in *Star Trek's* initial pilot, "The Cage" (1964), as the *U.S.S. Enterprise's* unnamed first officer, "Number One," opposite Jeffrey Hunter as the Captain and Leonard Nimoy as a pointed-ears alien named Spock. When NBC network executives bargained with Roddenberry to shoot another pilot with William Shatner as the Captain, they insisted on several other changes, one being the elimination of the role of "Number One" altogether. They didn't like that he had cast his girlfriend in such a key part. With his marriage to Eileen-Anita Rexroat (1942-69) on the verge of failing at the time, Roddenberry acquiesced to the demands of network executives and subsequently fired Barrett. He later wrote his girlfriend another part, supposedly a guest spot on the episode "What Are Little Girls Made of?" (Season 1.7, 1966). Nurse Christine Chapel was born and instantly became popular among the fans because of her love for Mr. Spock. Barrett was assured of continued work on *Star Trek*, as well as small parts in movies and television.

During lunch at the Fox commissary, Majel Barrett saw a younger version of herself in Angelique, and they became friends. Soon after, she started talking to Gene about Pettyjohn. Barrett thought she might be just right for a role they were developing for the second season, and the character was neither a stripper nor a go-go dancer. Pettyjohn beat her to the punch and met Roddenberry (1921-1991) all on her own a few months later, thanks in large part to a conversation her husband Otho had overheard.

More Women of Ill Repute

Angelique Pettyjohn continued to play women of questionable virtue in her next film roles. She played a secretary with a nose for trouble in *The Cool Ones*, a hooker in *Rough Night in Jericho*, a biker chick in *Hell's Belles*, an apartment hunter looking for fellow swinging singles in *For Singles Only*, and a go-go dancer in *The Odd Couple*. Casting directors didn't bother to look beyond her busty, statuesque physique to see if she could act, and merely plugged her into roles most any beautiful woman could have played. But she kept at it, working her craft. Little by little, Pettyjohn was becoming a ubiquitous presence in walk-on roles, and everyone who was anyone in the industry started to take notice of the hard-working blonde who had become part of the film's backdrop.

The Cool Ones (1967), directed by Gene Nelson, played like a spoof of the late sixties music industry as it followed the loopy tale of a young, millionaire rock promoter (Roddy McDowall) who decides to create a new boy/girl singing duo for his teen TV dance show by teaming an ambitious go-go dancer (Debbie Watson) with a has-been pop icon (Gil Peterson) to become everyone's favorite romantic pair. Originally developed as a vehicle to showcase the work of Nancy Sinatra. Sinatra

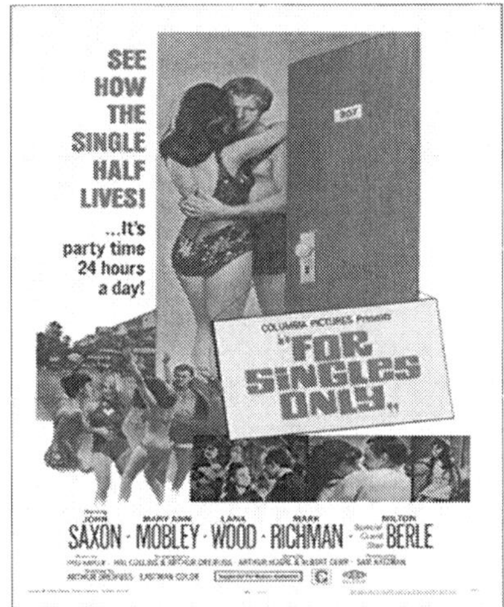

Figures 40 & 41. Posters for two other romantic comedies.

recorded several songs before backing out of the project. Her instincts were correct as the movie bombed big time at the box office.

American International Pictures' lightweight beach party movies, like *Beach Party* (1963), *Muscle Beach Party* (1964), *Beach Blanket Bingo* (1965), *How to Stuff a Wild Bikini* (1965), and *Ski Party* (1965) had gradually given way to edgier films featuring hippies, LSD, and motorcycle gangs, like *The Wild Angels* (1966), *Outlaw Motorcycles* (1967), *Hells Angels on Wheels* (1967), *Born Losers* (1967), and *Hell's Belles* (1969). The naïve, sweetly innocent tone of *The Cool Ones* was a huge embarrassment when compared to the type of films already being embraced by younger filmgoers. Gil Peterson was savaged by critics for appearing to be the living, breathing prototype for the Ken doll. Debbie Watson was similarly miscast as a former go-go dancer turned Malibu Barbie. Most notably in the cast, Angelique played a hip, young secretary who had tuned into what was "cool." Director Nelson would have fared much better if he had jettisoned the storyline featuring Watson and Peterson, and given Pettyjohn some biker leather and a hog in order to kick some rival motorcycle gang's butt. Now that movie would have been "cool!" *The Cool Ones* was far from being "cool."

In *Rough Night in Jericho* (1967), directed by Arnold Laven from a screenplay by Sydney Boehm, Dean Martin makes one of his rare appearances as a villain, Alex Flood, an ex-lawman who has taken over the town of Jericho and hired a band of ruthless gunmen to enforce his edicts. When Flood learns that Molly Lang (Jean Simmons) is determined to expand the stage line with a former Santa Fe lawman, Hickman (John McIntire), and a gambler, Dolan (George Peppard), he ambushes the stagecoach outside of town, wounds Hickman, and blames the attack of some outlaw gang. Molly knows he is lying, but can't prove it. After a few days, Dolan sees the odds are stacked against them and must organize the few men in town willing to put up a fight to oppose Flood. Finally, in a showdown, Flood and Dolan battle it out. Dolan wins, and restores freedom and order to the town of Jericho.

Figures 42. and 43. Dean Martin plays the villain; George Peppard is the gunslinger, and Angelique Pettyjohn is the hooker with the heart of gold, in *Rough Night in Jericho* (1967).

While things get increasingly violent during the final showdown, with lots of red blood flowing freely in the Technicolor release, the film managed to rise above its familiar and sometimes tired trappings to be quite entertaining. Dean Martin was quite good as the villain of the piece, as the hard-bitten and violent ex-lawman, a character vastly different from his familiar roles in *Rio Bravo* (1959) and *Five Card Stud* (1968). Western favorites, like Slim Pickens, John McIntire, and Don Galloway co-starred opposite Martin to add legitimacy to the production. Angelique had a walk-on role as one of the town's prostitutes. Beautiful, sexy, and highly desirable, she showed Dino how the West was fun.

Hell's Belles (1969), directed by Maury Dexter and written by James Gordon White and Robert McMullen, played more like a remake of Anthony Mann's Western classic *Winchester '77* (1950) than a motorcycle movie. When Dan (Jeremy Slate) wins a motorcycle worth $2,000, he plans to sell the bike for a down payment on a ranch and settle down. After the motorcycle is stolen by Tony (Michael Walker), Tampa (Adam Roarke) claims possession of it. Soon Dan is chasing after the thugs who took the bike as they make their way to Mexico.

Figure 44. Poster for *Hell's Belles* (1969).

Figures 45-47. Photos from *Hell's Belles* (1969).

One by one, Dan eliminates the crooks with boulders, fists, ropes, and even makes grisly and effective use of a pit of rattlesnakes to exact his revenge. Like sharp-shooter Lin McAdam (James Stewart), who chases the thugs who stole his Winchester '77 rifle across the frontier, Dan is not a bad guy. He just wants the motorcycle back and is willing to do anything to retrieve it from the motorcycle gang who stole it. Pettyjohn played a tough-talking biker chick named Cherry.

For Singles Only (1968) was an embarrassing rip-off of *Under the Yum Yum Tree* (1963) and other sex farces of the early sixties. Directed by Arthur Dreifuss from a screenplay he had written with Hal Collins, the story tells of an apartment building where the manager, Parker (Milton Berle), only rents to singles under thirty. Five years earlier, in 1963, Jack Lemmon had played the apartment manager, with Carolyn Lynley, Edie Adams, and Dean Jones as the swinging singles living in his building in *Under the Yum Yum Tree.* When Anne Carr (Mary Ann Mobley) and Helen Todd (Lana Wood, the younger sister of Natalie) move into the Sans Souci, they become unwitting targets of a swinging singles game. In the first game, Jim Allen (Charles Robinson) and Bob Merrick (Duke Hobbie), two tenants, bet playboy Bret Hendley (John Saxon) that he cannot seduce Anne within a week. He takes the wager in order to win enough money to complete his college education.

In the other game, Helen, an intellectual, is attracted to Gerald Pryor (Mark Richman), a married man living incognito as a swinging single in the complex. After a few close encounters, Bret becomes serious about Anne and rebuffs her rather than uses her. Anne learns about the wager and pretends to have been seduced in order to help Bret win money for his educational expenses. Hence, Jim and Bob must pay up. Bret and Anne profess their love for each other, and when they announce their plans to get married, Parker throws them out of the apartment complex.

Sadly, Helen also decides to leave the Sans Souci when she discovers Gerald is married. First, she tries to take her own life, and then later, she is raped by a group of waterfront thugs. Helen recovers and emerges as an unhappy woman who has experienced the rough side of life.

The movie played like a trashy soap opera, and was not nearly as clever as its precursor, *Under the Yum Yum Tree*, with Jack Lemmon. Angelique Pettyjohn had another one of her now famous walk-on roles as an "apartment hunter" looking for fellow swinging singles, and may well be the best part of the picture.

The Odd Couple (1968), the highest-grossing picture of her career, featured Angelique Pettyjohn as a go-go dancer at the Metropole Café in a sequence not scripted by playwright Neil Simon. Director Gene Saks felt it was important to introduce the character of Felix Ungar (Jack Lemmon), a neurotic neat-freak during the opening credits, so the humor of Simon's script could proceed without any melodrama. So, with the help of Angelique, Saks created a memorable sequence that plays without any dialogue.

Felix Ungar has just been thrown-over by his wife for another man. Despondent, he takes a room on the ninth floor at the Hotel Flanders and tries to throw himself out of the window, but he fails to open it and instead pulls a muscle in his back. Limping back on the Manhattan street, he enters the Metropole Café where beautiful go-go dancers are entertaining the largely men's-only crowd. Felix selects a chair on the bar where a sexy blonde (Angelique Pettyjohn), adorned in purple, is dancing. He tries not to notice her, but she is right in Ungar's face, gyrating to

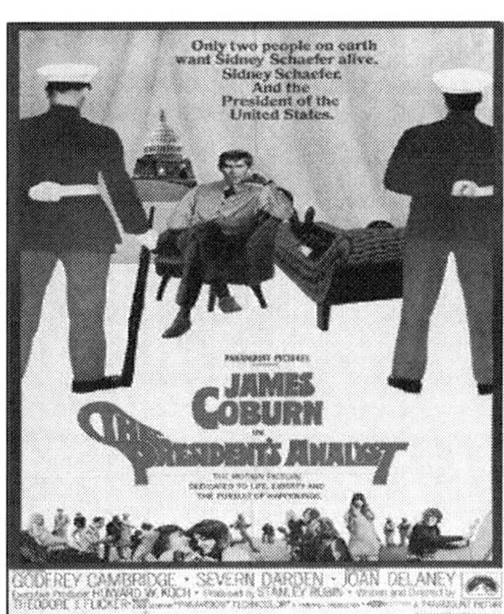

Figures 48 and 49. Posters from two of her successful comedies.

Figure 50. Poster from *Where Were You When…* (1968)

the music. Eventually, Felix starts to enjoy her nearly perfect "attributes," but when he throws down a shot of liquor while leaning back to watch her, he hurts his neck and slinks out of the bar a broken man.

Felix Ungar (as played by Jack Lemon) is a real mess. Even as he stands on a bridge, contemplating jumping into the river, he cannot summon the courage to commit suicide. He spends the rest of the film sparring with his best friend Oscar Madison (Walter Matthau), a fun-loving slob, trying to decide whether two completely opposite men can live together without driving each other crazy.

The film was highly successful with critics and audiences, grossing over $44.5 million in box office revenue, making it the fourth highest-grossing picture of 1968. Its success spawned a long-running television series with Tony Randall as Felix and Jack Klugman as Oscar. For her bit part in the film, Angelique was memorable as the go-go girl in purple.

As the period in her life of bit roles and walk-ons gradually came to a close, Pettyjohn looked for more substantive roles. She had already made a number of important contacts in the industry, now it was just a matter of networking and turning those contacts into speaking roles with the help of her manager-husband.

She played two more-bit roles in *The President's Analyst* (1967), opposite James Coburn, and *Where Were You When the Lights Went Out?* (1968), as the "Girl on the Subway Platform," then turned her sites on better roles in both television and movies.

Roles Not Taken or Offered

For all of the parts she got, Angelique Pettyjohn auditioned or screen-tested for at least a dozen other films she did not get. The first of these was *The Fat Spy* (1966), a Phyllis Diller comedy featuring sex bombshell Jayne Mansfield. She auditioned for the part of the "Treasure Hunter," which went to rival Linda Harrison. She tried out for a part that went eventually to sexy Sharon Tate (1943-1969) in the sex farce *Don't Make Waves* (1967) with Tony Curtis. With the popularity of the James Bond films, Angelique tried her hand at spy spoofs and auditioned for the part of Ingrid in *A Man Called Dagger* (1967), which went to Sue Anne Langdon, as well as one of the femme fatales in the spy spoof *In Like Flint* (1967), opposite James Coburn. Similarly, she competed for one of the "Slaygirls" who try to ambush Matt Helm in *The Ambushers* (1967) opposite Dean Martin, but lost out to Jan Watson, a friend she'd later play opposite in a *Batman* episode. Finally, she also tried out for the lead female in *Come Spy with Me* (1967), but lost out to Andrea Dromm, who's only other claim to fame was the role of Yeoman Smith in the second pilot for *Star Trek*, "Where No Man Has Gone Before."

When Fox announced the studio was going to hold an open casting call for its production of Jacqueline Susann's *Valley of the Dolls*, Angelique sought out the role of Jennifer North. Like most women in America, she had read the novel and identified with the role of the beautiful blonde with limited talent who starts as a showgirl and then is forced into making adult films before suffering with breast cancer and a mastectomy, and ultimately killing herself with pills. Angelique felt she could have played that role in her sleep, and auditioned, eventually losing the role to Sharon Tate, who did play the role in her sleep. Ironically, so much of what happens to Jennifer North in the novel as well the film adaptation anticipates events in Angelique's life in later years. The biggest role of her career, up to then, might have been a mute sub-human in *Planet of the Apes* if fate had taken a different turn.

Monkey Planet

On February 28, 1967, Angelique Pettyjohn was called by Associate Producer Mort Abrahams to do a screen test for the role of Nova in *Planet of the Apes* (1968) on the lot at 20th Century-Fox. Abrahams had first offered the role of Nova, the primitive sub-human who falls for Astronaut George Taylor (Charlton Heston), to Ursula Andress, and then Rachel Welch, but when neither woman expressed any interest, he turned to the up-and-comer Angelique. Besides, Welch had just played Loana, a primitive cave woman in *One Million Years B.C.* (1966).

Pettyjohn agreed to come into the studio and test for the role of Nova. Prior to the screen test, she devoured several books about primitives and cave women at the local library in Glendale as a form of preparation for the role. She also worked with a friend, who was a mime, in order to tap into that instinctual, still animal part of her brain. "I was a sophisticated young actress," Angelique recalled nearly twenty-five years later when we discussed the screen test, "and I had to make sure I didn't show any intelligence. My character's actions had to be based solely on instinct. I had to react, not act."

When Pettyjohn went in to do her screen test at 20th Century-Fox, she was initially disheartened by the whispered rumors she'd overheard from the crew, make-up, and wardrobe personnel. They all seemed to think the part of Nova had already been promised to the head of the studio's girlfriend. With the cameras rolling, Pettyjohn, billed as "Angelic Pettijohn" on the clapper, did the best job she could, working from an early script by Rod Serling with new material added by Michael Wilson. She read some dialogue (in the early version by Serling, Nova had dialogue) and then worked through a complicated action scene.

The screen test took roughly a half day to complete, particularly with time in make-up and wardrobe.

A few days after the test, she heard the studio had decided to go with another actress, and they wished her well. Angelique later read in *Variety* that Richard Zanuck's long-time girlfriend, Linda Harrison, had been cast as Nova. Ironically, Miss Harrison would turn out to be an unwitting nemesis for Angelique in the coming years as both women tried to build reputations as actresses. They were rivals for the part of a biker chick on *Felony Squad* (1967), a cheerleader on *Batman* (1967), and a major recurring role on *Bracken's World* (1969), all of which went to Harrison. They also competed for roles in bigger budget productions, like *The Fat Spy* (1966) and *A Guide for a Married Man* (1967), with Harrison winning key roles in both, and Angelique settling for a mere walk-on in one.

Figures 51 & 52. Screen test for *Planet of the Apes* (1968).

Planet of the Apes proved to be a surprisingly successful motion picture and inspired seven sequels, a short-lived television show, a Saturday morning cartoon series, a whole collection of tie-in books, comics and toys, and an inferior remake in 2001. The film was very well directed by Franklin Schaffner and provided winning performances from Charlton Heston, Kim Hunter, Maurice Evans, and Roddy McDowall. It also demonstrated that science fiction films could deal with very difficult and often profound subjects and still be extremely entertaining. In retrospect, *Planet of the Apes* was a classic work of cinema. Credit for its enduring legacy belongs clearly with the original novel by Pierre Boulle, the bold determination of producer Arthur P. Jacobs, and the inspired screenplay by Rod

Serling and Michael Wilson. The film endures today because it was one of the first films to explore relevant themes, such as the threat of nuclear war, the nature of man himself, and the direction in which humanity is headed as a species. At the time when it was released, most science fiction was characterized by films like *Fantastic Voyage* and *Voyage to the Bottom of the Sea*, but *Planet of the Apes* proved that audiences were ready for intelligent and well-thought-out entertainment, even if they did feature the studio chief's girlfriend in a key role

The LA Party Scene

Her model good looks and splashy personality made Angelique Pettyjohn a real natural for LA's Party Scene in the sixties. As a young starlet, seeking contacts to build her burgeoning career, she became the perfect party girl, and made sure she was seen with A-listers like Warren Beatty, Jack Nicholson, Mick Jagger, Bill Bixby, Ryan O'Neal, Michael Sarrazin, and many, many others. Even though she was married to an older man who worked as her personal manager, she spent many evenings out late at night, networking with fellow actors, often in the company of her two closest friends. Angelique got to know a lot of very famous people and had intimate relations as well as intimate knowledge of many of them.

In the mid-to-late sixties, the LA Party Scene was restricted to a mile-and-a-half stretch of Sunset Boulevard that passed through West Hollywood and extended all the way west to Beverly Hills, known as the Sunset Strip. The Strip was best known for its collection of boutiques, restaurants, rock clubs, and nightclubs that produced cutting edge entertainment nearly every night of the week. Since the Strip was situated just outside the Los Angeles city limits, within the jurisdiction of the County of Los Angeles, rules of behavior were a great deal more relaxed. Though still discouraged, public intoxication and the use of drugs were fairly commonplace. The Strip became a playground for the rich and the famous. Clubs like the Whisky-a-Go-Go, the Roxy, Pandora's Box, and the London Fog flourished, and bands like Johnny Rivers, Led Zepplin, The Doors, Sonny and Cher, The Byrds, Love, Frank Zappa, Joni Mitchell, Buffalo Springfield,

Figure 53. Hanging out, waiting to get into Whiskey-a-Go-Go.

James Taylor, and many others performed there. In 1965, go-go dancers first shimmied with their short-fringed skirts and go-go boots on the Strip, and were made a fixture at Gazzarri's in 1967 with the debut of the "Miss Gazzari Dancers." Nearby, the Hyatt West Hollywood (now known as the Andaz West Hollywood) featured a rotating door where wannabee starlets mixed it up with seasoned stars. Since many of the top celebrities of the day lived high up in the Hollywood Hills just above the Sunset Strip, they would join their friends, fellow celebrities, power brokers, and anyone else of significance down in the clubs for sex, drugs, and rock-n-roll.

"I remember her saying one time, 'Well, Ellie. I guess I was never meant to be a stay-at-home housewife." Eleanor Spencer (1943-2013 * Eleanor's last name was changed to "Spencer" to protect her family) was Angelique's lifelong friend. They met while both were auditioning for the role of Malibu, which ultimately went to Sharon Tate, in the Tony Curtis sex farce *Don't Make Waves* (1967). After the hour-long audition with Producer Martin Ransohoff, Angelique and her new-found friend commiserated together over a drink at the famous Rainbow Bar and Grill on Sunset Boulevard in West Hollywood. They found they had a great deal in common. Though she was not yet married, Spencer had worked as a go-go dancer at Whiskey-a-Go-Go and several other joints along the Sunset Strip, and had acted in a couple of underground movies in order to pay the bills on an apartment she shared in Venice Beach with a couple of other girls. Eleanor told Angelique about the clubs and night life along the Sunset Strip. while Pettyjohn had her reservations at first about getting involved in the LA party scene, she agreed to meet her friend for some fun. Soon, Angelique was one of the most popular party girls on the Strip.

"We were hanging out in clubs with Warren Beatty, Steve McQueen, Jack Nicholson, and Peter Fonda. If you were a beautiful enough starlet, you'd get to go to all of the in-clubs, so that's where we were usually hanging out," Spencer told me in a phone interview some years before her death. "The music was loud, the drinks were watered-down, but we were having a hell-of-a time. I mean, where else could you find dreamy guys, like Michael Sarrazin or Ben Murphy, who'd dance with you one moment and have their hands down your skirt the next."

On any given night, Angelique and her girlfriends would start with a light meal at the Rainbow Bar and Grill and then cruise down Sunset Boulevard in her Volkswagen Beetle, the row of nightclubs glistening off the hood of her car as they made a complete circuit. They'd cruise the Sunset Strip, looking for celebrities, working their way through the crowds of teenagers, hippies, bikers, longhairs, sailors, and party girls, and would pull into a club at the first sighting. Otherwise, they'd just cruise past Pandora's Box, The Trip, Ciro's, Bido Lito's, Gazzarri's, the Experience, and Whisky-a- Go-Go a couple of times before settling on their first club of the night.

They'd go into the night club, often avoiding the line outside because Angelique and her friends were hot chicks and they knew how to play the bouncers, then divide up in order to cover the floor, looking for celebrities. If they spotted an A-lister, like Beatty, or a B-lister, like Sarrazin, they'd get the guys to buy them a drink, then get cozy, grooving to the music or dancing with the guys on the dance floor. If the club was cold — devoid of actors or other celebrities — they'd pack things up after twenty-minutes and head to the very next bar on the circuit. They had a regular routine worked out and rarely deviated from plan, unless something unusual happened.

Figure 54. Jim Morrison & the Doors at Whiskey-a-Go-Go.

Jim Morrison and The Doors

When The Doors first started headlining London Fog, Angelique would beeline for it, passing up all the other night clubs in favor of the British-inspired club. But since it was such a small bar, they'd then have to fight their way through the line of teenage girls and their sailor boyfriends to get inside for a drink.

London Fog's dance floor was about the size of a queen-sized bed, and Jim Morrison and his band were sequestered above the bar on a tiny platform, no bigger than a kitchen table. All the little groupies worshipping Morrison had formed a stonewall around the bar, so the only way Angelique and her friends managed to score a drink was to muscle their way past the groupies who weren't drinking anyway. They were just dancing and grooving to the music; getting a contact high from all the marijuana smoke that filled the club like a typical London fog.

True to his character, Morrison not only sang but also provided the floor-show entertainment as he jumped around on top of the bar or rubbed the bulge in his leather pants against the mike stand in a very sexually suggestive way. Angelique just couldn't get enough of him and often had to be dragged out of the night club by her girlfriends, kicking and screaming.

> *I kept hearing about this singer named Jim Morrison and his group The Doors. They called him the Lizard King. Well, let me tell you something, honey, he was no lizard. He was a man-god. He was young and vibrant, and his moves reminded me of Elvis in the early days. They had been playing down at the London Fog and we caught several of their shows there before they moved to the Whisky-a-Go-Go. I couldn't take my eyes off the bulge in his leather pants. I don't think I ever wanted a man more than I wanted Morrison. The trouble was every woman gathered around the bar wanted him.*

As much as she tried, Angelique never did get the chance to meet Jim Morrison. He was always surrounded by dozens of young groupies — seventeen to twenty-one — who literally threw themselves at him, sometimes appearing topless or totally naked at his dressing room door or at parties; several even took their tops off at Whiskey-A-Go-Go and other clubs and tried to climb on stage. Of course, Pamela Courson, Morrison's red-headed girlfriend and later common-law wife, made damned sure nothing ever happened between her guy and his groupies. Pettyjohn would often see her sitting next to him or on Morrison's lap between sets, or interacting with Ray Manzarek or Robby Krieger, other members of the Doors, and wondered what Morrison saw in the waif-like Courson. She felt like she had more to offer him. After lusting after "the Lizard King" for a few sets, Angelique and her girlfriends would hit the road to see what else was happening on the Sunset Strip.

"It was always a great adventure whenever we'd go out," Darlene Jensen (1940- 2011 * Darlene's last name was changed to "Jensen" to protect her family) recalled in a phone interview. Along with Eleanor, Jensen was Angelique's other lifelong friend. She grew up in Milwaukee, Wisconsin, and while she had always dreamed of being a model in New York City, she got pregnant at seventeen, on the night of her prom, and delivered a baby girl a few months later out of wedlock. She never saw the baby's father again. Within a few months, the young and ambitious mother grew restless and took off to follow her dream. Taking the Big Apple by storm was a daunting task, made even more impossible with a toddler in tow, so Jensen left her daughter behind to be raised by her own mother. She landed a few jobs modeling, but after making friends with clothing designer Lenny Bryant, she followed him straight to Hollywood where she worked as a model and then later as a sales representative for his flamboyant line of clothes. Taking the Big Apple by storm was a

Figure 55. Wild in the Streets, along the Sunset Strip.

Figure 56. Rock-n-Roll on the Sunset Strip.

daunting task made even more impossible with a toddler in tow, so Jensen left her daughter behind to be raised by her own mother. She landed a few jobs modeling, but after making friends with clothing designer Lenny Bryant, she followed him straight to Hollywood where she worked as a model and then later as a sales representative for his flamboyant line of clothes.

Darlene Jensen met Angelique late one night at one of the clubs on the Sunset Strip and they became instant friends after exchanging stories about the children they had been forced to leave behind. "When I hung out with her, she'd always make me feel so important, so special. But that was really Angelique's gift. She had a way of doing that with each person in her life. She'd introduce me to Bill Bixby or Ryan O'Neal or Adam West as the Senior Vice President of Bryant Clothes. It was so hysterical because, in the beginning, I was just the front office girl who answered the phone and took all the sales calls for Lenny, but what did they know, or care? They were just there to have a few laughs, get drunk, and maybe get laid by one of us model types. But Angelique never let us forget it was always her show."

"If Angelique walked into a club," Eleanor Spencer revealed, being very candid about her best friend, "and not everyone had stopped to notice her, she would go out and come back in again to get it right." She said Pettyjohn was accustomed to being worshipped and adored by men; seemed to thrive in the spotlight of three or four good-looking men vying for her attention. "She was very driven. Very ambitious. She was the leader of our pack."

Figure 57. Outside Abbe Lane.

But then there were always plenty of handsome guys to go around for Eleanor and Darlene because Angelique always seemed to attract men, like moths to a flame. She had a very provocative lifestyle; often behaving more like a man. She had casual sex with no feelings involved, and often with multiple partners in one night. "Angie collected men, like most people collect rare stamps or antiques," Jensen added. "I'm not judging women who act like that. I may or may not have been just like her. But as much as my girlfriends and I act like we don't care, no one wants to feel like another notch on some guy's belt."

Pettyjohn had a lot of famous upscale friends; then she also had some friends on the seedy-size of life, street-wise people who could score her weed or pills, whatever she wanted, to get high. She also consumed a lot of vodka and gin making the rounds. She had a thirst for sex, drugs, and rock-n-roll that seemed to be totally unquenchable.

Keeping Score

"We had a saying between the three of us: 'All's fair in love and war,'" Eleanor explained. "And she lived by those words. Nothing would really stop her from getting what she wanted."

Pettyjohn was not only ambitious and adventurous, she also liked to keep score. Her two best friends claimed that during the time they were hanging out at the LA clubs, she'd kept a secret sex diary, complete with a ratings system, of the men she'd slept with. Darlene said, "What she did was give each man a rating, like 1-10, with ten being the highest score a man could achieve. So, for example, after she had sex with Warren Beatty, she would rate him in terms of longevity, technique, foreplay, and whether she had an orgasm or not. Warren naturally got all tens, but there were other men who did not fare as well."

Angelique Pettyjohn's celebrity-studded love life read like a who's who of the top Hollywood actors of the day — Beatty, Michael Sarrazin, Jack Nicholson, David Carradine, Bill Bixby, Ryan O'Neal, Ben Murphy, Mick Jagger, George Hamilton, Marty Milner, Peter Fonda, James Brolin, Doug McClure, Roger Smith, Pete Duel, Robert Logan, Edd Byrnes, Richard Long, Clint Walker, Roger Davis, and that was only chapter one. Many of them were one-night stands, but then there were others, like Bob Crane or Christopher Jones, who turned into long-term relationships, lasting months, even years. Her friend Eleanor concluded, “One day Angie was going to write a book and expose all of these people she had slept with as a part of the Hollywood scene. It was going to be a best seller.” Unfortunately, when Angelique died in 1992, the secret sex diary disappeared altogether.

Some thought Angelique might have sent the diary to Darlene Jensen or Eleanor Spencer for safe keeping, with strict instructions on what to do with it after her death. Others still believe (to this day) the diary was part of the estate that her two half-sisters, Diana Bourgon and Janice M. Salazar, supposedly inherited. Angelique showed me the diary in 1984, and I just glanced through it, taking note of the extensive list of names. I never saw it again, nor did I get a chance to write down any names and scores. After Angelique’s death, I did ask Darlene and Eleanor about the sex diary, but neither one knew or were willing to reveal what had happened to it. Neither Diana nor Janice responded to my inquiries. When I pressed the Clark County Court system for details about Angelique’s estate, I discovered there had been a legal battle in District Court between the two half-sisters. Like Angelique, her half-sisters are now both dead. For the sake of all concerned, perhaps it’s best one of them took it to the grave.

For the record, her friend Darlene warned her against keeping the diary. “I thought it was potentially dangerous. A well-known list of men she had slept with. I thought she was playing with fire.”

The Dark Side

Even though most people who met and knew Angelique Pettyjohn would agree she was a very kind and compassionate woman who always gave of herself and sought out the best in others, she also had a dark side. “Angelique was the role of her lifetime,” Darlene Jensen shared. “She loved the daily drama, especially when she was in full combat mode with someone she thought had slighted her.”

One of the women she had initially befriended, but then felt had betrayed her, was the beautiful and slightly-older Jennifer Gan aka "Ginny" Gan (1938-2000). Gan was a stage, film, and television actress who had appeared in sixteen film and TV shows in the sixties and early seventies. She was a member of The Actors Studio, playing in James Coburn's spy spoof sequel *In like Flint* (1967) and appearing in an uncredited role in the hit film *Valley of the Dolls* (1967), among other projects. She often competed with Angelique for roles which would have benefited both their careers.

Figure 58. Jennifer "Ginny" Gan..

Pettyjohn befriended Ginny Gan on one of her nights out with the girls, cruising the various clubs in search of celebrities. "In the beginning, we'd party together. We'd go to this party and that party," Angelique recalled, with a half-smile. "It was all very exciting. I'd introduce her around to some of the regulars, and if we got an invitation to go to a guy's house up in the Hollywood Hills, we'd take her along with us. But then she started meeting this actor I had in my sights or dating this other actor I wanted to date, and they'd be calling me for her number." Pettyjohn was so used to being in the proverbial spotlight she resented Gan for attracting more attention than her. She became more and more upset, watching Gan at the various parties with men she herself had found attractive. Finally, in an apparent fit of jealous rage, she cut Ginny Gan loose from her entourage.

Eleanor Spencer remembered the incident like it had happened yesterday. "She basically said you're out on your own. She [Angelique] didn't seem to care that it made her seem like such a small, shallow person." Pettyjohn later regretted her actions and did try to make amends with Ginny Gan, but by then, it was too late. In 1969, Gan changed her name to Jennifer Gan and began a professional association with Roger Corman that lasted through several B movies, one being *Naked Angels* (1969), where she got feature star billing as a biker chick, clad in leather and lace, and *Women in Cages* (1971), where again she got top billing. After playing Abbie in *The Great Northfield Minnesota Raid* (1972) opposite Cliff Robertson, Ginny Gan left Hollywood altogether, settled down, and then passed away at age sixty-two in 2000.

Figure 59. Linda Harrison.

Angelique had a similar dislike for Linda Harrison, the actress who won the much-coveted role of Nova in *Planet of the Apes* (1968). Their careers had also intersected in Gene Kelly's *A Guide for the Married Man* (1967), as well as on a number of television shows, and it always seemed Harrison got the upper hand, winning key roles Pettyjohn felt she deserved to play. She considered Harrison a rival, with never much regard for her, especially when they locked horns over men they were seeing, like Dennis Cole who dated both of them, or in bars where there just wasn't room enough for them both. Ironically, like Gan, Linda Harrison's career never went very far either. Harrison married (then later divorced) studio head Richard Zanuck, then largely retired from acting after *Beneath the Planet of the Apes* (1970), the sequel to the original Apes. She happily returned to her home in Berlin, Maryland to open a consignment shop and raise her sons. On the other hand, Pettyjohn continued working on stage, in film, and television right up until her death.

Figure 60. Sharon Tate.

Like Ginny Gan and Linda Harrison, Angelique Pettyjohn took an instant dislike to Sharon Tate, even though she had only run into her once or twice at clubs. They were born only a few weeks apart in 1943, both blonde and shapely, yet they could have easily been mistaken as sisters. During the 60s, they both played small television roles before appearing in films, and were regularly featured in fashion magazines as models and cover girls. After receiving positive reviews for her comedic and dramatic acting performances, Tate was hailed by critics as one of Hollywood's most promising newcomers. Pettyjohn received similar accolades, but nothing shouted,

"Star!" She disliked Tate because of the roles for which they had competed, and Tate always seemed to win. It started with *Don't Make Waves* (1966), then the occult-themed *Eye of the Devil* (1966), and continued on through *Valley of the Dolls* (1967). Later, when Sharon Tate earned the Golden Globe Award nomination from the Foreign Press Association for her performance as Jennifer North in *Dolls*, Pettyjohn held it against her, believing the award should have been hers. She carried her grudge against Tate right up until her death in 1969.

Both Eleanor Spencer and Darlene Jensen attributed Angelique's hatred of Sharon Tate to a completely different reason. "Christopher Jones," Jensen revealed in an interview sometime after Pettyjohn's death, "his charm and dark, brooding good looks were like an aphrodisiac to Angelique. The more she kissed him, made love to him, the more she wanted. She just couldn't seem to get enough of him. The trouble was that Jones was also seeing other women, in particular Sharon Tate." Spencer agreed with her. "Angie was head-over-heels for him. You know, over the years, we dated a lot of guys, but I had never seen her get so worked up about anyone of them, except Jones. He was like catnip to her. I suppose, if she had been single at the time, she might have married him. But then Tate came into the picture and ruined it all for her."

Ironically, Angelique's clandestine relationship with Jones paralleled the on-screen relationship Jones (as Major Doryan) had with Rose (Sarah Miles), even though she was married to the older, doting husband Charles Shaughnessy (Robert Mitchum) in David Lean's last great film *Ryan's Daughter* (1970). Obviously, in Angelique's case, her husband Otho Pettyjohn may well have suspected her of having sex with other men, but he never did find out for certain. She was all prepared to leave him, however, for Christopher Jones.

The Cowboy from Tennessee

Angelique Pettyjohn ran into Christopher Jones one night on the Sunset Strip, as she and her girlfriends were making the rounds. She had seen him in the title role of ABC's *The Legend of Jesse James* (1965-66) and thought he was a cowboy. Only much later did she learn he was actually from Jackson, Tennessee and had been born William Frank Jones in 1941. She also learned he had been an Army deserter who had served time in a military prison and played in Tennessee Williams' *The Night of the Iguana* on Broadway, opposite Shelley Winters. They had a couple of drinks together at one of the bars and she was totally smitten with him. When Jones excused himself to go to the men's room, Pettyjohn boldly followed him back to a private stall and gave him a blow job as other male patrons came and went. He was equally taken with her. Though married to Susan Strasberg, the daughter of method-acting forebear Lee Strasberg, at the time, Jones invited Angelique to join him for a private party at a small bungalow, actually his manager's guest house. (Fatefully, the bungalow was behind the house where Sharon Tate would later die.) Their private party turned out to be a well-orchestrated seduction, one Jones had played out a number of times with other women, but Pettyjohn didn't seem to mind. By morning, she and Jones had declared their love for each other.

After all thirty-four episodes of *The Legend of Jesse James*, produced by 20th Century-Fox, had run on ABC, Christopher Jones found himself out on the circuit auditioning for new roles Manager Rudi Altobelli found for him. Similarly, Angelique was also busy auditioning for roles her husband, Otho, had lined up for her. But Jones and Pettyjohn still managed to find time for each other. Their hot and steamy romance ran on-and-off throughout most of 1967 and part of 1968. Jones was also involved with a handful of other women, one being Pamela Courson, Jim Morrison's long-time girlfriend. Unfortunately, as Jones' star began to rise in Hollywood, appearing in one successful movie after another, he had less time for Pettyjohn, which she resented, canceling dates at the last minute and throwing herself at other Hollywood actors to get her revenge. When Jones accepted the title role in the 1968 movie *Chubasco*, opposite his wife Susan Strasberg, Pettyjohn was furious. She saw it as the ultimate betrayal. Over and over again, Jones had told Pettyjohn he no longer loved his wife, and yet here he was making a movie with her, playing her character's lover/husband.

Their marriage did not survive the filming, and they divorced in 1968.

Soon after news of their divorce made the pages of *Variety*, Angelique talked to her husband Otho about divorce. He had no clue she was so unhappy, even though he may have suspected a problem with all of her late-night outings.

Figure 61. Christopher Jones

When they did finally divorce in May 1968, Angelique was convinced Christopher Jones would ask her to marry him now that he was free of Strasberg. But then, just after the smashing success of *Wild in the Streets* (1968), Jones took up with Olivia Hussey, Juliet from Franco Zeffirelli's *Romeo and Juliet* (1968), dropping Pettyjohn like a rock. Jones saw Hussey on-and-off for over a year, and she even visited him in Ireland while he was filming *Ryan's Daughter*. Their relationship was a turbulent one, which soon became physically abusive, with Hussey later claiming (in 2018) Jones had raped her while they were dating. Those "well-acquainted" with Jones disputed Hussey's allegations.

As his relationship ended with Olivia Hussey, Christopher met Sharon Tate. She was already married to Roman Polanski and carrying his child, but because Polanski was a workaholic, he left her alone for long stretches of time. Jones took advantage of their separation and became a close friend of Tate's, taking it upon himself to look after her. Soon he began an affair with Tate, while Polanski was busy prepping his next film, which continued for several months. Jones became so close to her he had a premonition about her death and urged her to come with him to Europe. Christopher Jones' affair with Tate was the last straw for Angelique and so arranged to see him one last time. They rendezvoused at the same bar where they had first met. Pettyjohn had a twenty-minute tirade, then threw her drink in his face and stormed out on him. He never quite recovered from their final meeting, and Angelique apparently never forgave Sharon Tate.

Soon after *Three in the Attic* (1968), a sex farce in which Jones appeared with Yvette Mimieux, wrapped production, and he had been released from location shooting in Chapel Hill, North Carolina, Christopher Jones flew to Europe. He made two films with Actress Pia Degermark, *The Looking Glass War* and *Brief Season*, both in 1969. During the filming of *War*, Jones fell in love with his leading lady, and started a romance with Degermark. They remained together for the filming of *Brief Season* and the start of *Ryan's Daughter* for David Lean. Tired of Degermark, ending his relationship with her, he briefly considered going back to Susan Strasberg and wrote her a letter telling her how much he loved her; pleaded with Strasberg to give him another chance. Pamela Courson visited him in England and saw the letter, then dropped him flat, agreeing to return to Jim Morrison. (Courson caught back up with Morrison; was with him in Paris when he died mysteriously on July 2, 1971.)

Jones, seemingly desperate, spurned by several women, reached out to Angelique. They talked several nights on the phone, him begging her to give him that proverbial "last chance," but she also didn't want to have anything to do with him. She had trusted him once, which had resulted in her divorcing her husband, just so she could be free to marry him. Pettyjohn wasn't going to make that mistake again. Christopher Jones found himself alone and terrified at the prospect of being unloved and unwanted.

In August 1969, Jones' premonition came true when Sharon Tate was murdered by members of the Manson family. He suffered a breakdown soon after, and was involved in a horrendous car crash, destroying a silver 1969 365 GT Ferrari (a gift from producer Dino De Laurentiis), while drinking and drugging. According to Sarah Miles' first autobiography, *A Right Royal Bastard*, she and Robert Mitchum conspired to drug Christopher Jones during production on *Ryan's Daughter* in order to help him perform better as an actor. He continued taking drugs and drinking as a way to mask the darkness consuming him. Negative reviews of his acting, especially having his voice dubbed in two of the three films, took a personal toll on Jones. When he returned from Ireland to California, he crashed in his manager's bungalow for a few months, then vanished completely from the public eye.

"I'd had a nervous breakdown over Sharon Tate's death. I had done three pictures in a row in Europe, and had so many love affairs. I was exhausted. I was a tired, tired man," Jones explained in a 1996 interview.

With few offers for new film roles, Christopher Jones decided to abandon his acting career altogether. He kept a low profile, living a very quiet life as a painter and sculptor, first married to Carrie Abernathy, then Paula McKenna. He died in 2014 and was survived by his seven children, including his daughter Jennifer Strasberg. Pettyjohn never saw him again.

Jay Sebring (1933-1969)

During her nights out on the town, Angelique Pettyjohn liked picking up strays to add to her entourage. On one particular night, she picked up a fancy, new best friend, a flamboyant hair stylist, Jay Sebring (1933-1969), at Whisky-a- Go-Go. Born Thomas John Kummer in Birmingham, Alabama, Sebring spent four years in the Navy during the Korean War, before moving to Los Angeles where he changed his name to Jay Sebring (Jay, after the first initial of his middle name; Sebring after the famous car race in Florida.) Sebring had a real flair for men's hair, styling the hair of Warren Beatty, Steve McQueen, and other famous male celebrities of the time. At the request of Kirk Douglas, Sebring did the hair styling for the movie *Spartacus* (1960), thus becoming a member of Hollywood's elite. Sebring had a fondness for models; was actually married to the model Cami for three years in the early sixties. He dated Sharon Tate for several years, even later asked her to marry him. She declined, and soon met and fell in love with Roman Polanski during the making of *The Fearless Vampire Killers*, a horror spoof, in London in 1966. She played the role of the innkeeper's daughter. (Tate and Polanski were married in London on January 20, 1968.) He remained friendly with Tate and befriended Polanski until both he and Sharon Tate and three others were killed by members of the Manson family on August 9, 1969, in the home she shared with Polanski. At the time of her death, she was eight-and-a-half months pregnant with the couple's son. Polanski would later comment that despite Sebring's lifestyle, he was a very lonely person who regarded Sharon Tate and himself as his family.

"I always liked having him around," Pettyjohn said, with a shrug. "Jay was full of so much positive energy and had such a calming effect on me. When I'd go out with the girls at night, I could always count on running into Jay somewhere. And no matter what mood I was in, he'd always cheer me up."

Figure 62. Jay Sebring.

Jay Sebring did more than cheer Angelique up. Like he had done for Hong Kong martial artist Bruce Lee, whom he had met at the International Karate Championships in Long Beach in 1964, Sebring introduced Pettyjohn to his friend William Dozier, an actor and television producer. Dozier was best known for producing *Batman* and *The Green Hornet* for ABC, and would later cast Angelique Pettyjohn in small roles in each of the television series.

"She just had him around, like one of the girls," Darlene told me. "Feeding her sense of stardom, like a member of her entourage. I'm sure if she had made it really big, she would have had Jay styling her hair until the end."

Unfortunately, Jay Sebring's life was cut short, along with Sharon Tate and others, in what was considered to be the crime of the century.

The Manson Family Murders

In 1969, beyond the bright lights of the big city laid a seedy, desolate, dark side of Hollywood rarely glimpsed by the public; known only to those who lived and worked within the Industry.

Coke, as a recreation drug, was plentiful and cheap. Snorting was done out in the open by a lot of people working for the various studios. In fact, a major delivery company, and each of its offices in Hollywood, employed someone on the inside who sold coke with next-day delivery.

More sleazy directors and producers bedded starry-eyed newcomers arriving in Hollywood on the "casting couch" than at any other time in the history of the cinema. It was not uncommon to find some young starlet out washing a studio mogul's Maserati in a bikini as part of her audition, then giving the same studio boss a blow-job to solidify her next role. Sexually-transmitted diseases and the drugs to cure them were being passed around like Halloween candy. Pedophilia and homosexual behavior were quite common; something the big studios didn't mind terribly as long as the profits continued to pour in from that last picture. And since Hollywood was a company town, one call was all it took to get law enforcement or government officials to cover up crimes and criminal behavior of those in the public eye.

Figure 63. Roman Polanski and Sharon Tate on their wedding day, January 20, 1968.

In addition to the many mainstream problems, certain fringe elements made things even worse, as they contributed to the growing darkness at the edges of the Hollywood dream factory. Hippies and other members of the counter-culture flooded Los Angeles and other cities up-and-down the West Coast with their communes, radical ideology, rampant drug use, the growing peace movement and its opposition to President Richard Nixon's extreme Right-Wing values and the war in Vietnam. Satanism and occult practices challenged conventional religious beliefs, moving from the city limits into the middle-class suburbs. Unabashed racism and bigotry created an even greater divide between the rich and powerful living in their private gated communities and the poor and destitute squatting on land known as Death Valley. "Helter Skelter" was not just a song by the Beatles, but also a manifesto predicting an apocalyptic racial war between the "haves" and the "have-nots" of the world, ultimately leading to the end. Mainstream society seemed to be coming apart at the seams; the setting just right for what would become one of the most heinous crimes in America.

Angelique had seen both sides of Hollywood — the good and the bad — and the seedier side was one that she knew all too well, and sometimes it scared her. She maintained a respectful distance, except for those times when she needed a fix to chase away the demons in her head. She bought drugs regularly from her contacts on the societal fringe of Los Angeles, and on several occasions, even drove as far as the Spahn Ranch, an old movie-set ranch that had become a commune, to score LSD, Marijuana, and other drugs from the teenaged girls living there. Little did she know the girls all belonged to the Manson Family.

During the months leading up to the Tate/LaBianca murders in August 1969, Charles Manson was fighting demons of his own. He believed he was the fifth angel of Biblical prophecy, with the Beatles as the first four angels literally trumpeting the coming Apocalypse in their songs. His "chimerical vision," as it was termed by the court that heard Manson's appeal from his conviction for the murders, evolved from his own twisted misreading of the lyrics from the Beatles' *White Album* and scripture. His revelation contended that he and his followers had been tasked by God with precipitating the last great war, a racial war between blacks and whites. Two years earlier, the self-described cult leader had begun forming what would later become known as the "Manson Family," a group composed largely of young, naive women from middle-class families; runaways looking for a "father figure" to lead them. He sequestered them on a ranch, not far from Death Valley, then radicalized them with his teachings combined with a liberal prescription of hallucinogenic drugs. He often spoke to his cult members about Helter Skelter, boasting to others, some former inmates he had met in prison, that he would become more famous than God one day. In February 1969, he awoke with a "divine" vision, inspired by a reading of the New Testament's Book of Revelation, and told everyone in his compound the plan. He and his followers then worked for the next few months on every aspect of his plan.

Figure 64. Victims of the Tate/LaBianca Murders.

On the night of August 8, 1969, Manson directed his first lieutenant, Charles "Tex" Watson, to take three of his followers, in particular Susan Atkins, Linda Kasabian, and Patricia Krenwinkel, to a home located at 10050 Cielo Drive in Benedict Canyon, west of Hollywood, he had previously surveilled, and kill everyone there. Months earlier, Manson went there, looking for Terry Melcher (son of Doris Day) who had promised to make him a rock star, and learned from the owner, Rudi Altobelli, that Melcher (and his wife Candice Bergen) no longer lived there. Altobelli had recently rented the property to Sharon Tate and her husband Roman Polanski.

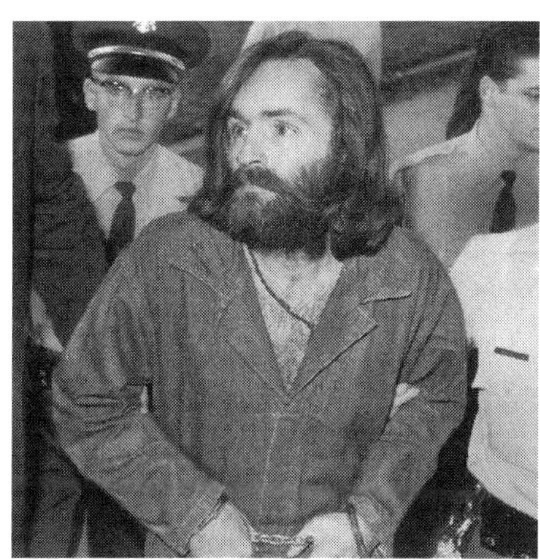

Figure 65. Charles Manson being jailed.

Enraged that he had been made a fool by Melcher, Manson decided the famous couple would be his first victims, and sent his followers to kill them. They killed Steven Parent, the property caretaker, in the driveway; then, soon after Watson, Atkins, and Krenwinkel had forced their way into the house, Manson's followers coerced Jay Sebring, Sharon Tate, Wojciech Frykowski, and coffee heiress Abigail Folger into the living room. (Polanski was away in Europe, working on *A Day at the Beach*.) They ordered them to lie face down on the floor, but when Sebring protested, reminding the intruders of Tate's advanced pregnancy, they shot him, kicked him in the face while he lay dying, then stabbed him several times. The Manson family members then murdered the other four, even Tate who was eight and a half months pregnant. As they left the home, Atkins wrote the word "pig" in blood on the front door.

On the following night, six family members — Leslie Van Houten and Steve "Clem" Grogan, along with the four from the previous night — drove out to the home of supermarket executive Leno LaBianca and his wife Rosemary, killing them, too. The murders created a nationwide sensation, and for one brief moment in time, Charles Manson's name was on the lips of everyone in the country.

When news of the senseless slayings broke, Angelique was beside herself with grief. She couldn't believe her gentle friend, Jay Sebring, was dead. She had always imagined they would be lifelong friends; joking with each other long after the bright lights of Hollywood were a distant memory. Five days later, Angelique and two of her girlfriends attended Sebring's funeral. Steve McQueen gave the eulogy.

Several months later, the Los Angeles Police Department arrested Manson and his followers who had committed the murders. They stood trial, and under the prosecution of Vincent Bugliosi, author of *Helter Skelter* and technical consultant on the *Helter Skelter* (1976) miniseries and 2004 film, were sentenced to death for their crimes. In February 1972, their death sentences were commuted to life in prison when the California Supreme Court abolished the death penalty in that state. Manson died of a heart attack and complications from colon cancer in prison on November 19, 2017. He was eighty-three years old.

In the summer of 2019, on the fiftieth anniversary of the tragic murders, Quentin Tarantino's ninth film, *Once Upon a Time in Hollywood*, debuted at the box office, featuring the "Manson Family murders" as a backdrop to his magnum opus about the dark side of Hollywood. Margot Robbie played actress Sharon Tate and Damon Herriman essayed the role of Charles Manson. Others in the cast included Rafal Zawierucha as Roman Polanski, Samantha Robinson as Abigail Folger, and Emile

Hirsch as Jay Sebring. Of course, as written and directed by Tarantino, the film plays loosely with the facts as set forth in the historical record, and turns the tragic story into a fairy-tale, not unlike Daniel Farrands' *The Haunting of Sharon Tate* (2019), released several months earlier with Hilary Duff as Tate.

The *Playboy* Mansion

"I got my first invitation to go to the *Playboy* Mansion from Pompeo Posar (1921-2004), a magazine staff photographer who shot many of the centerfolds. He was a lovely and very talented man," Pettyjohn recalled. "Later, after I had done a few television episodes, one of which was 'Love and the Modern Wife' for

Figure 66. The Playboy Mansion.

Love, American Style (1969), Bob Crane took me as his guest to the Mansion. I didn't know it at the time, but I soon learned Bob was a regular there and had bedded half of Hef's bunnies. Whether his wife Sigrid knew or didn't know, I can't say. It was the swinging sixties and Bob was a real swinger."

The 22,000 square-foot *Playboy* Mansion was described in a *Forbes* magazine article in 2007 as "Gothic-Tudor" style, with equal parts owing to a revival of the Gothic and the Tudor styles. Designed by Arthur R. Kelly in 1927, it has twenty-two

Figure 67. Hugh Hefner and His *Playboy* Bunnies.

rooms, a wine cellar, a game room, a zoo and aviary (and related pet cemetery), tennis courts, a waterfall and swimming pool area, in addition to a patio and barbecue area, a grotto, a sauna, and a bathhouse. A dozen bedrooms with connecting bathrooms make up the rest of the Mansion. Described in a 2010 memoir, *Bunny Tales*, by former girlfriend and *Playboy* bunny, Izabella St. James, the house was in need of some serious renovation. "Everything in the Mansion felt old and stale, and Archie, the house dog, would regularly relieve himself on the hallway curtains, adding a powerful whiff of urine to the general scent of decay."

Pettyjohn recalled visiting the Mansion for the first time, "A spectacular home! Absolutely enormous. I had never seen anything like it. The first place I'd ever seen that had quarters for the servants. Hef [Hugh Hefner] came down the stairs with several of his girls and greeted me with a kiss on the cheek. I felt like royalty. Then he went about his business, seeing to his other guests."

Angelique and her two girlfriends got themselves a couple of drinks at the bar and started mingling with the other party guests; the usual actors and producers, casting directors, singers, and politicians they had seen nightly on the Strip. At one point, Pompeo Posar acted as Angelique's personal guide, introducing her to others as an up-and-coming actress. First, she met China [pronounced "chee-na" to rhyme with "Tina"] Lee, *Playboy's* Playmate of the Month for the August 1964 issue, and the first Asian-American Playmate. Since Posar had photographed her centerfold, she treated him and newcomer Angelique with a great deal of courtesy. She introduced the two of them to comedian Mort Sahl, whom she was dating and would later marry in 1967. China Lee had just completed filming Woody Allen's *What's Up Tiger Lily?* (1966) in which she had performed a striptease, one she discussed at length with Pettyjohn when she learned that Angelique had been a stripper in Las Vegas.

Figure 68. Fantasy Artist Frank Frazetta.

Figure 69. Science Fiction Author Ray Bradbury.

Next, Angelique was introduced to artist Frank Frazetta (1928-2010), who had worked with Al Capp on his "Li'l Abner" comic strip before joining *Playboy's* art department to illustrate its own parody strip of "Li'l Abner," "Li'l Annie Fannie." Frazetta had just broken into the mainstream, drawing book covers for the re-issues of the *Tarzan* and *Conan* books, as well as movie posters for several big Hollywood movies, like *What's New Pussycat?* (1965), *After the Fox* (1966), and *Hotel Paradiso* (1966). She and Frazetta flirted on-and-off throughout the evening, and he even offered to paint Angelique in the nude, which she discussed with him, although nothing ever came of the offer. Unbeknownst to all, Frazetta's fame as a fantasy illustrator was still ten years away with his famous posters for the *Mars* books by Edgar Rice Burroughs.

One of the people Angelique met later that night was a forty-five-year-old writer with a crew cut and thick, horn-rimmed glasses who wrote poetry and science fiction. Pettyjohn found him "very interesting." Ray Bradbury (1920-2012). She confessed of having never heard of him before and asked him somewhat naively about the books he had written. Rather than bore her with a list of his stories and novels, he told her the true story of how a young editor once called upon him for a favor. The young editor was starting up a new magazine that would have a certain appeal to men, and he needed good, thoughtful material to fill it. Bradbury told her he sold his short novel, *The Fireman*, for $400 to run in the magazine. The young editor was Hugh Hefner; the magazine, the first issue of *Playboy*. The novel was later published by Ballantine Books under the name *Fahrenheit 451* (1953). She vowed to go out and read it the first chance she got, but alas, the closest she ever got to Bradbury's work was buying a ticket to the 1966 film version by François Truffaut, starring Oskar Werner and Julie Christie. The movie version was immensely popular and did justice to Bradbury's dystopian novel.

Later that evening, sitting on the couch and listening to music with some of the other guests, she happened to glance across the room. The huge party was starting to wind down. As fewer and fewer people danced, most others had begun pairing up for their own intimate mingling. With lots of refer smoke in the air, Angelique strained to keep her focus. She recalled, "I just kept staring at this person's lips. They were the most fascinating thing I had ever seen. I just stared and stared and stared. It was Mick Jagger, sharing a 'doobie' [a hand-rolled marijuana cigarette] with one of Hef's *Playboy* bunnies. I must have been stoned myself because I could barely keep my eyes open."

Working the Various Corners of Hollywood

Tom Gries (1922-1977), film director, writer, and producer, said, "There were a lot of girls like Angelique who seemed to work their way through the various corners of Hollywood."

Gries met Angelique and her girlfriends one night at one of the clubs. He had been having a drink with a few friends when she approached him at the bar and insisted they knew each other. Although flattered by the younger woman's interest in him, he had met enough up-and-coming starlets to know she was just "working" the room, looking for a contact. Having started in television in the fifties as a writer, he had directed several low-budget movies before concentrating his attention on television. He had created *The Rat Patrol*, a very popular series that followed the exploits of a group of Allied soldiers during the North African campaign in WWII for ABC Television in 1966. He gave her his business card at the bar and asked her to come in and read for the role of Gabrielle, Moffitt's ex-girlfriend, for second season episode "The Fatal Reunion Raid." The role eventually went to Louise Sorel, who had played the role of Rayna Kapec on *Star Trek* before headlining the long-running soap opera, *Days of Our Lives* (1992-2000).

Over the years, Gries kept in touch with Angelique and recommended her to several fellow show-runners; two being Bruce Geller for *Mission Impossible* and Sheldon Leonard for *I Spy*. Ironically, Tom Gries directed the two-part television movie *Helter Skelter* (1976), which detailed the gruesome murder of Sharon Tate and her friends by the Manson family. Gries collapsed and died of a heart attack while playing tennis at age fifty-four in 1977.

While Angelique partied in Hollywood, her husband Otho stayed at home, planning her career. He worked tirelessly for her, calling casting agents, producers, show runners, basically anyone who would listen to him. She'd come home after two or three in the morning, and he would have her schedule for the next day all laid out for her. Otho Pettyjohn had no interest in her party lifestyle. He preferred just staying home, having a beer and watching television. Angelique felt it was essential to her career to network with other actors, so her celebrity-studded lifestyle became the only reality she knew.

5
Cold Readings, Warm Heart

It was about three years into my career, after I had done a number of different films and was a working actress in Hollywood, that I did my first television show. I had a small part here, and then a larger part there. There were so many it's difficult to recall which came before and after Star Trek. *I did a* Batman *episode, thanks to a friend who had a connection with the producer. I was on* Get Smart!, The Girl from U.N.C.L.E. *(where I had a fairly large part),* Felony Squad, Good Morning, World, *and a number of those television shows from the sixties. The work was steady, the pay was good, not great, and I think it helped to raise my profile. Of course, today, a lot of well-known actors do television, but back in those days, it was a place to get discovered and to hone your talent as an actor.*

In 1967, thanks in part to the hard work of her husband and personal manager Otho Pettyjohn, Angelique started popping up on the small screen, that little box in the majority of homes Americans turned to for their entertainment. She had just the right look for making TV guest appearances on a number of the fantasy, spy, and science fiction series debuting on the big three networks. Though probably best known for her role on *Star Trek*, Pettyjohn also made memorable appearances on other sixties television shows, like *Batman*, *The Green Hornet*, *Mister Terrific*, *Felony Squad*, *Good Morning*, *World*, *The Girl from*

U.N.C.L.E., *Love, American Style*, and *Bracken's World*. One of her more popular roles was playing spy Charlie Watkins on *Get Smart!* The male spy goes undercover in the form of the shapely Angelique Pettyjohn as a Las Vegas cigarette girl who aids Don Adams' bumbling Maxwell Smart on several missions. With residuals from repeat episodes, Pettyjohn might have done well to stay in television, to have followed the example of her friend Joan Collins, but Angelique was determined to make it big in Hollywood, considering television a stepping stone to a career in features. Ironically, after nearly a twenty-year absence from television, she returned to play a hooker, Lotta Gue, on two episodes of the award-winning *Hill Street Blues* in 1984.

Television in the Sixties

Television in the sixties was considerably different than television most people watch today. Instead of having hundreds of channels at your fingertips, which is what cable television has brought to most Americans (and the world) today, viewers in the sixties had only three channels to watch, ABC, CBS, and NBC. For those fortunate enough to live near a major metropolitan area, like New York or Chicago or Los Angeles, viewers may have also had a local channel, like WOR, WGN, or KTLA, that broadcasted shows in syndication or re-runs of cancelled first-run shows. Television reception wasn't obtained through a cable or dish, but rabbit-ear antenna located on top of the television or an aerial antenna attached to the roof of the house. The big three networks determined what American viewers were going to watch, based on the important Nielsen Ratings Systems that calculated how many viewers were tuned into a particular television episode. For instance, the final episode "The Judgment: Part II" (Season 4, Episode 30, or 4.30) of TV's long-running series *The Fugitive* (1963-1967) was the most-watched television series episode at that time, with 25.70 million households (45.9% of American households with a television set and a 72% share) tuned in. Immediately after the episode aired, problems with water pressure were reported in several major cities, like Chicago, as people got up to use the bathroom all at the same time.

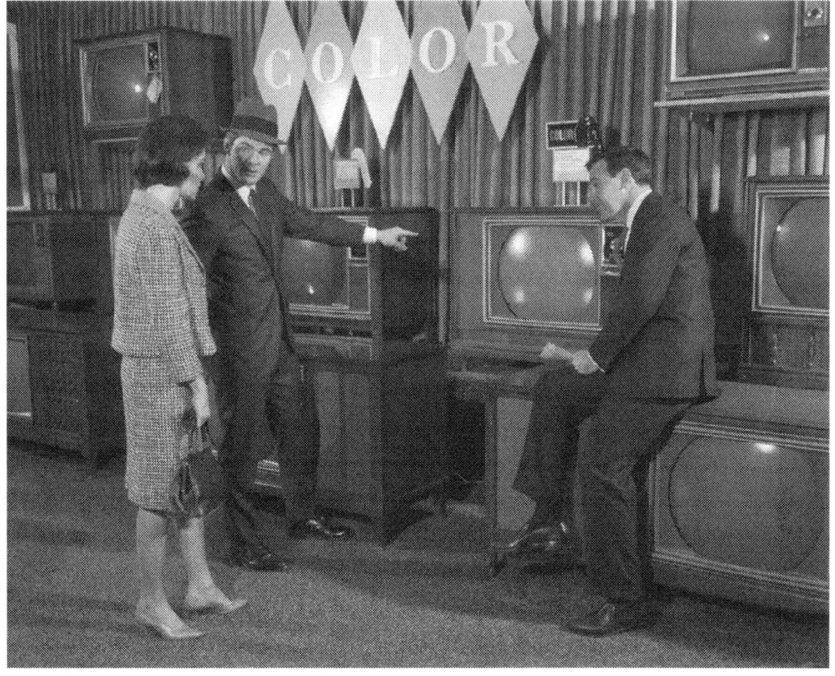

Figure 70. Television turns from B&W to Color in the Sixties.

The all-important Nielsen Ratings determined whether a show would end prematurely and be replaced mid-season (in January), run one season, or stretch out to eight or ten years (or more). *Gunsmoke* (1955-1975), the longest running show in television's history, ran for twenty seasons on CBS Television. Ratings helped advertisers determine which shows to support, and even though we saw fewer commercials in the sixties (compared with the shows of today), advertisers like Ford, Kellogg's, Hunts, Coca Cola, or Del Monte really controlled what Americans watched on our television sets. Shows typically ran twenty-eight to thirty episodes per season, not like the ten to twenty typical of today. Episodes for a one-hour show ran fifty-one to fifty-two minutes, while for a thirty-minute show, it ran twenty-five minutes. Today, even with the cable market, episodes run forty to forty-five minutes for a one-hour or eighteen to twenty minutes for a thirty-minute, which leaves more time for advertisers to promote a product. The top shows by network were the ones most Americans watched. *Gunsmoke*, *Perry Mason*, *Gilligan's Island*, *The Beverly Hillbillies*, and *The Andy Griffith Show* were popular shows on CBS in the sixties. *Bonanza*, *The Bob Hope Show*, *The Virginian*, *The High Chaparral*, *I Dream of Jeannie*, and *The Man from U.N.C.L.E.* ran on NBC, and *The Fugitive*, *Marcus Welby, M.D.*, *The Flintstones*, *My Three Sons*, *77 Sunset Strip*, and *American Bandstand* ran on ABC.

Television of yester year was also entertainment families watched together as a whole. A typical Friday night consisted of the family watching their favorite show on television, sitting on the sofa with a bowl of popcorn, and each person with his or her favorite beverage. Popcorn was cooked on the stove in a large kettle, shaken as it popped; only later did families have access to Jiffy Pop Popcorn. Pizza was rare, but if family members had a taste for pizza, it had to be picked up. Back then, there was no such thing as pizza delivery . Most families in the United States

Figure 71. Families watched television together.

never owned a color television (until the seventies), so shows, even if they were broadcast by the networks in color, were watched in monochrome on the old black and white television set. The cost of purchasing a color television was out of reach for most mainstream Americans until well into the next decade when advances in transistors replaced the old tubes. [I didn't see my first show in color until I visited a rich friend. I marveled at the cool colors while watching a second season episode of *Lost in Space* (1966). The first season was telecast in black and white.] And since most families couldn't afford two televisions, everyone watched the same show, even if there were detractors in the house who wanted to watch something other than *Peyton Place* (1964-1969), sometimes as many as three nights a week.

In simplest terms, television in the sixties played an important role in the lives of most Americans, and had as great an impact on popular culture as did the rise of cable in the eighties, the Internet in the nineties, and the development of alternative forms of media in the new millennium.

Most Americans who watched television in the sixties remember the decade started out when Westerns were king and comedy/variety shows were clean fun. *Bonanza*, *Bronco*, *Cheyenne*, *Death Valley Days*, *Gunsmoke*, *Have Gun-Will Travel*, *Rawhide*, *Wyatt Earp*, *Wagon Train*, and *The Rifleman* were all carry-overs from the fifties. And just as the Western had begun to wane at the Motion Picture Box Office, televised Westerns for the small screen dominated the airways. Similarly, comedy/variety shows featuring Bob Hope, Carol Burnett, Andy Williams, Jackie Gleason, Red Skelton, and Ed Sullivan were all the rage when the decade began, but by the close, they had been supplanted by shows like *American Bandstand*, *Hootenanny*, *Hullabaloo*, *Shindig*, and others with subversive elements, like *Sonny and Cher* and *Laugh-in*.

Networks continued to crank out the usual crime dramas, comedies, and attorney and medical shows, but they also experimented with shows set during WWII, like *Combat!*, *The Rat Patrol*, *Hogan's Heroes*, and shows set in the future, like *Voyage to the Bottom of the Sea*, *Lost in Space*, *Star Trek*, *The*

Invaders, and *The Outer Limits*. Finally, the networks also took a cue from the huge success of James Bond at the Box Office and created a handful of popular series set against the backdrop of international intrigue and espionage, like *Get Smart!*, *The Man from U.N.C.L.E.*, *Mission: Impossible*, *The Wild, Wild West*, *Honey West*, and *Amos Burke-Secret Agent*. It was into this milieu of television shows Pettyjohn sought to hone her craft as an up-and-coming actress and get discovered by the TV-watching public.

Cold Reading

Cold readings were a common practice in Hollywood in the sixties, and are still frequently employed by producers or casting agents today as a way to audition actors in order to get a general idea of their performing capabilities. Essentially, a cold reading is reading aloud from a script or other text with little-to-no practice or rehearsal. A good actor or actress who has learned their stagecraft relies on acting techniques to develop and communicate the scene with confidence and precision, even though he or she may be new to the materials. He should be able to project speech rhythms and rhymes as well as bring out the intent, mood, and characterization of a piece through appropriate articulation and body language. Cold readings tend to separate good actors from the fairly new, and often make a huge difference in terms of who is hired to play a particular role and who goes home without a contract. They were not unlike the huge cattle calls Pettyjohn had already experienced in Las Vegas, but instead of showing off her dance steps, she was demonstrating her acting skills.

> *As you may know, when you go in for an interview for a part in a television series, you're in an outer office and a secretary gives you a script, which has the description of the character you're to play and some dialogue, and you have about ten minutes to look through it. Then you go into an inner office where you have a casting director, the director, the producer,*

and various people. Then you'll sit there and read it. It's called a cold reading. Nine times out of ten, they'll expect you to perform the scene brilliantly, even though you've only looked at the lines for a couple of minutes.

Pettyjohn recalled that most cold readings she did for producers or casting agents were not as frightening as they could have been considering the industry. Ninety percent of the time, she was given a few minutes on her own to read through the lines and come up with the character for her scene. For the other ten percent, she simply dug in tight, fearless in her pursuit. Typically, Pettyjohn would read the script over once or twice since it was short, underline her lines and memorize them.

Comic Book Superheroes

Jay Sebring introduced Angelique Pettyjohn to his long-time associate, William Dozier, an actor and television producer, at a private house party in the Hollywood Hills in 1966. Previously, Sebring had brought Hong Kong martial artist Bruce Lee to Dozier's attention, who hired Lee to be one of the two leads (along with Van Williams) for a new series he was developing at ABC as a spin-off of the hugely popular *Batman* (1967). The series, *The Green Hornet*, featured the exploits of playboy-media mogul Britt Reid (Williams), the owner and publisher of *The Daily Sentinel*. As the masked vigilante Green Hornet, Britt fights crime with the assistance of his valet Kato (Lee), a martial-artist, and his weapons-enhanced car, the Black Beauty. On police records, the Green Hornet is wanted as a criminal, but in reality, the crime fighter pretends to be a criminal in order to infiltrate the dark underbelly of the underworld. *The Green Hornet* debuted on ABC television on September 9, 1966, and while the adaptation of the comic book character had proved to be a critical success, the show had yet to find its audience by the first week in October. Unlike the heavy-camp, semi-comedic storytelling that characterized *Batman*, *The Green Hornet* took a more serious and realistic approach to masked crime-fighting. However, this approach may have actually hurt the show as its rival debuted one outlandish villain after the other, such as the Joker and the Riddler. *The Green Hornet* played things so straight, it turned out to be deadly dull by contrast.

Dozier knew he needed to do something to shake things up a bit in order to rescue the show from cancellation, and was willing to consider anything, possibly even giving the young starlet a shot. He cast Angelique in a small, walk-on part as the "Girl" in Episode 1.18, "Corpse of the Year: Part 1." She worked several days on the set just after the Halloween holiday in 1966, and the episode aired two and a half months later on Friday, January 13, 1967. During its nighttime rounds, a *Daily Sentinel* delivery truck is fired on by an imposter Green Hornet, driving an exact duplicate of the Black Beauty. Attacks on the paper's employees continue throughout the night. It appears someone has declared war on the *Sentinel*. Britt Reid is soon contacted by Dan Scully (Tom Simcox), a reporter for the rival *Daily Express* paper, claiming his boss Sabrina Bradley (Joanna Dru) is out to

Figure 72. Angelique is the "girl" on *The Green Hornet* (1967).

destroy the *Sentinel* using any means necessary. That goal seems close to fulfillment when Reid attends a party of *Daily Express* publisher Simon Neal. As he and Neal (J. Edward McKinley) stand outside, the Green Hornet poser drives up, announces his intentions to kill Britt Reid, and fires his gun. By the time the episode aired, the fate of *The Green Hornet* had already been decided by network executives. While Van Williams as Britt Reid survives the gun-shot attempt on his life, ABC had nailed *The Green Hornet's* coffin shut. The series ran through March 17, 1967, lasting twenty-six episodes. ABC repeated the series after its cancellation by the network, until July 14, 1967, when *The Green Hornet* had its last broadcast on network television.

Figure 73. *The Green Hornet.*

Despite its only lasting one season, *The Green Hornet* amassed a cult following of fans, most likely because of martial arts legend Bruce Lee, who made his American television debut on the show. Since Angelique Pettyjohn appeared as the "Girl" in Episode 1.18, later in the season, William Dozier gave Angelique her second chance to play in his world of televised superheroes, and cast her in another walk-on role in Episode 2.51 — "A Piece of the Action" on the *Batman* series. She received credit as "The First Model," and shot for less than a day in February 1967. The episode she shot featured Batman and Robin in a team-up with the Green Hornet and Kato. Angelique had her own team-up of sorts with Jan Watson (December 1942-), the actress who played

"The Second Model." Watson was actually a friend Angelique had met while auditioning for the role of a "Slaygirl" in *The Ambushers* (1967), then later introduced her to the LA party scene. Jan Watson had also played in *Dr. Goldfoot and the Bikini Machine* (1965), several Matt Helm pictures, and later married the prodigious director Henry Levin. Angelique Pettyjohn and Jan Watson looked awesome as the two models in the *Batman* episode.

In "A Piece of the Action," which aired on March 1, 1967, the Green Hornet and Kato (Van Williams and Bruce Lee) have come to Gotham City to bust a counterfeiting stamp ring. Believed to be arch-criminals by nearly everyone, their midnight visits to Colonel Gumm (Roger C. Carmel) at the Pink Chip Stamps Factory stirs alarm. Even Batman and Robin (Adam West and Burt Ward) believe they are out for a piece of the action.

The next day, Pinky Pinkston (Diane McBain), owner of the Pink Chip Stamp Company, calls the police who, in turn, hands the case to Batman. Meanwhile, Bruce Wayne gets a call from his boyhood friend, Britt Reed. They're both scheduled to have lunch with Pinky at a swanky restaurant, where they agree to behave like gentlemen, rather than rivals for her affection. The two playboy millionaires take turns flirting with two lingerie models (Angelique Pettyjohn and Jan Watson). Figuring the Green Hornet's goal must be the Gotham Gothic, a rare and valuable stamp, Batman and Robin trail him and Kato to the Pink Chip Stamps Factory. But when Colonel Gumm and his men make giant stamps out of the visiting crime fighters, it appears Batman and Robin will soon be doomed to the same fate. The episode was written by Charles Hoffman and directed by Oscar Rudolph. The great Edward G. Robinson has an uncredited cameo as himself, and watch for Alex Rocco, the actor who plays Moe Green in *The Godfather* (1972), in a small role as Block.

Batman was a sixties American, live-action television series, based on the DC comic book character of the same name, which starred Adam West and Burt Ward, as Batman and Robin, respectively, two crime-fighting heroes who defended Gotham City from an assortment of super villains, like the Joker, the

Figure 74. *Batman* TV show (1966).

Riddler, the Penguin, and Catwoman. It aired on the American Broadcasting Company (ABC) network for two and a half seasons from January 12, 1966 to March 14, 1968, airing twice weekly for its first two seasons and weekly for the third, with a total of 120 episodes produced by William Dozier during its run on network television.

The popularity of comic-book inspired shows like *Batman* and, to a lesser extent, *The Green Hornet* spawned a couple of imitators on the rival networks in January of 1967. *Mister Terrific*, from the creative talents of Jack Arnold and Budd Grossman, debuted on CBS Television, and *Captain Nice* premiered on NBC Television. They were both created to take advantage of the Bat-mania sweeping through the country. Dozier wasn't the least bit concerned with the two young upstarts and decided there was enough room on the airwaves for more than one silly superhero. Both were largely ignored by the public, generating only a handful of fans, and were gone by the fall. In between shooting episodes for *The Green Hornet* and *Batman*, Angelique took time off from her work with William Dozier to play Carol in *Mister Terrific*, a thirty-minute sitcom shot at Universal Studios in November 1966. Episode 1.3 — "I Can't Fly" aired on January 23, 1967. And, Angelique continued to flirt with William Dozier, Adam West, and other male actors out on the Sunset Strip at night.

The premise for *Mister Terrific* was a unique one for network television, in part due to issues raised by Standards and Practices regarding the use of pill-popping. Stanley Beamish (Stephen Strimpell) is a mild-mannered weakling who labors as a gas station attendant at a Washington, D.C.-area gas station, but that is merely his secret identity. In reality, he also fights crime as a top-secret super-agent for the Bureau of Secret Projects. When the Government Agency needs Stanley for a mission, he takes a "power pill," candy coated, resembling a giant jawbreaker, which gives him the strength of a thousand men and enables him to fly, much like Superman, albeit by furiously flapping hi

Figure 75. Angelique climbing steps of fame.

arms. There was a catch, however; the pills only lasted an hour, and he could only take one pill per day. Later, as the producers worked out all the kinks, he was allowed to have, in a pinch, a pair of booster pills that would give Mister Terrific an extra twenty minutes of power. To his friends, even best pal and fellow gas station attendant Hal Walters (Dick Gautier), Stanley was still just plain old Stanley. But to Bureau of Special Projects chief Barton J. Reed (John McGiver), Stanley was the caped superhero, known as Mister Terrific. Unfortunately, the fact that Stanley got his power from drugs made the show an unpopular one among many adults who were trying to teach their children about the evils of illegal drug use, and thus, when the show went off the air, it never resurfaced in syndication.

Mister Terrific Episode 1.3 — "I Can't Fly" finds one of Air Force One's landing wheels stuck in the "up" position during a cross-country flight, putting the president's life in jeopardy. The Bureau of Special Projects summons Stanley Beamish to make the necessary repairs in flight as Mister Terrific, but unfortunately, the power pills have stopped working for our hero. Reed (McGiver), Trent (Paul Smith), and Dr. Reynolds (Ned Glass), inventors of the "power pill," scramble to identify the problem, while Stanley's continued efforts to fly eventually land him in a psychiatric ward under the care of a psychiatrist (David Opatoshu) and his nurse (Eileen Wesson). Reed and Trent work against the clock to free Stanley, now confined to a straitjacket, and administer a re-formulated pill before the president's plane runs out of fuel and crashes. The episode aired on January 23, 1967, featuring Pettyjohn in the role of a sympathetic girlfriend named Carol.

Charlie Watkins and *Get Smart!* (1967)

Even though she was probably best known for her role as "Shahna-the Girl in the Silver Bikini," on *Star Trek*, Angelique Pettyjohn's favorite part was Charlie Watkins, an undercover male agent and master of disguise. Agent 38 appeared as a scantily clad, glamorous woman in two of season two's episodes. He also appeared once in season four, with a different actress (Karen Arthur), as Angelique was unavailable. As part of his clever disguise and the fun in playing the character, Watkins had the ability to switch to a feminine voice, which makes for an interesting scene when the lead asks for an update and Charlie quickly switches to his masculine voice.

"My professional manager, my husband Otho at the time, got a copy of the script for that particular week of *Get Smart!*, read through it, and saw a part with a description he felt suited

Figures 76 & 77. Pettyjohn as Charlie Watkins, *Get Smart!* (1967).

Figure 78. Angelique, opposite Ted Knight, on *Get Smart!*

me, so he arranged for me get an interview," she remembered. Arnie Rosen and Jess Oppenheimer invited Angelique to come into their offices at Talent Associates to do a cold reading. Pettyjohn recalled not doing a very good reading for them, but when they reviewed her physical assets for the part of Charlie Watkins, they agreed they could always dub her voice for the female lines. They ended up dubbing her only for the masculine lines. The two hired her on the spot, and after the episode aired, she got so much fan mail and critical acclaim her character was written into the script for a second appearance later that same season.

Get Smart! (1965-1970) was an American television comedy series that poked fun at the secret agent genre made popular by the James Bond films and had spawned a whole host of imitators, such as *The Man from U.N.C.L.E.* (1964-1968) and *The Wild Wild West* (1965-1969). Created by Mel Brooks with

Buck Henry, *Get Smart!* starred Don Adams as Agent 86, Maxwell Smart; Barbara Feldon as Agent 99, Smart's partner and love interest; and Edward Platt as the Chief of CONTROL, a secret American government counter-espionage agency. Henry said he and Mel Brooks created the show at the request of Daniel Melnick, who, along with Leonard Stern and David Susskind, were partners in Talent Associates, the show's production company. They wanted to capitalize on "the two biggest things in the entertainment world today," which was the James Bond films and Inspector Clouseau from *The Pink Panther* (1963) and *A Shot in the Dark* (1964). Brooks referred to *Get Smart!* As, "An insane combination of James Bond and a Mel Brooks comedy. I was sick of looking at all those nice sensible situation comedies. They were such distortions of life. If a maid ever took over my house like *Hazel*, I'd set her hair on fire. I wanted to do a crazy, unreal comic-strip kind of thing about something besides a family. No one had ever done a show about an idiot before. I decided to be the first." (Oddly enough, this was the only Mel Brooks production to feature a laugh track.)

Figure 79. Sexy Charlie Watkins.

With Mel Brooks' premise in mind, he and Henry created a series centered on a secret agent who was basically an idiot, and how his need to do things by-the-book often put him at odds with his boss and fellow agents. Maxwell Smart, also known as Agent 86, was the bumbling fool who worked for a secret counter-intelligence agency, known as CONTROL. Teamed with a female partner, always known as Agent 99, and a whole lot of

Figure 80 & 81. Fans of *Get Smart!* wanted more Angelique.

gadgets that never seem to work for Smart, the two dealt with threats posed against to the United States by KAOS, an international organization of evil. The goofy enemies, like Conrad Siegfried (Bernie Kopell), and world-takeover plots were typically parodying those found in the James Bond films. Even the gadgets, like the Cone of Silence, the shoe phone, the button laser, and the soup-bowl camera were parodies of the gadgets in the Bond films.

In Episode 2.22 — "Smart Fit the Battle of Jericho" (February 18, 1967), government buildings constructed by the Jericho Construction Company keep blowing up. While on assignment in Las Vegas following Frank Lloyd Joshua (William Chapman), a CEO and government contractor, Maxwell Smart (Adams) runs into his fellow CONTROL agent Charlie Watkins in disguise as a beautiful cigarette girl at a casino. Smart has been flipping a coin with a miniature transmitter inside it, and accidentally flips it into her tray full of coins and cigarettes.

Cigarette Girl: What do you think you're doing?
Maxwell Smart: Well, I'm looking for my silver dollar. You gave me the wrong one.
Cigarette Girl: What's the difference? A dollar's a dollar.
Maxwell Smart: Well mine is a very special silver dollar. Oh, here it is.
Cigarette Girl: How can you be sure it's yours?
Maxwell Smart: Eh... yes, well it has my name on it.
Cigarette Girl: Oh, is that so? Well, what's your name? [Grabs dollar to examine it.]
Maxwell Smart: Eh. E pluribus unum.
Cigarette Girl: Wise guy.
[She promptly puts the coin between her cleavage.]

Neither Max nor the audience has any clue she is really a man until Watkins reveals it himself by talking in a deep, masculine voice. Watkins then saves Smart's life by clobbering the KAOS agent over the head, sending Smart after the real bad guys. Then 86 returns to Washington and goes undercover as a worker at the Jericho Construction Company to learn how KAOS is destroying important government buildings. He discovers they are puttying nitroglycerin inside the bricks, then detonating them when the buildings are completed and full of people. With the aid of a sandwich phone, Smart calls in his findings to CONTROL and is rewarded for a job well done. Written by Arne Sultan and directed by Bruce Bilson, the “Smart Fit the Battle of Jericho” was classic *Get Smart!* in one of its best episodes. Pettyjohn scored high marks with one of the best roles, to that point, in her career, and felt great when CBS television told her about all the fan mail she received. Barbara Feldon who played Agent 99 felt threatened by all the attention Angelique got, and warned them she’d walk if they continued to showcase Watkins’ character with better lines. Feldon was the co-star, not Pettyjohn!

Figure 82. H.M. Wynant threatens Angelique Pettyjohn.

In the follow-up episode, Episode 2.27 — "Pussycats Galore" (April 1,1967), a take-off of the character "Pussy Galore" from the James Bond film *Goldfinger* (1964) (itself parodied in Episode 2.42 — "Bronzefinger"), CONTROL agent Charlie Watkins returns to aid his fellow agents by going undercover as a gorgeous Pussycat at the Pussycat Club (a takeoff on the old *Playboy* clubs). When a beautiful woman (Pamela Courtney) comes to Max's apartment to reveal that important scientists have been abducted from the club, the Chief (Edward Platt) arranges for Max (Don Adams) and 99 to work with Watkins. Barbara Feldon, as Agent 99, plays her reaction to Charlie Watkins' picture perfectly. She bubbles over and says, "That's a fantastic disguise!" They decide to go in disguise themselves as Fritz and Greta Braun, married German scientists, in order to try and get kidnapped. Hans Fromme (Ted Knight) of the German Embassy invites them out to the Pussycat Club, where KAOS attempts to drug them. They are ably assisted by CONTROL agent Charlie Watkins, who learns how they are getting the victims in and out of the club.

Maxwell Smart: Anything to report Watkins?
Charlie Watkins: I've turned this place inside out to find a secret passageway for them to smuggle out their victims.
Maxwell Smart: Did you find it?
Charlie Watkins: Finally.
Maxwell Smart: Where is it?
Charlie Watkins: There's a back door in the kitchen that leads to the alley.
Maxwell Smart: The old backdoor to the alley trick. What'll they think of next?

Figure 83. *Get Smart!* (1967).

With the plan revealed, Max and 99 pretend to be drugged, but get the upper hand on the KAOS agents and save the day. In the epilogue, Max invites 99 to go dancing, but also says sexy Watkins can join them. Written by Arne Sultan and directed by Sidney Miller, the episode became a popular one. It also gave extremely sexy Angelique Pettyjohn another outing as the male CONTROL agent Charlie Watkins whose expertise with female disguises was top drawer. Pettyjohn recalled seeing Don Adams again at the *Playboy* mansion, after she had started dating Bob Crane, and was told Adams was a close friend of Hugh Hefner's.

The show, which debuted on September 18, 1965, on NBC, ran for five seasons, four on NBC and the final season on CBS, and ended on May 15, 1970, with a total of 138 half-hour episodes produced during its run. Four feature-length movie versions were produced, following its demise in 1970. Those follow-ups included *The Nude Bomb* aka *The Return of Maxwell Smart* (1980), released theatrically; *Get Smart, Again* (1989), a made-for-TV sequel, which aired on ABC; *Get Smart!* (2008), starring Steve Carell and Anne Hathaway; and *Get Smart's Bruce and Lloyd: Out of Control* (2008), a made-for-DVD spin-off. The series was also briefly revived on FOX in 1995, with Adams and Feldon in their key roles.

More Secret Agents

In another one of her favorite roles, Angelique Pettyjohn played an ardent blonde heiress opposite Michael J. Pollard on an episode of *The Girl from U.N.C.L.E.* (1967). The part was a real juicy one for Pettyjohn for it afforded the actress the most screen time she had had and gave her the chance to work with an actor who was soon to win an Academy Award for Best Supporting Actor for his portrayal of C.W. Moss in the 1967 crime film *Bonnie and Clyde*. The two of them would sneak off between takes, smoke marijuana together, and have some laughs. Angelique also got the opportunity for a little romance, both on-screen and off, with dreamy Noel Harrison (1934-2013), son of Rex Harrison. Those kisses on the set with Harrison as Mark Slate were merely a preview of what she had waiting for him in her dressing room during her short tenure with Arena Productions. Nearly every woman in the United States was charmed by the handsome Brit, a former Olympic skier and singer before he won the coveted role as the U.N.C.L.E. agent. Angelique was similarly charmed by him and worked very hard to make her character on the show a believable one, with the added benefit that she had private rehearsal time with him. Two years later, he recorded "The Windmills of Your Mind," the theme song from *The Thomas Crown Affair* (1968), which won the Academy Award for Best Original Song in 1968. Pettyjohn loved the song, and often hummed the tune in later years in remembrance of Harrison. She enjoyed making that episode of *The Girl from U.N.C.L.E.* for many reasons. Ironically, the series almost didn't make it on the air in its familiar form.

In 1966, when *The Man from U.N.C.L.E* was at the peak of its popularity, Creator Norman Felton suggested a spin-off series to the executives at NBC featuring a female U.N.C.L.E. agent and her partner. NBC wanted to see a pilot, so Felton wrote a special episode, "The Moonglow Affair," of *The Man from U.N.C.L.E.,* which debuted on February 25, 1966. Felton picked the name April Dancer from Ian Fleming's original notes for the television spy series. Fleming had suggested April Dancer as the name for the secretary to Napoleon Solo's boss, but Felton preferred to use the name for his female lead. Mary Ann Mobley, a former

Figure 84. Ian Fleming.

Miss America from Mississippi, was the actress selected to play Dancer in the pilot. She was assigned a partner/mentor, a character named Mark Slate (played as her senior, Norman Fell). Slate, in the pilot, was supposed to be over forty years old, which was the official age for retirement from field work for U.N.C.L.E. enforcement agents, and was paired with Dancer, age twenty-four and new to field work, to break U.N.C.L.E.'s first female enforcement agent into the job. Apparently, Slate had been Napoleon Solo's mentor as well when he first started as an U.N.C.L.E. agent. At their first meeting with Waverly, Dancer raises the issue of Slate's age, but Waverly pretends to ignore her. Later, when Waverly sees how well the two work as a team, he agrees to let them continue as partners, and insists that Slate correct the error of his age in his personnel files.

The pilot received favorable ratings, but the popularity of *Batman* with its quirky sense of humor and its swinging sixties style persuaded NBC executives to suggest a few changes to the series. The younger woman/older man pairing was dropped in the final version of the series, and it was decided the series would aim to attract the same young, hip audience watching *Batman*. Mary Ann Mobley was dropped in favor of the sexy Stefanie Powers who would play April Dancer as a mod sixties woman with long red hair, bright-colored miniskirts, go-go boots, and berets. Mark Slate was re-imagined as a hip, young Brit, and Noel Harrison was hired to play a trendy dandy who adopted a Carnaby Street look,

Figure 85. ***The Girl from UNCLE*** **(1967).**

wearing such popular fashions as corduroy suits, turtlenecks, and jaunty hats. The leads would never be romantically involved, but would be friends in a brother-sister relationship. This freed them to flirt with different characters in future episodes, but like Solo and Kuryakin, neither had a steady love interest. Their U.N.C.L.E. superior, Mr. Waverly, would be played by Leo G. Carroll, a role he also played on *The Man from U.N.C.L.E.* He was the first actor to be in two series simultaneously. *The Girl from U.N.C.L.E.* made its debut as a weekly series on September 13, 1966, at the beginning of the third season of *The Man from U.N.C.L.E.* It ran Tuesday nights at 7:30 on NBC, and had twenty-nine episodes in its first and only season.

Figure 86. Angelique Pettyjohn spied *The Girl from U.N.C.L.E.*

In Episode 1.27 — "The U.N.C.L.E. Samurai Affair" (March 28,1967), written by Tony Barrett and directed by Alf Kjellin, Alexander Waverly (Leo G. Carroll) believes a notorious Japanese war criminal is active again and may help U.N.C.L.E. locate a stolen submarine. He dispatches two of his best agents,

April Dancer (Stefanie Powers) and Mark Slate (Noel Harrison), to Hawaii to follow up on their only lead, the war criminal's sister Sumata (Signe Hasso). When their only informant turns up dead, Mark and April realize the sister is involved. But before the assignment is over, the two agents have become entangled in a seemingly unrelated murder, including a fire dancer, an all-too-affectionate heiress, Cora Sue (Angelique Pettyjohn), her idiot paramour Herbie (Michael J. Pollard), a man-eating plant, and a human-sized knife-throwing statue. Ultimately, April and Mark recover the stolen

Figure 87. April Dancer (Stefanie Powers) & Mark Slate (Noel Harrison).

submarine, and Mark ends up fighting a cleverly disguised Sumata in a sword duel, Samurai-style.

Although NBC thought they had a real winner on their hands with *The Girl from U.N.C.L.E.*, the show floundered in low ratings. Norman Felton tried to inject more humor, and when that didn't seem to work, he injected plots involving crossovers, Napoleon Solo and Illya Kuryakin from *The Man from U.N.C.L.E.*, but that was simply not enough. The show ran for one season, then was canceled. But alas, the one Pettyjohn did was a good, and has survived to this day as one of the better episodes produced. She also came away from the show with many happy thoughts.

A couple of years after appearing on *The Girl from U.N.C.L.E.,* Angelique was told by her agent that two producers, representing a certain secret agent with a 00-license to kill, were scouting locations in Nevada for an April-August 1971 shoot. EON Productions, producers of the James Bond films, had decided to film *Diamonds Are Forever* entirely in Las Vegas. With her experience as a showgirl and dancer, Angelique should try to audition for the role of a Las Vegas showgirl, even if she had no lines, but alas Cubby Broccoli and Harry Saltzman never called. Ironically, prior to his death in 1964, Ian Fleming had been responsible for creating *The Man from U.N.C.L.E.* for NBC, in particular the characters of Napoleon Solo and April Dancer. Had Pettyjohn been to audition, the symmetry of her performance would have been a unique one indeed.

The James Bond craze of the 1960's produced yet another spy series, *It Takes a Thief* (1968), which employed Pettyjohn. Produced as a mid-season replacement show by Gene L. Coon (writer for *Star Trek*) and Glen Larson (creator of *Battlestar Galactica*, 1978), the show debuted on January 9, 1968 and ran three seasons. *It Takes a Thief* was created by television writer Roland Kibbee, and featured Robert Wagner as Alexander Mundy. Convicted cat burglar Mundy gets an offer he can't refuse from the United States Government: If he puts his formidable talents as a thief to work for the SIS (Secret Intelligence Service), he'll be released from prison early. Munday is puzzled, and asks, "Let me get this straight. You *want* me to steal?" His SIS handler Noah Bain (Malachi Throne) replies, "Look, Al, I'm not asking you to *spy*. I'm just asking you to *steal*." Munday agrees, and tries to return to his sophisticated, playboy lifestyle. Unfortunately, many veteran character actors of the James Bond movies, like Martine Beswick, Karin Dor, Adolfo Celli, Cec Linder, and Richard Kiel, have other nefarious plans for him! The show was hugely popular for the first two seasons, but when producers moved the production to Italy and added Fred Astaire as Munday's father, viewers tuned it out.

A week before *It Takes a Thief* debuted on network television, on January 2, 1968, ABC-TV brought in Angelique Pettyjohn, along with a dozen other girls, dressed her in a silver bikini, and photographed her with Robert Wagner in a tuxedo. The shots were supposed to suggest 007 and his Bond girls as part of a publicity campaign to launch the show and ran in newspapers around the country. Pettyjohn agreed to

Figure 88. Photo shoot for *It Takes a Thief* (1968).

do the shoot with the hopes she might land an important role on the new show, but nothing ever came of her one-day's work. She was paid well for her time, and as an added bonus, Angelique was pictured in the entertainment section of dozens of daily newspapers, but she never got the call back from the casting director to do an episode of the show.

A couple of months later, she ran into Robert Wagner, enjoying a cocktail at a night club out on the Sunset Strip and thought about flirting with him, maybe even taking him to bed. But when Wagner's wife Marion (Marshall) walked into the bar and sat down on the stool next to him, Angelique lost her nerve. She merely smiled, nodded her head at the happy couple, and kept walking. Grief-stricken, years later, when she heard the news that Natalie Wood had drown near Catalina Island, she called her friend Lana Wood, with whom she had worked on *For Singles Only* (1968), to commiserate the loss of her sister, and listened to Lana, for more than an hour, explain how Robert Wagner had been responsible for his third wife's murder. At that time, the police ruled Natalie Wood's death was accidental; stating Wagner was never a suspect. In 2018, the Los Angeles County Sheriff's Department re-opened the case at the insistence of Lana Wood, naming Wagner a "person of interest" in the death of Natalie Wood.

Dennis Cole and *Felony Squad* (1967)

Angelique Pettyjohn played a mobster's wife on *Felony Squad* (1967), a half-hour crime drama created by Richard Murphy for ABC, and ran from September 12, 1966 to January 31, 1969, a span encompassing seventy-three episodes.

One night on the Sunset Strip, Pettyjohn was introduced to handsome Dennis Cole (1940-2009), the second lead opposite stern Howard Duff on the show, by a friend, and had a few drinks and some laughs with the eligible bachelor. (Cole was divorced from first wife, Sally Bergeron, who shared joint custody of his son, Joe.) Angelique thought he really liked her, because they had flirted madly throughout the night at one of the clubs, but Dennis Cole never asked her back to his place for a late-night drink and sex. He did recommend she come into Fox for an audition with the casting director for *Felony Squad*, and she was hired to play Felicia Majeski, based largely upon the word of Cole.

They remained friends, and Angelique later worked with him on *Bracken's World* (1969), in which he played stunt man Davey Evans, but Cole never found his way into her sex diary. Dennis Cole later married Jaclyn Smith in 1978, after a guest appearance on *Charlie's Angels* (1976), and then found himself divorced from her in 1981. He died tragically in 2009 of renal failure at age sixty-nine.

Felony Squad, originally titled *Men Against Evil*, followed Sergeant Sam Stone (Howard Duff) and Detective Jim Briggs (Cole) as they investigated crimes in an unidentified West Coast city as part of a Major Crimes Unit. In Episode 1.24 — "Target!" (February 20, 1967), Sam is suspicious when deposed syndicate leader Harry Majeski (Will Kuluva) offers to testify against his successor, Vic Durant (Steve Ihnat), who uses a plant nursery as his cover. But Majeski is abducted from police custody during an ambush by syndicate enforcers sent by Durant. Majeski turns the tables on Durant, and manages to take him down before he is killed. Felicia, his wife, (Angelique Pettyjohn) seeks the help of Stone and Briggs, but it is too late. Written by Frank L. Moss and Tony Barrett, and direct by Allen Reisner, the episode was edgy in parts and concluded with a thrilling shoot-out in the plant nursery, but alas, Pettyjohn's character had little to do with the plot and so she appeared in a thankless role.

Two Television Worlds

Angelique Pettyjohn played characters on two other television shows in the sixties with the word "world" in the title, *Good Morning, World* (1967) and *Bracken's World* (1969). In *Good Morning, World*, Episode 1.24 — "Here Comes the Bribe" (February 27, 1968), Pettyjohn played scatter-brained Mitzi, the love interest of Larry Clarke (Ronnie Schell), who tries to help Clarke (and his fellow disk jockey) avoid a crooked record promoter and his payola scam. She has recorded a song that crooked record promoter Mickey Mouze (standup comedian Jan Murray) attempts to bribe Clarke (and his fellow disk jockey) to play on the air with his payola scam. Clarke and his partner

David Lewis (Joby Baker) are early morning disc jockeys in Los Angeles. David is happily married, while Larry thinks of himself as a lady's man and "swinger." Their boss Roland Hatton, Jr. was played by Billy De Wolfe, as a stuffy, humorless station manager, while Girl Friday, Sandy Kramer (as played by Goldie Hawn, prior to Rowan and Martin's *Laugh-In*) seemed to be the brunt of most of the jokes. The thirty-minute sitcom, which aired twenty-six first-run episodes between 1967 and 1968 on CBS, was played very broadly for laughs, and anticipated, in many ways, the behind-the-scenes shenanigans that would make *WKRP in Cincinnati* (1978), such a sensation a decade later. The character of Mitzi, as played by Angelique, was imagined as a frequent guest player, but when the show was canceled after less than a year, all plans for her character went out the window.

On *Bracken's World* (1969), Pettyjohn played a "recurring" character, Elizabeth "Ellie" Plover, who appeared as a young actress under contract at Century Studios (a fictionalized 20th Century-Fox). The role wasn't much, and amounted to little more than a couple lines in two of the episodes of the series, but she got to work with Hollywood's best and brightest — Eleanor Parker, Peter Haskell, Warren Stevens, Dennis Cole, Ray Milland, and even rival Linda Harrison on the show.

Figure 89. *Bracken's World* (1969)

Bracken's World was a drama series created by Dorothy Kingsley and broadcast on NBC from September 19, 1969, to December 25, 1970. The series was centered on a powerful producer and his studio's group of up-and-coming starlets. During the first season, Eleanor Parker received top billing as Sylvia Caldwell, executive secretary to Century Studios head John

Bracken (Warren Stevens), who was sometimes heard but never seen. Warren Stevens provided the voice of the unseen Bracken. When the second season began, Parker was gone and Leslie Nielsen took over as Bracken. Other cast members included Elizabeth Allen, Jeanne Cooper, Karen Jensen, Madlyn Rhue, and Laraine Stephens. Many of the active film stars of that time made cameo appearances as themselves to Make the series seemed real. *Bracken's World* was later cancelled halfway through its second season because of low ratings.

Figure 90. *Good Morning World.*

In Episode 1.8 — "Don't You Cry for Susannah" (October 10, 1969), young actress Susannah Ray (Diana Ewing) shows up vying for the lead in a forthcoming production. The lady believes she's so perfectly suited for the role she assumes the identity of her character in real life. Producer-writer Kevin Grant (Peter Haskell) is very impressed with pretty Susannah Ray and arranges for her to read for the lead in his new film. Ray does a brilliant reading for the lead character, but Grant is concerned Susannah Ray may have lost complete perspective and does not hire her. But when a mysterious illness overtakes Diane Waring (Laraine Stephens), the new lead, several studio executives express concerns Ray may have poisoned Diane on the set in order to get the part. As Diane recovers in the hospital, she also grows concerned Ray may commit suicide because that's exactly what happens to the character. Written by Robert Presnell, Jr. and directed by Paul Henreid, the story is a familiar one most moviegoers would recognize as a rift on *All About Eve* (1950). Like her idol Marilyn Monroe in *Eve*, Pettyjohn has a modest walk-on in this episode.

Allen Reisner directed Episode 1.12 — "Move in for a Close-Up" (December 12, 1969), based on a script by writer Oliver Hailey. Marjorie Grant (Madlyn Rhue) attempts to save her failing marriage to Kevin (Peter Haskell) by getting a job as an assistant script supervisor at Century Studios. But Kevin is annoyed, feeling Marjorie's place is at home with their young son, Mark, and other staff are concerned Marjorie will serve as a spy for the other non-working wives. She takes the job seriously, but fouls up nonetheless; comments aloud on the scenes, forgets to replace important props, and resents Kevin's relationships with the other actresses. When Bracken (Stevens) learns of her employment, he dispatches Sylvia (Parker) to fire her.

Tempted to drink on her way home, Marjorie decides to buy a bottle of wine and keep her husband's attention with a black negligee and a candlelit dinner. The romancing seems to do the trick, for Kevin actually leaves the studio early to take his wife on a three-day weekend up the California coast. The episode was simply dreadful, rising to the level of melodrama typical of an afternoon soap opera. Angelique again had very little to do as Ellie, other than appear to be a young starlet on the rise at a major studio, exactly what it must have been like for Marilyn Monroe in her early days in the business.

Bob Crane and *Love, American Style* (1969)

Love, American Style (1969) was a very hip, modern anthology show about dating and mating in the swinging seventies, featuring a weekly collection of romantic vignettes drawn from the comedic side of life. Produced by Paramount, the ensemble cast changed from week to week and employed an impressive guest roster: Milton Berle, Sid Caesar, Sonny and Cher, Ozzie and Harriet, Tracy Reed, Stuart Margolin, Phyllis Davis, James Hampton, and other icons of the era. Loosely derived from the 1961 Italian comedy *Divorce, Italian Style*, the show was popular, playful, and never taken even remotely seriously. *Love* ran for five seasons on ABC from September 29, 1969 to January 11, 1974 and inspired a 1985 remake, *New Love, American Style*. The original series was also known for its ten-to-twenty second, drop-in silent movie-style "joke clips" between the featured segments, in which an acting troop played with then-risqué, burlesque-style comedies of manner.

In Episode 1.5a — "Love and the Modern Wife" (October 27, 1969), Director Alan Rafkin and Writer Allan Burns crafted a

Figure 91. Angelique Pettyjohn and Bob Crane from *Love, American Style* (1969).

juicy little tale about a husband, Howard (Bob Crane), who thinks his wife, Laurie (Patricia Crowley), doesn't need to take a pop psychology course on modern marriage. When she says it's necessary because she suspects him of cheating, he decides to make her suspicions come true. He heads to a swinging singles bar and tries to pick up a beautiful blonde (Angelique Pettyjohn), but ultimately discovers he doesn't have the courage to go through with an affair despite his more than willing pick-up. He loves his wife, but things get complicated when she sees the two of them together and thinks the worse. The episode was sweet and sentimental, and featured Pettyjohn in one of her signature roles. It also proved to be a very ironic one for actor Bob Crane (1928-1978).

Star of *Hogan's Heroes* (1965), family man, churchgoer, and lead actor in two Disney pictures, *Superdad* (1973) and *Gus* (1976), Bob Crane was also a sex addict who manifested an unusually strong compulsion to have sex. He was hungry for "the act" all the time and was publicly open about his status as a swinger, even though he was married to Anne Terzian. (He divorced Anne in 1970, then married his *Hogan's Heroes* co-star Sigrid Valdis, aka Patricia Olson.) Crane enjoyed flirting with other women, telling racy, sexually-explicit jokes, watched pornography, had a proclivity for blondes with very large breasts, and also spoke very openly about the number of women he had bedded, keeping a sex diary of his own; often recording the sex with the help of a videographer from Sony. His desire to have sexual intercourse

Figure 92. *Love, American Style* (1969).

with as many different women as possible was insatiable. Often, after Crane had slept with them, he would dehumanize them with crude and offensive language. He spent a lot of time in night clubs and strip clubs along the Sunset Strip, and had a fondness for group sex, often leaving with two or three women at a time. He was also into BDSM and financed "dungeons" in the homes of some of his swinger friends. In 1978, he was found dead, bludgeoned to death with a weapon that was never found, and had an electrical cord tied around his neck in an apartment in Scottsdale, Arizona. His murder was never solved, even though John Henry Carpenter, his videographer, was arrested and charged with his murder. He was later found not guilty.

At the time when "Love and the Modern Wife" was shot for *Love, American Style*, Angelique had frequently flirted with Bob Crane at night clubs, but did not know him very well. She thought he was hugely desirable, but knew nothing about his addiction to sex. To all outward appearances, he was a devoted family man, who liked to flirt with young starlets. On the set, the sparks between Pettyjohn and Crane flew, which started a long-term love affair lasting several years. He often took her to the *Playboy* mansion, where they enjoyed a free-willing sexual relationship, encompassing all manner of sexual activities — threesomes and group sex with other actresses, bondage and discipline, and other forms of kinky sex, like making X-rated movies together. Angelique said she learned nearly everything she knew about sex from him, and would have married him and settled down if he hadn't already been married. She was truly devastated by his tragic death in 1978 and attended Crane's funeral at St. Paul the Apostle Catholic Church in Westwood, California. She was there with fellow actors Patty Duke, John Astin, and Carroll O'Connor.

Bob Crane's life and unsolved murder became the subject of a 2002 film, *Auto Focus*, directed by Paul Schrader and starring Greg Kinnear as Crane. Roger Ebert described the film as "brilliant," as it attempted to connect the happily-married family man to the Hollywood celebrity lifestyle that just spiraled out of control into nonstop partying and sexual excess. His son

Scotty Crane and widow Sigrid Valdis had shopped their own script, alternately titled *F-Stop* and *Take Off Your Clothes and Smile*, but when the Schrader film came out, no one else in Hollywood seemed interested.

Roles Not Taken or Offered

For all of the parts she got, Angelique Pettyjohn auditioned or screen-tested for at least a dozen other shows she did not get. One of her earliest auditions was for *The Rat Patrol* (1966), thanks to Tom Gries, a director and producer whom she met at one of the night clubs on the Sunset Strip. He asked her to come in and read for the role of Gabrielle, Moffitt's ex-girlfriend, for second season episode, "The Fatal Reunion Raid," but the role eventually went to Louise Sorel, who had also played a part on the original *Star Trek* (1966).

Gries was also instrumental in getting auditions for Pettyjohn with several fellow show-runners, Bruce Geller for *Mission Impossible* and Sheldon Leonard for *I Spy*, but those cold readings did not amount to any work. She read for the part of "Berlin Betty" (a parody of "Axis Sally") on *Hogan's Heroes* (1965), but lost the part to Antoinette Bower, who actually wound up playing three different characters during the series.

Thanks to friend and former co-star Bill Bixby, from *Clambake*, she got an invite to read for James Komack, creator and executive producer of *The Courtship of Eddie's Father* (1969), but did not land a role. And lastly, she auditioned for *The Wild Wild West* (1965) for the role of Countess Zorana, but lost out to unknown actress Lisa Pera.

Angelique returned to television in 1984, playing the character of Prostitute Lotta Gue in two episodes of *Hill Street Blues* (1984). Had she stayed in television, Pettyjohn might well have carved out an interesting niche for herself and maybe found herself a recurring role or series, like Joan Collins, but stardom in motion pictures was her next big goal.

6
Star Trek Siren

> *I really loved working on* Star Trek. *It was really delightful to work with such a group of talented actors, especially William Shatner. I found him to be friendly, gregarious, kind of mischievous with a twinkling-eyed little smile, and a really marvelous person around the set, comfortable to be around.. He made me feel very comfortable because, at first, when I came in I was very much in awe of working with him. He wasn't pretentious at all but was very friendly and welcoming to me.*

Star Trek was an American, science fiction television series, created by Gene Roddenberry and first produced by Lucille Ball's Desilu Productions (1966-67), then later Paramount Television (1968-69), and ran for three seasons on NBC. Sold as a kind of Western in outer space or a so-called "Wagon Train to the Stars," Roddenberry simplified his high-concept show to language studio chiefs and television network executives would understand.

In 1964, Westerns still dominated NBC, CBS, and ABC. *Gunsmoke* (CBS, 1955-1975), *Bonanza* (NBC, 1959-1973), and *Wagon Train* (NBC, 1957-1965) were three of the most popular shows on television at the time, while dozens of other Westerns also played in prime time. Like the familiar *Wagon Train*, each episode of Roddenberry's Space Western was to be a self-contained adventure story, set within the structure of a continuing voyage through space.

In his original concept, the protagonist was Captain Robert April of the starship *Yorktown*, which later changed to

Captain Christopher Pike of the starship *Enterprise*. When Roddenberry presented the *Star Trek* draft to Desilu Productions, Herbert F. Solow, Desilu's Director of Production, saw promise in the idea and signed a three-year program-development contract with Gene. Lucille Ball, the Head of Desilu, was not familiar with science fiction, but she was instrumental in getting the pilot produced.

Two pilots were actually shot for *Star Trek*. In 1964, with the help of Grant Tinker at NBC, "The Cage" was made with Jeffrey Hunter as Pike and Leonard Nimoy as a pointed-ears Martian (later changed to Vulcan). NBC turned the pilot down, stating it was "too cerebral." However, the executives at NBC were impressed enough with the concept to order a second pilot. "Where No Man Has Gone Before" featured an almost entirely new crew: Captain Kirk (William Shatner), Scotty (James Doohan), and Sulu (George Takei). The single hold-out from the first pilot was Nimoy's Spock, now clearly defined as a half-human, half-Vulcan science officer. The second pilot proved to be satisfactory to NBC, and the network added *Star Trek* to its schedule for 1966.

With the success of the second pilot, Roddenberry added a handful of characters we now associate as series regulars: Deforest Kelley as Doctor Leonard McCoy, Nichelle Nichols as Lieutenant Nyota Uhura, the communications officer, Grace Lee Whitney played the captain's yeoman Janice Rand for half of the first season, then was let go; Majel Barrett (Christine Chapel) and Walter Koenig (Chekov) rounded out the rest of the cast. The show's production staff included art director Matt Jefferies, designer of the starship *Enterprise* and most of the sets, William Ware Theiss worked as the costume designer and made all of the uniforms and costumes for the characters on the show, and Wah Chang, an artist who had worked for Walt Disney Productions, made all of the props and devices used on the show.

Once the show was green-lighted by NBC, production of the series' episodes moved to Desilu, the former studio complex for RKO Pictures. Midway through its three-year production run, the executives at Paramount Pictures bought out Desilu and

Figure 93. ***Star Trek*** **"Where No Man Has Gone Before" (1966), original illustration from TV Guide.**

added the sound stages used for *Star Trek* into those on the Paramount lot.

Star Trek ran for three seasons on NBC and was cancelled three times: once in 1966, then again in 1967, and finally in 1969. A letter-writing campaign and protest by thousands of fans saved the show twice from extinction. After the third cancellation, the series went into syndication, then Kaiser Broadcasting ran the show five times a week during the late afternoon or early evening time slot. Through syndication, *Star Trek* found an even larger audience than it had on NBC and became television's first bonified cult classic.

Episode Synopsis and Review

Season 2, Episode 17: "The Gamesters of Triskelion" was written by Margaret Armen and directed by Gene Nelson. Production number 60346, the episode aired on January 5, 1968. When the scene opens on Star Date 3211.7, the starship *Enterprise* has arrived at Gamma II, an automated communication and astrogation station on which they are doing a routine maintenance check. Kirk, Chekov, and Uhura are preparing to beam down to Gamma II when they're suddenly plucked from the transporter chamber and whisked away to another location, before Scotty can even activate the transporter. They quickly find themselves on the planet Triskelion in a gladiatorial arena where their phasers don't

Figure 94. "The Gamesters of Triskelion" (1968).

work, *and* they cannot contact the ship. Then they are confronted by four warriors — two men and two women — carrying spears and knives. Kirk, Chekov, and Uhura fight hand-to-hand with the warriors, but are ultimately subdued by the far superior force.

Meanwhile, on board the *Enterprise*, Spock, McCoy, and Scotty conclude there was no equipment malfunction; that the Captain and his party may have been taken by some alien force. Their only clue is a fluctuating energy reading in a nearby hydrogen cloud that has left an ionization trail.

The Master Thrall, Galt (Joseph Ruskin), appears in the middle of the arena; a tall humanoid with white powdery skin, bald with a goatee but no mustache, wearing a black robe with a high, red, sparkly collar. He welcomes Kirk, Chekov, and Uhura to the world Triskelion, telling them they are to be trained as gladiators in the arena for the pleasure of the Providers. Collars are placed around their necks, similar to the ones on the other combatants, and Galt as well. The "collars of obedience" are only meant to warn and punish, as when a thrall is slow to respond to a command, and they appear to choke the wearer when activated. Members of the landing party quickly learn they must obey or be choked to death by their collars.

According to Starfleet records, Triskelion is a planet over twelve light years from Gamma II, in the trinary star system M-24 Alpha, and has a dark blue sky and sparse vegetation. The inhabitants live in the southern hemisphere. It was home to an advanced race, now known to their subjects simply as the "Providers," but they evolved beyond humanoid form to devote themselves exclusively to intellectual pursuits. They now find athletic competition to be the only challenge. In order to keep the gladiatorial games new and fresh, they kidnap lifeforms from other places and force them to become "thralls," fighting each other for the entertainment of the Providers, tri-colored glowing brains — red, yellow, and green. The Providers live a thousand meters below the surface and gamble with quatloos (their form of money) on the competitions for their amusement. The symbol of Triskelion appears to be an inverted triangle with the corners cut off, surrounding a stylized triskelion.

Figure 95. End Titles card for "Gamesters" on *Star Trek* (1968).

Back on the *Enterprise*, Spock is pursuing the ion trail with hopes of finding the landing party, while Scotty and McCoy claim he is behaving most "illogically."

As new thralls, Kirk, Chekov, and Uhura are assigned drill thralls to teach them what they must know before they fight in gladiator-style battles for the amusement of the Providers. Lars (Steve Sandor), a combatant from earlier, tries to train Uhura, but she'll have nothing of his mistreatment of her. Chekov is assigned Tamoon (Jane Ross), a friendly, female drill thrall who truly wants to get to "know him," but she is overweight and disgusting-looking. Kirk is assigned Shahna (Angelique Pettyjohn), the drill thrall wearing the silver bikini. She is gorgeous, and the Starfleet captain is very attracted to her. He flirts with her, makes a pass at her, and tries to convince Shahna they should practice some of Triskelion's mating habits. Naively, she claims not to know anything about mating or sex. Kirk is about to show her when he and the others are called to the arena to strike a living practice dummy for training. They all refuse to strike a defenseless person, then Kirk is made the *new* practice dummy at the hands of Kloog (Mickey Morton), a massive brute-like creature with limited intellect. When Captain Kirk easily defeats him, the Providers, who have not been heard from so far, start squabbling over the newcomers. Provider One outbids his fellow Providers in order to possess the newcomers. Kirk, Chekov, and Uhura are given the red collar of their Provider and are told they will wear that color collar until death. They are now considered full-fledged thralls.

The next day, Kirk (now shirtless) goes out jogging with Shahna in her silver bikini and go-go boots. (Presumably, Kloog's whip shredded his Starfleet-issued uniform.) They decide to take a breather, and the Captain goes all out to win the

Figure 96. Angelique Pettyjohn as Shahna, Kirk's Drill Thrall.

trust of Shahna by telling her about freedom and love, two concepts utterly foreign to her. Kirk also tries to find out more about the Providers, but his questions are so provocative the Providers choke Shahna into submission. He begs the Providers to spare her life, and now intrigued by the notion of "compassion," the Providers decide to stop their torture of Shahna. When she stops writhing in pain, Kirk moves in for a kiss, and she kisses him back. Later, when Shahna brings him food (and a lot of questions), he punches her out and tries to escape with Chekov and Uhura. But they only get as far as the arena, before Galt appears and punishes them.

The *Enterprise* finally reaches Triskelion. But before Spock and McCoy can beam down to look for the landing party, the Providers take control of the ship. The Providers have already decided to destroy the starship in such a way that the Federation won't come looking. But Kirk makes a deal. If he can defeat three of the Providers' thralls, then the ship and the crew will be free to go, and the remaining thralls will be set free and taught to self-govern. If he loses, then the entire crew will become thralls under the Providers. Kirk wins, the thralls are set free, and the *Enterprise* continues on her way. In the final moments of the episode, Shahna looks up into the star-studded night and promises to follow Kirk to the "lights in the sky" one day.

From Margaret Armen's beautiful script, Captain Kirk's final words with Shahna:
KIRK: I'm sorry, Shahna. I didn't lie. I did what was necessary. Someday, I hope you'll understand.
SHAHNA: I understand, a little. You will leave us now?
KIRK: Yes.
SHAHNA: To go back to the lights in the sky?
KIRK: Yes.
SHAHNA: I would like to go to those lights with you. Take me?
KIRK: I can't.
SHAHNA: Then teach me how, and I will follow you.
KIRK: There's so much you must learn here first. The Providers will teach you. Learn it, Shahna. All your people must learn

Figure 97. Angelique as Shahna & Shatner as Captain Kirk..

before you can reach for the stars, Shahna. (He gives her a farewell kiss) Scotty!
SCOTT [OC]: Aye, sir.
KIRK: Beam us up.
(The crew disappears in a twinkle.)

SHAHNA: Goodbye, Jim Kirk. I will learn, and watch the lights in the sky, and remember.

Originally titled “The Gamesters of Pentathlon,” “The Gamesters of Triskelion” was the first of several scripts written by Margaret Armen for *Star Trek*. She also wrote or co-wrote the third-season episodes “The Paradise Syndrome” and “The Cloud Miners” as well as two animated episodes “The Ambergris Element” and “The Lorelei Signal.” She also wrote an unproduced script, “Savage Syndrome,” for the abortive Phase II *Star Trek* series. The episode received uncredited rewrites from Gene L. Coon and John Meredyth Lucas.

The character of Shahna was revived for Phaedra M. Weldon’s sequel, “The Lights in the Sky,” published in *Strange New Worlds*. Around the time of the *Star Trek: Generations* prelude, Shahna is welcomed as Triskelion’s ambassador to the Federation. Armen’s original script called for Sulu instead of Chekov, but George Takei was away filming *The Green Berets* (with John Wayne) at the time. Similarly, the original story finds Kirk, Sulu, and Uhura being taken off the *Galileo* shuttlecraft while in orbit of Gamma II, but the kidnapping was changed to eliminate any similarities to the episode “Metamorphosis.”

Detractors of the original *Star Trek* series were particularly critical of “The Gamesters of Triskelion.” They criticized the episode’s stupid clichés, terrible dialogue, and outlandish costumes, especially Shahna’s silver bikini and go-go boots. They referred to it as a “misbegotten piece of crap.” Fans of the episode, however, embraced it, and regarded Angelique’s Shahna as one of their favorite guest stars.

“Shahna—The Girl in the Silver Bikini”

In 1967, Angelique Pettyjohn was making the rounds of the various networks and television shows, when her agent/husband Otho Pettyjohn called, saying he had found something very special. Otho told her he had read a script for an upcoming episode of *Star Trek*. “My husband, who had been working as my agent, got the script from a script girl he knew at Desilu Productions. He read through it and saw a part with a description

Figure 98. Shahna and Kirk in the arena, behind the scenes. (Notice the blurred image of the clapper in the shot.)

he felt suited me, so Otho arranged an interview with the front office. But I've got to be honest with you. There really wasn't much of a character there, and she was *nothing* like me. She had green hair and looked like some gigantic Amazon on steroids. Her first action in the script was to leap out from behind a rock and pin the lead on the show [William Shatner] to the ground with a spear. I laughed out loud the first time I read it. But since Otho had already set up the meeting, I thought I'd go in and see if they had anything else for me to read."

When Pettyjohn first arrived at Gene Roddenberry's office at Desilu Productions, the office secretary told her things were running late that day. She gave Angelique a copy of the script for "The Gamesters of Triskelion" and a short description of the character, then asked her to sit down and wait. Patiently, she read through the materials and realized nothing had changed.

Figure 99. Publicity Shot: Shahna means business with Kirk.

She was just not right for this "green-haired, green-eyed Amazon." She waited for about forty minutes and was just about to leave when she was called into Roddenberry's office. John Meredyth Lucas, Gene Coon, and Roddenberry were waiting for her. When she walked through the door, the first thing Pettyjohn said was, "Gentlemen, before I waste my time and yours, I really don't feel I fit the description of this character."

Gene Roddenberry looked at Angelique from head to toe. She was a very beautiful woman, and as a ladies' man who used to boast he had slept with every woman on *Star Trek*, he liked what he saw. She was everything Majel Barrett, his long-time girlfriend and soon-to-be wife, had told him. He glanced at Lucas and Coon, who were sitting comfortably in his office, and said, almost in unison with the other men, "Well, why not?"

Nervously, she replied, "Well, I've got the green eyes, and I'm sure you can fix me up with green hair, but I'm hardly an Amazon. I'm only five foot six. Maybe a bit taller in heels."

Roddenberry laughed out loud, followed by a chorus of belly laughs from Lucas and Coon. When they all finally stopped laughing, Gene Coon said, "Look, honey, next to Shatner, you'll look like an Amazon. Go ahead and read the script."

Pettyjohn didn't realize he was a shorter man since he looked so tall on the television, so she went ahead and read the script. They liked her cold reading and called in Fred Phillips, the make-up supervisor. Angelique had always worn bangs to hide her very high forehead. When Phillips pulled the hair away from her forehead for a moment, she complained, "No, no. I don't look good that way." But they said, "Please," and she pulled the hair back from her forehead, so Phillips could see if the green wig would fit. It did. Satisfied, Phillips gave his bosses the heads-up, and they asked her to wait in the outer office for a minute more.

She waited for what seemed like an eternity, but in those fifteen minutes, they had called Otho and finalized a contract with him as her agent. When she finally returned to Gene Roddenberry's office, Roddenberry smiled, and said, "You're hired, go to wardrobe."

Pettyjohn was initially surprised by how quick the process was, but then she later learned the producers were anxious to start filming around the middle of October 1967. The original airdate for "The Gamesters of Triskelion" was set for January 5, 1968, less than three months away. The production had been held up, awaiting a suitable actress to play Shahna. Many other actresses had read for the part, but she was the one they selected.

"That was how I got the part," Angelique explained. "I got my script, and we had several rehearsals scheduled before we started shooting [the episode]. These rehearsals were with the stunt coordinator, Dick Crockett [who also played the blue-skinned Andorian]. Crockett was actually the stunt coordinator for all of the *Star Trek* episodes. He handled the stunt work and taught us all how to fight with the poles as he choreographed the fight scenes between William Shatner and me. Part of the reason, I think, I got that particular role was because of my past experience as a ballet dancer. I had ballet training from the time I was six years old and was a professional dancer before I became an actress. Because I had started my career as a dancer, it was relatively easy for me to follow his stunt choreography. So, we had a couple days of rehearsal with the stunt coordinator, then we started filming. I also learned, for the first time, how to throw a punch and do a stunt punch, be on the receiving end of a punch."

Figure 100. Rittenhouse Archives featured Angelique Pettyjohn in the *Women of Star Trek Card Set*, #5--Shahna and James Kirk

Behind the Scenes

"The Gamesters of Triskelion" was filmed October 17-24, 1967, on Desilu Stage 9, which held the sets for the Bridge and the Transporter room; Desilu Stage 10, which was the combat arena and the Provider's ancient city; and two Paramount Test Stages, which held the Provider's chamber, cell corridors, and three cells (one each for Kirk, Uhura, and Chekov).

Shortly after production on *Star Trek* closed for the year 1967, Lucille Ball sold all of her shares of Desilu to Gulf+Western for $17 million (a value of $125 million in 2017). Gulf+Western then transformed Desilu into the television production arm of Paramount Pictures, rebranding the company as the original Paramount Television. Desilu's entire library was owned by CBS through two of its subsidiaries. Even though CBS owned *Star Trek*, as a result, the television series continued to run on NBC.

The call sheet for Tuesday, October 17, 1967 listed Angelique Pettyjohn, even though she had no scenes to shoot that day. She was asked to come in a day earlier to work with wardrobe and make-up, and to meet her co-stars for the episode. Sometime just after 6:00 a.m., on the first day of filming, Pettyjohn reported to work at the main gate to Desilu Productions and was shown by a security guard where to park her car on the lot near Stage 9. She walked directly onto the soundstage and reported to make-up, where Fred Phillips applied her "green" hair and makeup for the first time. Phillips had just completed the complicated Vulcan makeup for Leonard Nimoy, which meant she most likely passed him in the corridor on his way to the Bridge. Angelique was so nervous about her first day on the *Star Trek* set she could very well have walked by an all-brass marching band and not noticed a thing. She later remarked to me, "I thought Leonard Nimoy was marvelous, intelligent, kind of quiet, a very polite man. I respected him very much."

After a short trip to wardrobe, donning her trademark silver bikini and silver go-go boots, Angelique reported to Gene Nelson, the director, who quickly approved the costume and briefly introduced her to the cast. The cast and crew were in the

Figure 101. Publicity Shot: "Shahna, Let's Get Physical!"

middle of shooting a scene in the Transporter room on Desilu Stage 9, and the momentary break in the action came at a good time. They were all very professional, welcoming Pettyjohn aboard the starship *Enterprise*.

Some years later, Pettyjohn recalled that day as well as her first impressions of the cast, "I loved Nichelle Nichols. I thought she was just a doll. We got to be good friends on the set, and after I finished shooting, I saw her on a personal basis a couple of times. Walter Koenig was a really nice guy. Very nice. Very Friendly. Kind of quiet. He seemed a little on the shy side. William Shatner made me feel very welcome. When I first walked out on the set, wearing that preposterous costume and green 'fright' wig, I was a little bit uptight meeting him. You might just say I was very much in awe of him as an actor. But he instantly made me feel very comfortable and just like a friend and fellow actress."

For the remainder of the day, Angelique rehearsed with Dick Crockett, the stunt coordinator. He wanted her to be proficient with the Triskelion spear she carried as a warrior, so he demonstrated its use as a spear as well as its three-pronged hooks for ensnaring a combatant's feet. They worked on Desilu Stage 10 in the combat arena built specifically for the episode. The floor of the stage was divided into the three parts of the Triskelion world symbol, so she had to practice staying off her opponent's colors as she moved around the arena. (In the episode, a combatant in the arena must surrender one of his or her weapons if they accidentally step on the colors of their opponent.)

She learned her routine quickly and efficiently. Sometime after lunch, in the commissary, William Shatner joined them on the set and was walked through the stunt coordinator's fight choreography. He nailed the steps and began rehearsing with Pettyjohn. They continued working on the choreography throughout the week whenever they had a free moment, and in no time at all, they both looked like gladiators in the Triskelion arena. The actual fight scenes were filmed on Friday, October 20th, through Tuesday, October 24, 1967. A former dancer, Angelique looked fantastic in the dailies.

The "love scenes" between Captain Kirk and Shahna needed work, however. Pettyjohn looked very competent as a warrior, but she appeared shy and awkward during the romantic scenes. Actually, audiences might have expected such a response from Shahna, who had spent her life training to be a gladiator, but for those aware of the Captain's proclivity for romancing his co-stars, they wanted Shahna to melt into his arms and give him anything he wanted. But the scene was simply not working. Shatner and Pettyjohn did endless takes, some of which made it to the blooper reel. Most of the retakes were due to her stiff, almost wooden performance. Again and again, they tried to get the kiss right, and again and again, the two actors struggled to make it seem natural and not forced. Finally, during one take when they were holding each other, she stopped struggling with him, and just let him kiss her. Mark and print? Well, almost. There was a mishap with Angelique's silver bikini. Her 38-inch bust had broken free of the large cup and was clearly visible on screen.

"I had never kissed a leading man before," Angelique confessed to me years later. "I was very shy at the time, and I was married. That's where I got my name, Pettyjohn. I was married to Otho Pettyjohn, who unfortunately has passed away since then. A super nice guy. I had been married to him a couple of years, and Hollywood was a very new adventure for me. I had several kissing scenes in that particular episode, which for me was unique since Shatner was the star of the show, and I had never really had love scenes with a star before. The script called for me to kiss a leading man. I was very shy, but I enjoyed it. Shatner kisses wonderfully. A marvelous kisser!" But not without a lot of rehearsal time and Saurian brandy.

After lunch, on the second-to-the-last day of shooting, William Shatner invited Angelique to his dressing room to go over their "kissing" scene together. He poured her a brandy from the same bottle that often stood in for Saurian brandy on the television show and they read through Margaret Armen's beautifully-written love scene together. Shatner then poured her a second brandy, and they discussed several ideas of how to bring out the tenderness these two people from different worlds felt towards one another. By the time he poured her a third brandy, she was feeling *very* relaxed and comfortable in his arms. She had stopped struggling. He then leaned in and kissed her for real. She responded by wrapping her arms around his neck and returning his kiss, also for real. They started necking like two teenagers, then whatever awkwardness she had felt with him simply disappeared. It took the better part of the next day to set up the shot with the cameras. Then, with the entire crew holding their breath, the two actors delivered a very memorable scene in one take.

Figure 102. Publicity Shot: Angelique Pettyjohn, the Girl in the Silver Bikini.

Star Trek Cancellation and Rebirth

During the filming of "The Gamesters of Triskelion," on Friday, October 20, 1967, a producer came in during lunch time and made an announcement to the cast and crew. He was sorry to say that NBC had cancelled the series. This was the second time NBC had cancelled *Star Trek*. One year earlier, NBC had cancelled due to low Nielsen ratings, but the fans, lead by author Harlan Ellison, writer of the top-rated "City on the Edge of Forever" episode, and super-fans Bjo and John Trimble launched a letter-writing campaign of 29,000 fan letters that ultimately saved the show for a second season. Much of the mail came from doctors, scientists, teachers, and other professional people. They all seemed to agree *Star Trek* was the most literate of any show.

When Gene Roddenberry learned *Star Trek* had again been cancelled, he secretly funded an effort by the Trimbles and other fans to launch another letter-writing campaign. Using 4,000 names from the mailing list for the World Science Fiction Convention, the Trimbles asked fans to write to NBC and to ask other fans to do so as well. NBC received almost 116,000 letters for the show between December 1967 and March 1968: more than 52,000 in February alone. The letters supporting *Star Trek*, whose authors included New York State Governor Nelson Rockefeller, convinced NBC to renew the show for a third season. In an unprecedented way, a spokesperson for NBC announced during the closing credits of the March 1, 1968 episode "The Omega Glory" that *Star Trek* had not only been renewed but fans could stop writing letters now. Little did they know, *Star Trek* would continue to a third season.

Angelique recalled being "depressed" by the news. "I loved shooting my episode. Just before we finishing shooting, three or four days after we started filming, a producer came in and told us all the show had been canceled. Now this was before the marches and everybody changed things around. And so, during the last two days of shooting, everyone was kind of down around the set because they all loved working together so much. On my last day of shooting,

I had a speech where I said, 'Goodbye, Jim Kirk. I will watch the lights in the sky and remember,' and I had tears in my eyes, and those tears were real at the time because I was thinking it seriously was goodbye *Star Trek.* 'I will watch the films and the lights in the sky, and I will remember this experience with all of you.' It meant a great deal to me. I really cried because I knew the series wasn't going to be shooting any more. Later on, I understand, a lot of fans got together, wrote letters, marched on the network, and the show was kept on for another season before being canned. But that's how my experience ran during the week of shooting."

During the filming of the original *Star Trek* series, the cast and crew observed a weekly tradition, the Friday night wrap party. Actually, rather than a wrap party, the weekly Friday night party was more like a Thank-God-Its-Friday. It was almost always held on Desilu Stage 9 at the end of shooting, whether they wrapped an episode or not. Every member of the cast and crew, studio executives, and even occasionally a network suit would gather to celebrate the work done during the week. They would have a few drinks, laugh, tell stories, and simply cut themselves free of the pressures of the week. Production always came to a halt at 7:00 p.m., then the big hangar doors to the sound stage were opened, sometimes flooding Stage 9 with the bright sunlight of the day. Cast members still wearing their costumes headed for the dressing rooms to change. The studio commissary staff would then wheel a huge wet-bar onto the soundstage, laden with soft drinks and liquor, a big bowl of ice cubes, salted nuts, chips, veggies and dip, and shrimp on ice. The party was usually in full-swing by 7:15 once everyone had turned out to cut loose.

On Friday, October 20, 1967, the mood was much more somber. The cast and crew only had two more days of work before "The Gamesters of Triskelion" wrapped, and they were all happy about their work on that particular episode. But the reality of cancellation and subsequent unemployment was staring at most of them in the face. To the cast and crew, Pettyjohn was really the lucky one; she still had another two days of shooting, and then onto her next assignment. But most of the rest of them had, at best, only a few months remaining. They had given over their talent and the best days of their lives to a sinking ship named *Enterprise*. Pettyjohn was tearful because she felt like she was losing her *Star Trek* family. She had grown close to

Figure 103. Publicity Shot: How dare NBC cancel *Star Trek*?

Nichelle Nichols, and even closer to William Shatner. She and Shatner would remain friends throughout the rest of her career in pictures.

When Gene Roddenberry finally arrived at the party, with Majel Barrett, he was smiling, far more optimistic than the cast and crew. He complimented everyone for the outstanding work they had done and said, "Things always appear darker before the dawn." Secretly, Roddenberry was already plotting with Trek fans for another letter-writing campaign and march at Berkeley and MIT, which proved to be even bigger and more far-reaching than the first one.

Majel remembered Angelique from the lunch they had at the Fox commissary when they were filming *A Guide for the Married Man* (1967) and introduced her to Gene. He liked her very much and suggested the three of them should get together informally some time. Pettyjohn agreed, but then nothing ever came of his invitation. Perhaps all for the best. Gene Roddenberry was known as quite the lady's man. Most likely, Gene and Majel had something very intimate in mind for the unsuspecting Angelique.

"The Gamesters of Triskelion" debuted on January 5, 1968 to its largest ratings, and became a fan favorite.

NBC finally relented and green-lighted *Star Trek* for a third season. Unfortunately, the network also got even with Roddenberry (and the fans) by moving the show to the undesirable time slot of 10:00 p.m. on Friday night. The last day of filming for *Star Trek's* third season was January 9, 1969. After seventy-nine episodes, NBC finally canned the show in February 1969. In 2011, the decision to cancel *Star Trek* by NBC was ranked # 4 on the *TV Guide Network* special, *25 Biggest TV Blunders*. *Star Trek* returned to the big screen in 1979, ten years after its cancellation, and eventually spawned a franchise, consisting of six additional television series, twelve additional feature films, hundreds of books and magazines, toys, games and collectibles, and millions of fans worldwide. It is now considered to be one of the most popular and influential television series of all time.

Like *Star Trek*, Angelique Pettyjohn's fortunes would take a turn, imperceptibly at first, for the better, as the *Star Trek* convention circuit gathered steam, bolstered by the release of *Star Trek: The Motion Picture* (1979). Because "The Gamesters of Triskelion" was a fan favorite, Pettyjohn found herself in increasingly high demand as a guest at *Star Trek* conventions. She used to wear a button on her silver bikini that read, "Coming Soon: *Star Trek X: The Wrath of Shahna!*" While largely a joke, she knew the importance of marketing herself to the *Star Trek* fans, and they loved her for how savvy she was. Her new-found fame on the convention circuit attracted the attention of independent filmmakers, which also led to roles in features, such as *Repo Man* (1984), *The Lost Empire* (1984), *Biohazard* (1985), *The Wizard of Speed and Time* (1988), and many other movies.

Figure 104. Star Trek X: The Wrath of Shahna!

7
Scream Queens & Femme Fatales

As much as I had enjoyed working in television, my real love was features. I was on Get Smart!, Batman, The Girl from U.N.C.L.E., Felony Squad, Good Morning World, *and a number of other television shows. I had also continued to work in film. I'd done a variety of different things, and I looked different in so many different roles. I was sometimes blonde, sometimes brunette, sometimes a redhead and in* Star Trek *I had green hair. [She laughs.] Some people had seen me in things and couldn't quite put it together because I didn't always play the same person, but did different types of characters. I felt the most comfortable playing characters, and I thought of myself as a character actor. I looked forward to playing more character roles.*

All throughout her tenure working on the small screen, Angelique Pettyjohn continued to seek work in feature films. She considered her walk-on roles a thing of the past, and now sought parts with real substance. The training and discipline of working on weekly television series, even as the guest star of the week, had not only provided her with the necessary skills she needed as an actress, but had also rewarded her with a new-found confidence she hadn't possessed before. Angelique might have continued to work another ten to twenty years in television if her desire to work in the movies hadn't been so overwhelming.

As she entered this next phase in her career, trouble was brewing at home. She had always known her marriage to Otho

Pettyjohn had been one of convenience. Even though she loved him, like the father absent from her life, and he had worked so tirelessly on her behalf, she loved the business of Hollywood even more. She had built a network of contacts in the industry through all the hard work she had done at night, and now sought to work with quality film directors and producers who wanted her for something more than just a walk-on. Pettyjohn was determined to show them she was a working actress with a SAG card and looked toward a break-through in A-list feature films.

Childish Things (1969)

In 1966, not long after Angelique Pettyjohn had moved to Glendale with her new husband Otho, she met John Derek (1926-1998) at one of the night clubs on the Sunset Strip. Derek got his start in bit parts as a teenager; his first role came in the wartime tear-jerker *Since You Went Away* (1944). He worked as an actor in the forties and fifties, playing in a number of high-profile films, some of which were: *All the King's Men* (1949), *The Ten Commandments* (1956), *Omar Khayyam* (1957), and *Exodus* (1960), among others. With his matinee-idol looks, he had also starred in plenty of "B" pictures, cast as either the cardboard cut-out hero or the cardboard cut-out villain. Derek had grown disappointed with the kind of parts being offered, and so turned to film directing. About to start work on a new film, *Childish Things*, with his girlfriend, Linda Evans, in the female lead, he was also waiting for the ink to dry on his divorce from second wife, Ursula Andress, so he could marry Evans. Evans was on hiatus from shooting her role on *The Big Valley* (1965). Derek told Pettyjohn about the film, offering her a small but pivotal role in the movie. She agreed to take it, and was soon working with the great John Derek on a new motion picture.

Childish Things (1969) was a vanity project for actor Don Murray (1929—). Murray had written the screenplay, raised most of the money himself with his then-wife, Hope Lange, and starred in the true-life drama of one of Hollywood's most famous stunt men, Tom Harris, and the incredible changes that took place in his life after he embraced Christianity. A former street-fighter and alcoholic, Harris (Murray) returns from the war without a real occupation or means to support himself. The ex-GI cons his way into the boxing racket where his savage fists eventually lead him to working for the mob as an enforcer, collecting debts and committing various crimes. He even rapes an innocent young woman Pat (Linda Evans), but rather than turn on Harris, she prays to God for forgiveness for his crime and works to rehabilitate him. Tom Harris has a spiritual awakening, thanks to Pat, and turns his back on the mob and decides instead to devote his life to helping other alcoholics. Produced far from the Hollywood mainstream, this inspirational indie (independent film) may well have been one of the first religious films of its day to deal with such a difficult subject. Others would soon follow, but few were touched with such intimacy and grace.

Figure 105. Poster for *Childish Things* (1969).

When John Derek completed the picture in 1966 (with help from David Nelson), he had hoped to find an interested distributor, in order to capitalize on Linda Evans' fame and success on the TV western series *The Big Valley*, but he did not get any takers. Most studios were not interested in "message" pictures, especially ones with a religious tone. He continued to edit the film, and even shopped his project around for several years, changing titles several times, from *Childish Things* to *Tale of the Cock* and finally *Cock-a--doodle--doo--Do*. The motion picture was released with the title *Confessions of Tom Harris* in 1969. Although many filmgoers thought Murray's performance, as well as that of the entire cast was truly exceptional, most found the message a bit heavy-handed. John Derek continued to make films, but his best-known work as a director were the films he made with fourth wife, Bo Derek, who appeared in four of his movies. He also photographed Andress, Evans, and Bo Derek for*Playboy.*

Figure 106. *The Love God* (1969).

Pettyjohn's role in the film was a small one *and* her character was named ironically Angelique. There was really not much for her to do but play a convincing drunk who was part of the seedy underbelly of the mob. Her character as the mobster's wife, Felicia Majeski, on *Felony Squad* was actually far deeper. Unfortunately, Pettyjohn's next role was an equally small one.

In *The Love God?* (1969), Angelique had yet another walk-on as a model. Written and directed by Nat Hiken (1914-1968), who died shortly after the motion picture was shot but before it was released, the film was little more than an extended episode of *Love, American Style*. Abner Audubon Peacock IV (Don Knotts) is so worried that his beloved bird-watcher's magazine, *The Peacock*, may fold due to financial difficulties he agrees to take on a new partner, Osborn Tremain (Edmond O'Brien), who has a plan to turn the magazine around. Tremain re-imagines the publication as a sexy gentleman's magazine. Abner is against the plan, but before the hapless bird-watcher can prevent Tremain, the next issue of *The Peacock* sells over forty million copies. The financial crisis is over! Abner is dubbed "the love god" by the press and becomes an unwitting playboy nearly overnight, settling uneasily into the swinging single's lifestyle. Of course, he also has to deal with Darrell Evans Hughes (James Gregory) who advocates moral reform and the removal of *The Peacock* from newsstands because it opposes good, old-fashioned family values. The rest of the film devolves into a discussion about First Amendment rights. The Universal Pictures film was released in August 1969, and while it featured funnyman Don Knotts, the attempt to assimilate him into the adult-themed movies dominating the late sixties and early seventies was a complete misfire. Predictably, Angelique played a model destined to be the next centerfold.

Divorce, American Style

After just two years of marriage, Angelique Pettyjohn divorced Otho A. Pettyjohn, Jr. on May 31, 1968. She cited "irreconcilable differences" as her reason, filing in Clark County, Nevada, but truthfully, in her mind, Otho had become very jealous and controlling, and she was too much of a free spirit to put up with a man who had started monitoring her every move. Often, he would accuse Angelique of having clandestine affairs with other men behind his back, and when she lied and told him he was wrong, he demanded to know why she found it so necessary to spend nearly every night out on the town with her girlfriends. One could argue Otho had every right to be upset with her. He was being cuckolded, rather blatantly night after night, as Angelique made the rounds, fucking every swinging dick that raised her brow. She called herself a "free spirit" and blamed her uncontrollable behavior on an addiction to sex. But for him, it was all just "bullshit," psychological "mumbo-jumbo" people used to subvert the truth. Even though he never out-and-out called her a "slut," he soon came to acknowledge the truth about his wife; she was a promiscuous woman with very loose sexual morals.

Otho Pettyjohn thought when he married his "little princess," they were going to have a very traditional marriage. But alas, that's not at all how she saw it. Angelique had always seen her marriage to Otho as a marriage of convenience. She did spend most of her nights out, and on those rare occasions when she was at home, Angelique was busy reading a script or working on her career in some other way. She had never wanted to be a traditional housewife, and when her in-laws began siding with Otho and calling her names, like "floozy" and "hussy," she retreated even further from the relationship. Eventually, she could no longer take it from any of them, and filed for a quickie divorce in Las Vegas. She decided to keep his last name for her stage name. She remained in contact with him throughout his life, and always thought highly of him, but she just couldn't remain married to him. Otho Pettyjohn died twelve years later at age fifty-eight on October 9, 1980.

"Otho was a great guy, and he actually did a lot for my career," Angelique recalled many years later. "But when you're a working actress in Hollywood, you can't afford to be married to someone jealous and possessive. I loved him, but I just couldn't stay married to him. I could see the toll my long working hours had made on him, and it just wasn't fair." Deep down inside, I think Pettyjohn knew she had done him wrong. After all, here was a man who had given her everything — a home, a car, a whole new way of life — and had worked tirelessly as her manager as well. Otho certainly deserved better than what he got from her. If there was an unsung hero in Angelique's story, Otho Pettyjohn was that man; a determined advocate largely responsible for launching her career in Hollywood.

Not long after her divorce, Angelique Pettyjohn hired John C. Harris (1918-2003), a well-known producer, writer, and talent agent, to represent her in Hollywood, and Sol Goodman (1911-??), a famous booking agent in Las Vegas, to represent her in Vegas. The two men managed her career for most of the rest of her life. After Pettyjohn's death in 1992, Harris worked with Elvis Junior on several projects, and spoke often with her son about his never-realized plan to pair Angelique with British comedian Benny Hill in a comic farce, titled *The King of Burlesque*.

Figure 107. Angelique Pettyjohn in *Heaven with a Gun* (1969).

Heaven with a Gun (1969)

"I did a Western with Glenn Ford, called *Heaven with a Gun*," Angelique told me. "It was very well received, and may have been my favorite of the A-list pictures I did."

Heaven with a Gun (1969) was an old-fashioned Western that shot it out at the box office with several revisionist westerns, such as *Butch Cassidy and the Sundance Kid* (1969) and *The Wild Bunch* (1969). Released on June 11, 1969 by Metro-Goldwyn-Mayer, the film was a violent tale that made a strong argument for non-violence and co-existence between rival groups.

The script was written by blacklisted writer Dalton Trumbo (1905-1976), author of the critically acclaimed 1939 anti-war novel *Johnny Got His Gun*. A staunch advocate of labor unions, Trumbo joined the Communist Party in 1943 to support the labor movement, but was later indicted as one of the "Hollywood Ten" for being a Communist. When Trumbo refused to testify before the House on Un-American Activities Committee in 1947, he was fired by MGM and forced to serve a ten-month prison sentence in Ashland, Kentucky. After his release from prison, Trumbo found himself blacklisted from Hollywood, but that did not prevent him from writing. He wrote eighteen screenplays for a fraction of his former asking price, selling them under the byline of fellow writers unaffected by HUAC. He actually wrote the Academy-Award-winning screenplay for *The Brave One* (1956), which was credited to Robert Rich. By the time *Heaven with a Gun* went into production, Trumbo had been reinstated as a big-ticket screenwriter, with the support of Otto Preminger and Kirk Douglas.

Based loosely on Victor Hugo's sprawling epic *Les Misérables* (1862), *Heaven with a Gun* sends a reformed-gunslinger-turned-frontier-preacher, Jim Killian (Glenn Ford), into Vinagaroon, Arizona, a town embroiled in a range war between cattlemen and sheep herders. He could easily put an end to their feuding, but as a man of the cloth, he must minister to the town's needs without yielding to the temptation to put on a pair of six-shooters again.

The local half-breed Leelopa (Barbara Hershey) looks up to Killian. But when her father is hanged and she is raped by one of the local cowhands, Coke Beck (David Carradine), Killian is tempted to take justice into his own hands. He is reminded to seek God's justice, and merely tries to mediate the conflict by meeting with the rival factions. Later, Coke Beck, the son of a rich cattle rancher, Asa Beck (John Anderson), is stabbed to death through the neck, and his father and former co-workers suspect Jim Killian had something to do with it. Madge McCloud (Carolyn Jones), the whiskey-drinking madam of the town's saloon and brothel, and one of her saloon girls Emily (Angelique Pettyjohn) act on Killian's conscience. They remind him he is going to have to make a choice between Heaven and Hell, between being a gunslinger or a preacher. After a hired gunman working for Beck tries to kill Killian and four cowhands burn the church, Killian makes his choice. He straps on his gun one last time and prepares to act alone.

Despite its limited budget and the hiring of TV director Lee H. Katzin, *Heaven with a Gun* had an excellent cast and looked like an "A" picture when it was released by Metro-Goldwyn-Mayer in the summer of 1969. Central to the cast was fifty-three-year-old Glenn Ford (1916-2006), wearing the role of Jim Killian like an old ranch hand comfortable with Westerns. More than twenty years after his important work in Charles Vidor's *Gilda* (1946) and Fritz Lang's *The Big Heat* (1953), Ford was still active making mostly Westerns, with pal Henry Fonda in Burt Kennedy's *The Rounders* (1965) and *Day of the Evil Gun* (1968). Ford was supported by an able cast of familiar character actors — John Anderson, J.D. Cannon, Noah Beery, Jr., and Harry Townes — who had all played in Westerns, as

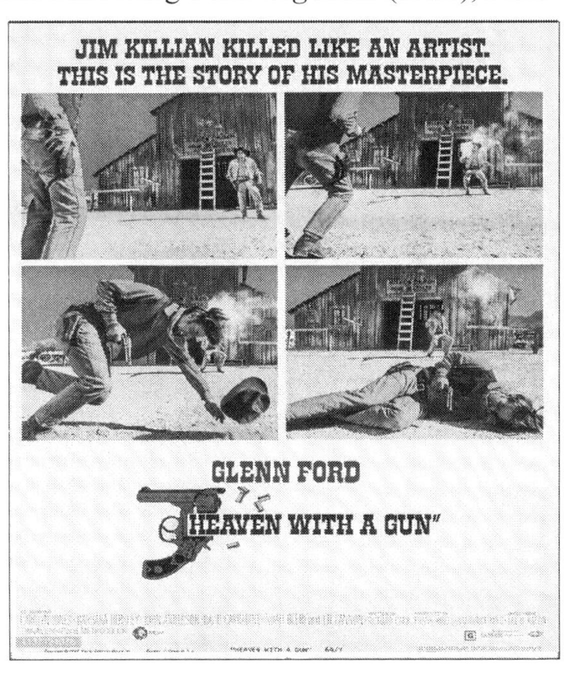

Figure 108. *Heaven with a Gun* (1969).

well as newcomers Barbara Hershey, David Carradine, and Angelique Pettyjohn.

And while part of the film was shot on the backlot at MGM, the location shoot in Arizona proved to be interesting in terms of the off-screen high jinx of several of the cast members. David Carradine and Barbara Hershey fell in love mid-production, and married a few years later. Ford approved of the couple's off-screen romance, but got the wrong idea when he saw Carradine and actress Pettyjohn sneak off to smoke a joint. Pettyjohn was attracted to Carradine, but also knew there was real chemistry between he and Hershey. She kept things playful, almost naughty, in keeping with her character, but she never crossed the line. Ford, however, thought Carradine was two-timing Hershey with Pettyjohn and gave the actor the cold shoulder for the rest of the shoot.

Richard Carr was brought aboard to punch up parts of Trumbo's script, which he did brilliantly, but he was also interested in promoting himself as a screenwriter. During principal photography, Carr pitched Carradine on an adaptation of Henry Norton Robinson's 1945 novel *The Perfect Round.* David Carradine liked the idea and bought the rights from the Robinson estate. He then spent the next ten years with Carr trying to get *Americana* (1983) made and released.

Heaven with a Gun performed solidly at the box office, but was easily eclipsed by the two revisionist Westerns in 1969, *Butch Cassidy and the Sundance Kid* and *The Wild Bunch*. Even *True Grit*, with John Wayne's Academy-Award-winning role as Rooster Cogburn, made *Heaven* seem old-fashioned by comparison. But the motion picture represented a non-violent Western at a time when violence was what sold the Western as a genre and art-form.

The final scene in the film when Killian and the town's people, including the women, march to the watering hole and confront the cattlemen whose guns are drawn is a classic. For the potentially violent confrontation to turn out peaceably was clearly a reflection of the motion picture's time. Young people who were a part of the counter-culture movement of the sixties were advocating peace instead of war. Perhaps that's all Ford needed to do — and ultimately does — was give peace a chance. A solid message for a solid film.

Tell Me You Love Me, Angelique

Angelique Pettyjohn continued her quest for parts in A-list feature films, and auditioned for the great Otto Preminger (1905-1986) to land a role in *Tell Me That You Love Me, Junie Moon* (1970) opposite Liza Minnelli. Preminger, well known as a film director who pushed the boundaries of censorship and good taste, cast Pettyjohn against type. While she still appears bare-assed naked opposite a gay artist (Leonard Freyywho is painting her nude, Preminger makes her wear a red wig, plays down her good looks, and casts her as Warren's abusive mother. This was the first time in her career Angelique was taken seriously as an actress; her meaty role as Melissa fooled most audience-goers who didn't even recognize Pettyjohn at all. She appeared to be completely submerged in the small but so critical role. The flashback scene is played somewhat for laughs,but is critical to establish character of Warren's mother.

> *I landed a plum role in* Tell Me That You Love Me, Junie Moon*, with Liza Minelli. There's a scene in the film in which a red-headed man who's been confined to a wheelchair describes in a flashback what his mother was like, and I played his mother who was supposed to be a crazy red-headed lady. When the movie came out [in 1970], not one of my friends recognized it was me. That character was worked out in rehearsals with Otto Preminger, and it turned out to be a difficult job to do because he was quite a hard director to work for. But the results do speak for themselves. Melissa was a great character to play.*

Throughout his career as a director, Austrian-born Preminger had worked with a great number of actors and actresses, and he himself had started out as an actor in Austria, then later in the United States.

Otto Preminger directed the relatively unknown Gene Tierney in the title role of *Laura* (1944), singer Alice Faye in a dramatic role in *Fallen Angel* (1945), Frank Sinatra in *The Man with the Golden Arm* (1955), James Stewart and Ben Gazzara in *Anatomy of a Murder* (1959), Paul Newman as a blonde-haired Jew in *Exodus* (1960), and Henry Fonda in *Advise & Consent* (1962).

Preminger himself played a number of memorable characters, including the World War II Luft-Stalag Commandant, Oberst von Scherbach of the German POW camp in *Stalag 17* (1953), directed by Billy Wilder, and the comic book villain Mr. Freeze in the sixties *Batman* television series. He was known in Hollywood for pushing the boundaries of censorship by dealing with topics considered taboo, such as drug addiction in *The Man with the Golden Arm*, rape in *Anatomy of a Murder*, and homosexuality in *Advise & Consent*. In his personal life, he was romantically involved with burlesque performer Gypsy Rose Lee, and tried to make Lee's transition from stripper to movie actress as seamless as possible. But alas, Hollywood refused to take Lee seriously and cast her in "B" pictures, in less-than-minor roles.

Years later, when he began working with Pettyjohn on *Tell Me That You Love Me, Junie Moon*, Otto Preminger saw a great many similarities between his former love, Lee, and Pettyjohn. He worked very hard with her, often losing his famous temper over little things because he had hoped to shape the former showgirl and stripper into an actress. Their hard work paid off because Angelique does deliver the finest performance since the beginning of her career. She would remain friends with Preminger, and got to know his third wife, Hope Bryce, well, until his death in 1986 at age eighty.

In Otto Preminger's beautiful and moving *Tell Me That You Love Me, Junie Moon*, based upon the short novel by Marjorie Kellogg, three gallant, self-styled "freaks" agree to move into a broken-down bungalow, and set up housekeeping together. Their new home comes complete with its own assortment of unusual characters: a peeping Tom who lives next door; a rich, but spooky landlady (played by Minnelli's godmother, Kay Thompson) who dresses like a World War I flying ace with the leather jacket, tinted goggles and long, flowing white scarf; a roly-poly fishmonger (James Coco) who is so lonely he befriends Junie Moon and her friends; a hoot owl that lives in the banyan tree in the back yard; and a scroungy old dog who needs a home. But the story is really about the complicated relationships that develop between the three lead characters, Junie Moon (Liza Minnelli), Arthur (Ken Howard), and Warren (Robert Moore). Each are wounded in some way and need each other in order to survive the cruel, dispassionate world they face.

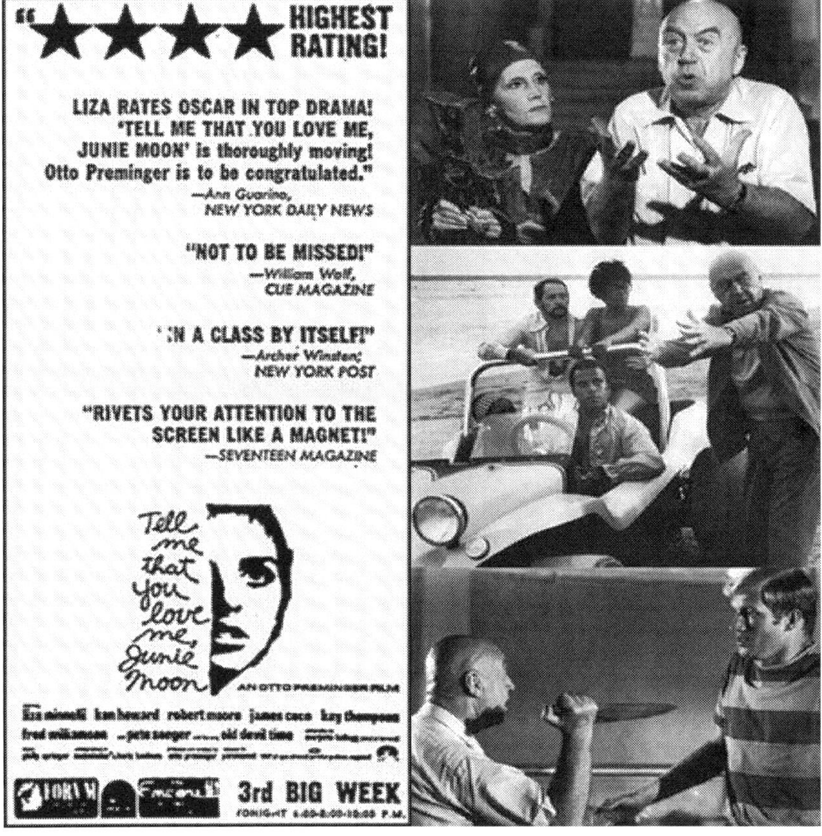

Figure 109. Otto Preminger directs *Tell Me…Junie Moon* (1970).

For Junie Moon, half of her face is scared by acid, like Lon Chaney's *Phantom of the Opera*, thanks to a traveling salesman who, when she refused his sexual advances, topped off their date by pouring battery acid all over her. She has spent years seeking relief, working with dispassionate doctors who only see her as part of their experiments but not a real person. Arthur is a tall, handsome, blonde young man who suffers with epilepsy. Even though he manages to keep the occasional seizures in check, he is also fighting a progressive neurological disorder that is gradually turning his body into mush. And Warren, the most pathetic member of the three, is a red-bearded, barrel-chested homosexual who has been confined to a wheelchair since he was seventeen. He'd dared to make a pass at a friend during a hunting trip, who then promptly shot him in the spine. He suffers with nightmares of past events that reveal he was tortured and psychologically abused by his own mother Melissa (Pettyjohn), who didn't want a queer for a son.

All three of them are disabled, but not down. They live together like a family, determined to prove themselves and to help each other out. When love does ultimately come to Junie, in the form of the aging bachelor played by James Coco, they rally around her, and are pleased by her choice.

Released by Paramount Pictures on May 11, 1970, just in time for Mother's Day, *Tell Me That You Love Me, Junie Moon* was a critical success, and performed moderately well at the box office. Otto Preminger was nominated for the Golden Palm at the 1970 Cannes Film Festival, and then later charged (but not convicted) of desecrating the graves at the Braintree, Massachusetts cemetery for shooting the nude scene in which Minnelli and the salesman have their date. During production of the film, Minnelli's mother, Judy Garland, passed away, causing her a period of mourning. Most critics cited this reason as the source of her highly-charged, poignant performance.

Pettyjohn received the best reviews of her career for the very raw and emotional portrayal of Warren's mother. She should have been nominated for a Golden Globe or an Oscar for her excellent performance.

Love, Computer Style

Pettyjohn didn't know Paul Rapp personally. She didn't meet him in one of the night clubs on the Sunset Strip or at one of the parties in the Hollywood Hills, nor had she ever been formally introduced to him by one of her friends or contacts, but she had heard about him. Everyone in the industry had heard about Paul Rapp (1937—).

While attending the film school at the University of Southern California in 1958, he wrote an influential paper about the use of three cameras in shooting sitcoms that went onto revolutionize how situational comedies were shot. Shortly after graduation, Rapp went to work for Roger Corman, the low-budget studio chief who launched the directing careers of Martin Scorsese, Jonathan Demme, Ron Howard, James Cameron, and many others. Paul became the head of production on many of Roger's films, both as a writer and director. He worked as an assistant director or a unit production manager for nearly every major studio in Hollywood, yet continued his association with Corman developing new technologies, like the use of a hand-held camera and other ways to cut production costs. He shot some of Corman's earliest films, like *The Terror* (1963), with Boris Karloff and Jack Nicholson, in five days or less. While still working for Roger Corman, Paul tutored Scorsese, Demme, and others in how to shoot films economically, and was instrumental in helping Scorsese make his first film *Mean Streets* (1973). Rapp was certainly well-known in the industry, and when he decided to make his very first feature film, everyone expected big things from him.

He chose to make a science fiction movie.

In 1969, for the first time since the early fifties, science fiction movies were enjoying a renaissance at the box office. Thanks to the critical success of *2001: A Space Odyssey* (1968) and the phenomenal box office returns for *Planet of the Apes* (1968), nearly every studio had a science fiction film in production or in release. Universal was readying *Journey to the Far Side of the Sun* for release; Warner Brothers had Ray Bradbury's *The Illustrated Man* in production; Metro-Goldwyn-

Mayer was set to follow up *2001* with *Ice Station Zebra* and *Captain Nemo and the Underwater City*; and Columbia had produced *Marooned* for a 1969 release date. Even Pettyjohn had just starred in a low budget sci-fi film, *Mad Doctor of Blood Island*, scheduled to come out later in the year. With Paul Rapp's decision to make a science fiction film, plus his stellar reputation in Hollywood, Angelique was convinced he would produce a real masterpiece. But she turned out to be very, very wrong.

> *[Paul] Rapp started out to make a science fiction film,* Love, Computer Style. *There was supposed to be this Master Computer teaching a bunch of young people in the future that actually used to be virgins. And then it told the story of these three young women in the sixties. There was a very lovely black girl, a short red-haired girl, and myself that were the three stars of it. It told how all three of us were friends in college and we were virgins. We were the last three virgins in our school, and it dealt with what we were going through in order to try and get rid of it. That's not much. I did a lot of films, and I did a lot of films I was very proud of. That particular one was not thrilling. In fact, it was a real stupid movie. At the time, it was rated X only because it had frontal nudity. That's how many years ago it was. Needless to say, it wasn't a very good science fiction movie.*

Love, Computer Style (1970) was set in the sexually-liberated but totalitarian world of 2177 A.D. The Master Computer rules the lives of its people with an iron fist. It has created a society that is devoid of love, romance, emotion, family ties, and any notions of 20th Century morality. Sex for its own sake is now the social norm, and it is prohibited to have sex as an expression of love. Furthermore, the concept of virginity is completely foreign to the computer-run society as every girl is sent to be deflowered by an "older man" at the age of thirteen. That also means that certain motion pictures from the past have been completely banned, but that doesn't stop an underground film club in Los Angeles (now an island after a great quake) from

Figures 110-112. Scenes from *The Curious Female* (1969).

meeting clandestinely in a cave to watch these forbidden features and discuss their social significance.

Two rebels within the totalitarian state, Liana (Bunny Allister) and Jorel (David Westberg), have agreed to host *The Vacuum Salesman*, a college campus film, which is particularly popular among the club members. They know they are breaking the Master Computer's law, but all agree to do so in order to find out what love was like in the distant past. One of the films, a 1969 release, *The Three Virgins*, turns out to be the most popular feature of the night. It tells the story (within the larger context of the film) of three women, the only virgin students at a university, and how they are counseled by a computer named CUPID to work through their problems. Joan (Allister, in her second role) has broken up with medical student Paul (Westberg) because of his demand for pre-marital sex in return for a vague promise of marriage; Pearl Lushcomb (Charlene Jones), a beautiful African-American girl, is frigid because of her lecherous uncle assaulted and tried to rape her, and Susan Rome (Angelique Pettyjohn) has been reared by her conservative parents to resist sex without love. The three virgins want to shed their inhibitions, and so act in accordance with their own individual desires. Pearl finds herself attracted to a white woman and tries her first lesbian encounter. Susan learns to loosen up with some recreational drugs and wild behavior, and Joan breaks up with her boyfriend when he has sex with a prostitute. By the end of the movie, Liana, Jorel, and their club members are discovered and arrested, and the Master Computer decides to re-run the film for its own enlightenment.

The idea was a good one — and might have made an interesting movie — but the execution was not very satisfying. Paul Rapp did a great job with his extremely limited resources, but there was really no mistaking what kind of picture he had made. It was basically a late-sixties softcore porn movie disguised as a science fiction film, with the wrap-around sequences involving the Master Computer.

The title was changed to *The Curious Female* for its world-wide release on November 10, 1970 to take advantage of the salacious headlines regarding the Swedish adult film, *I Am Curious (Yellow)* (1967), which was seized by customs, banned in numerous cities, and finally released in the United States in 1969 after a heated court battle dealing with American censorship. Like *I Am Curious (Yellow)*, Rapp's motion picture was immediately slapped with an X-rating and did not get much of a showing outside of art houses. It still remains a cult film in Europe and outside the United States. Regrettably, it did very little to advance Pettyjohn's career in Hollywood. It was more like a step backwards to the kinds of movies she made with Doris Wishman and Joe Sarno.

In 1973, Rapp worked with Gene Roddenberry as a producer on Gene's follow-up to *Star Trek*, titled *Genesis II*.

Had CBS picked up the series about a NASA scientist from the 20th century, trying to help rebuild Earth in the 23rd century after a nuclear holocaust, Rapp had promised Angelique a guest spot on the new show, but alas CBS green-lit its juvenile version of Planet of the Apes instead. An episode in development was titled "Poodle Shop," in which men are captured and sold as domestic pets by the females in charge; Pettyjohn would have played one of those females. Unfortunately, when Roddenberry reworked the script for the second pilot, titled Planet Earth (1974), she was not available, and Gene cast Star Trek alumnus Diana Muldaur in the part instead. Angelique would have been amazing!

Figure 113. Poster from *The Curious Female* (1969).

More Childish Things

One day, out of the blue, Angelique's co-star from *Childish Things* (1969), Don Joslyn (who played Kelly) called her to find out what she was doing. She had just finished playing Susan Rome in *Love, Computer Style* and had a fairly open slate. He had written a screenplay, *The Seduction of a Nerd*, and was being given the opportunity to direct as well as produce it. Joslyn had written a role with her in mind, the character of "Honeysuckle," and he wanted to know if she'd be interested in playing the part in his movie. Pettyjohn agreed, even though it was far from the kind of A-list pictures she wanted to make, simply to help her friend out.

The Seduction of a Nerd (aka: *Up Your Teddy Bear* and *Mother*, 1970) featured the meek, soft-spoken Wally Cox, the larger-than-life Victor Buono (from *What Ever Happened to Baby Jane?*, 1962), and the luscious Catwoman herself, Julie Newmar, in an oddball, R-rated sex comedy. Honestly, when anyone thinks of an R-rated sex comedy, two names that don't instantly come to mind are Wally Cox and Victor Buono. Perhaps, if you had mentioned Julie Newmar and Angelique Pettyjohn, but then again, there was something truly unique about Don Joslyn's screenplay.

Clyde King (Cox), a toy store employee whose hobbies include making wooden toys and stalking women, makes some of the finest toys ever produced by hand. "Mother" (Newmar), who owns "one of the biggest toy companies in the world," wants Clyde to work for her company, where she plans on mass-producing his delicate, hand-carved toys. She delegates her second-in-command, slimy Lyle "Skippy" Burns (Buono) to put Clyde under contract. However, King will not join her company as she reminds him of his mother. She then becomes the subject of bizarre fantasies in which "Mother," the toy company owner, as imagined by King, brow-beats and humiliates him. Discovering Clyde King's predilection for leaving work at odd times to stalk random women, Skippy first tries to entice Clyde with sexy Honeysuckle (Pettyjohn), then tries to trick him into signing an employment contract by supplying him with women, even going as far to dress himself up in drag as a hooker. But every time he sets King up with a woman, the encounter ends disastrously, so Skippy finally decides to kill him.

This totally bizarre concoction of the weird and wild seventies never quite lives up to its promise as a farcical romp, but it is worth a single viewing, if only to see Angelique get naked in a non-porno movie. Cox is supposed to be funny, but comes off as creepy. Scantily-clad Newmar is supposed to be sexy and beguiling, but comes off as an over-protective mother. Buono, who's supposed to be creepy, is hilarious, going for broke no matter how lame the joke is. In the course of the film, Buono sports a sleazy mustache, a bad comb-over, tons of sweat, an oversized wetsuit, and a drag costume of the fattest and ugliest prostitute in New York City. He's like a human cartoon character from a Chuck Jones looney-toon who is always slipping or falling or going berserk in order to satisfy his boss, and hire Clyde King.

Released two days before Christmas, December 23, 1970, *The Seduction of the Nerd* turned out to be a real box office bomb. Even with hip music by Quincy Jones, Don Joslyn couldn't give tickets away to his stinker. Perhaps Joslyn should re-edit *The Seduction of the Nerd*, and try re-releasing it today as *Toy Grabbers*.

Figure 114. *The Seduction…Nerd* (1970).

The timing of the film's release was also difficult for Angelique. Ever since she had been forced to give up her son, Elvis, Jr., on Christmas Eve 1961, nine years earlier, she wondered what he was thinking and doing, and if he would ever want to know her reasons for giving him up. It made it even more painful to be making a movie about toys, a toymaker, and children.

Making "B" Movies, Again

After working so hard to establish her career in "A" pictures, Pettyjohn found herself working in "B" movies again. Not only was the money generally good, but she also had more of an opportunity to headline a "B" movie. She might have worked for ten years or more to get the chance to star in another "A" picture, whereas "B" movie directors often sought her out because of her notoriety on the small screen. They weren't looking for someone who could act, they were looking for someone audiences would recognize as well as someone they could afford. Also, the time it took to shoot a "B" movie was nearly half that of a first-class, quality production. Pettyjohn found the opportunities for travel to be far better with the low-budget films as well. The bottom line was she just wanted to keep working.

Filmed in the Philippines by Directors Eddie Romero and Gerry de Leon, *The Mad Doctor of Blood Island* (aka *Tomb of the Living* Dead, 1968) was a throwback to the kind of horror/science fiction films made in the thirties and forties, specifically *The Island of Lost Souls* (1932). In that classic film, Charles Laughton played an obsessed scientist who was conducting profane experiments in evolution on the natives of a remote island. Nearly forty years later, the titular "mad doctor" was still conducting profane experiments on the local natives in a *Weird Tales*-inspired story. Only this time, he has turned his faithful lab assistant into a green-blooded, Chlorophyll "plant monster" that rampages around a small island, killing natives in one of the goriest splatter films of the seventies. The Filipino scare fest did offer Pettyjohn her best screen opportunity to romance handsome John Ashley and a rather meaty plotline about an alcoholic father she must save from the mad doctor and his monster. She also had a great opportunity to get out of Hollywood and take part in a really international kind of production. She acquitted herself marvelously, and achieved true cult status worldwide along the way.

I would say I had a most wonderful experience working on The Mad Doctor of Blood Island. *I had a great leading man. Well, John Ashley kissed really good, too. Both on screen and off. And the movie had a great monster! But it wasn't without its hardships. I mean, you've got mosquitoes the size of your thumb and everything is soaking wet. The humidity is so heavy that you curl your hair and it goes straight in five minutes. It was really uncomfortable. We would drive in jeeps to the location and then we'd get out and carry equipment and hike in another mile to get to some of the beautiful locations, so it had its difficulties. Very long shooting hours. But it was one of the most memorable experiences of my entire life because the Philippine jungle, and some of the area's locations we shot in, were the most exotically beautiful I have ever seen in my entire life. The tropical flowers are as big around as a tire wheel and the butterflies are as big as your head. These are things that this gal from the western United States would never have seen possibly in my entire life. So, just that part of the experience — the memory of the waterfalls and some of the beauty in nature I saw on location there — are the best things I remember from a picture I shot twelve or thirteen years ago. Maybe more. What I remember most is the beauty of it all.*

When natives living on a remote tropical island in the Philippines start reporting man-eating plants and animal mutations caused by some strange form of radioactivity, local officials call the United States for help. Dr. Bill Foster (John Ashley), an American government scientist, travels to the remote island to investigate rumors of strange deaths among the locals. There, he meets Dr. Lorca (Eddie Garcia), a scientist who has

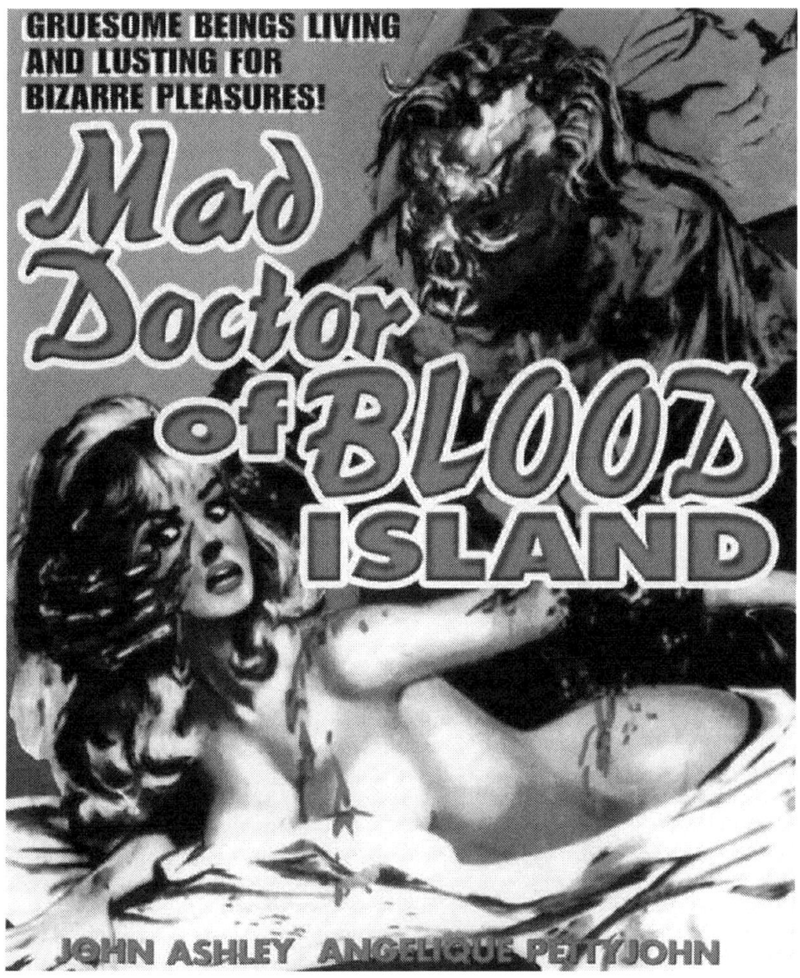

Figure 115. Poster for *The Mad Doctor of Blood Island* (1968).

been experimenting on the populace using chlorophyll as a means of curing leukemia. At the same time, Sheila Willard (Angelique Pettyjohn) and Carlos Lopez (Ronaldo Valdez) have come to the island, looking for their loved ones. They agree to work together after the captain of the ship that brought them claims the island is cursed and tells a story about a man they picked up on a raft who bled green blood.

Sheila eventually finds out her father is a hopeless alcoholic, and Carlos can't seem to convince his mother the place is haunted, even though her husband, Don Ramon Lopez died there recently under mysterious circumstances. When they exhume the grave of Don Ramon, it is empty. Suddenly, rumors abound about a green-skinned monster with chlorophyll for blood is responsible for deaths among the natives. Sheila is attacked in the jungle by the monster and only survives because an unfortunate native was killed trying to save her. Foster is relieved that Sheila didn't die, and confesses he is in love with her.

Everything seems to point back to Dr. Lorca.

Foster soon learns that Lorca's experiments have mutated Don Ramon into the green-blooded monster wreaking havoc on the villagers. It kills his wife and almost kills his son, Carlos, but at the last moment, a glimmer of humanity returns to the creative. It attacks Dr. Lorca in his hidden lab. A fire breaks out in the lab,

Figure 116. Sheila and Foster share a moment of passion.

Figure 117. Dr. Foster confronts Sheila with news of her father..

resulting in a huge explosion that presumably destroys Lorca and his monster.

Dr. Foster, Sheila, her father, and Carlos all return to the ship, relieved to be leaving "blood" island behind them. But as the ship leaves port, a grisly hand appears from underneath a boat tarp, dripping green blood.

Over the years, fans of low-budget horror-science fiction movies have made *The Mad Doctor of Blood Island* one of their cult classics. They seem to love the chlorophyll monster, though decidedly lacking the technical wizardry of a Stan Winston. The monster is very much like the invisible hunter in *Predator* (1987) as it stalks the natives through the jungle, killing them one at a time. They are also very fond of the softcore scenes which feature Angelique Pettyjohn and Alicia Alonso as they romp naked through the jungle, and then get together with the former teenage heartthrob John Ashley for a tryst in the overgrowth. Pettyjohn is truly luscious in every one of her scenes. It's clear her talents are wonderfully exploited here. She enjoyed all her scenes with Ashley who reminded her of Elvis; while their sex scenes were supposed to be simulated, she confessed she was so smitten with Ashley, and he with her, they decided to make all the sex scenes real. (Ashley had just left his wife Deborah Walley, after two years of marriage, and returned to his bachelor ways during his time in the Philippines.) Pettyjohn continued to steam things up with John Ashley both on-and-off-the-set, and even talked about continuing their affair back in the States. But the minute their plane landed at LAX, Ashley stepped into the arms of the woman who would be his next wife, Nancy Moore. Disappointed, Angelique returned to her home alone.

Frequently screened on the drive-in theater circuit with *Blood Demon* (1967), *The Mad Doctor of Blood Island* was actually released under a variety of titles in the seventies and eighties, such as *The Mad Doctor of Crimson Island* and *Tomb of the Living Dead.* The film also enjoyed some notoriety thanks to a ridiculously bad, pre-credit sequence devised by Independent-International head Sam Sherman, also the producer of the motion picture. Each patron was given a free packet of colored liquid, labeled "green blood," and urged to drink it, prior to the movie, in order to ward off the effects of Dr. Lorca's experiments. Shot entirely at Clark Air Force Base in Manila, using American teenagers, the prologue was a goofy gimmick which harkened back to the fifties when studios relied on 3-D and "Percepto!" to trick audiences into thinking the events in the movie were actually real.

> *I've seen* The Mad Doctor of Blood Island *many, many times on television. Unfortunately. Though I think they changed it to* Tomb of the Living Dead. *They changed it to that title just for television only because the censors at the time wouldn't allow them to use the word "blood" in the title. Isn't that something? They changed any title that had the word "blood" in it. Yes, they're*

> *still re-running that thing and I even have a tape of it at home in case any of my friends wanna laugh. I think the best thing of the whole picture, just as I said, was the beauty of the photography. The sets weren't sets; they were there. The huts were real huts the natives lived in. They stepped out and we took over. It was so authentic, and the color was beautiful. When I watched it for the first time after it was done, I remember sitting there — it was in a drive-in theater — and I thought, "Well God, the story was bad enough before they edited it. Now it doesn't make sense at all. But boy, it's beautiful."*

One year later, the chlorophyll creature returned in *Beast of Blood* (1970), along with Ashley, Romero, and Garcia, but minus Pettyjohn. *The Revenge of Doctor X* (1970, aka *The Devil Garden, Venus Fly-Trap*) was a movie made in the sixties, from an unproduced screenplay by Ed Wood, cross-pollinated with scenes from *The Mad Doctor of Blood Island.*

Remarkably, in some video versions of *The Revenge of Doctor X*, the opening credits have been swapped out and replaced with the credits from *Mad Doctor*. Regal Video of New York actually featured an illustration of a screaming, naked blonde, who looks suspiciously like Angelique Pettyjohn, on its VHS box, with a summary that reads (in part): "A pretty woman journalist enlists the aid of an American adventurer to set sail with her on a cargo ship with a ruffian crew. Her mission: find her father who mysteriously disappeared in the jungles of an uncharted island—cursed with EVIL…" The box lists the cast as John Ashley, Ronald Remy, and Angelique Pettyjohn. The actual story features James Craig as a burnt-out NASA scientist taking a week's vacation off to go to Japan. He finds rest and romance along the way with a hillbilly snake charmer, topless pearl divers, and a Japanese hunchback assistant, but ultimately must fight a man-sized Venus flytrap monster. No female journalist. No

American adventurer. No ruffian crew. Please don't be fooled by this video! Pettyjohn had nothing to do with it, but someone who promotes grade-z videos must have thought enough about her talent to list her. One day, MST3K (Mystery Science Theater 3000) should get to work on this piece of shit.

Her Mother's Death

Maia Irene "Micky" Enke Herbert died at home of natural causes on July 29, 1972. She was only fifty years old. She was buried at Wasatch Lawn Memorial Park in Salt Lake City, Utah, surrounded by her family. When news of her mother's death finally reached her on the set, Angelique Pettyjohn was in the middle of production on *Bordello* (1974). She took a few days off for bereavement leave and flew home. Because she had not been home in years, Pettyjohn received a chilly reception from her half-brother Jerald and her two half-sisters Janice Marie and Diana Kay. They'd seen her on television and followed the other parts of her career, but she might as well have been a stranger to them. Her step-father Claude Herbert didn't even get out of his favorite chair to greet her. He was almost comatose with grief for his beloved "Micky."

On the next day, Angelique visited her mother's plot at the cemetery. The earth was still fresh and they had not yet installed the headstone. She looked down at the grave, but she could not even summon a single tear. She had always sought out her mother's approval, but when she was alive, German-born Maia was a stern woman with little humor or warmth. She had managed to keep a roof over her daughter's head and paid for singing and ballet lessons. Maia didn't know what more was required of her, such a busy woman, perhaps too busy.

> *Even before she died, I was never able to talk to my mother about anything; my dad, my pain and suffering, my desire to be loved. She was always too busy. Most of her life, it seemed like she lived in this little bubble, unaffected by anything around her, and no matter how hard I cried or tried to get her to notice me, she never did. How was I supposed to reach her now that she was buried eight-feet down*

> *in a cemetery plot? I went to Wasatch Lawn Memorial Park, where she was buried, and I threw myself down on her grave. I was wracked with guilt, shame, and pain. I took out a bottle of booze and drank it down.* Did you ever once love me? *I hungered for your love and affection.* Did you ever once notice me? *I listened and waited for her answer. It never came. Finally, when all my grief was spent, I got up and went home.*

For the next few months, following her mother's death, Angelique searched for her father throughout the Southwest. She didn't know whether he was alive or dead, but was determined to find him. In November 1972, she found Richard Lee Perrins living a solitary life in Long Beach, California. Pettyjohn tried several times to contact her father by letter, phone, and telegram, but he had no interest in knowing her. He simply wanted to be left alone. Period. End of story.

Her worse fears had all come true. As a child, Angelique had always suspected her father was so aloof and uncaring because he didn't really love her. Now, tragically, she knew that for certain. Her issues with low self-esteem, drinking, and meaningless sex were all tied to the fact that she got no love at all from the two people in her life who mattered the most, her mother and father.

"As that realization hit me, I just came unglued, right then and there. I cried and I cried. I couldn't stop," Pettyjohn explained much later to me.

Bordello (1974)

She returned home from the funeral to complete work on *Bordello* (1974), a movie that turned out to be completely unfilmable. Set in Paris during the 19th Century, *Bordello* was supposed to have been an erotic, gender-bending slice of the swinging sixties (the 1860s) that followed a number of characters into the world of Toulouse-Lautrec and his left-bank entourage, but was instead a softcore porn film, masquerading as an art-house film. Poster art claimed it was banned in Denmark.

Figure 118. Pettyjohn works in a brothel.

Pettyjohn is the highest paid courtesan in all Paris, and so spends most of her screen time naked with other girls in the titular bordello. Characters come and go; courtesans dress and undress for their patrons; a young man with no money begins a passionate but ultimately doomed love affair with Pettyjohn, who dies in the end. The story anticipates Baz Luhrmann's *Moulin Rouge* (2001), a vastly superior film. Good luck in finding this 1974 disaster, which was retired from domestic release and cut up into a dozen, X-rated shorts released on 8mm film.

G.I. Executioner (1975)

Co-written and directed by Joel M. Reed, based on a short story by Keith Lorenz and Ian Ward, *G.I. Executioner* (aka *Wit's End, Dragon Lady*, 1975) was an action-adventure thriller based loosely on the classic *Casablanca* (1943). The idea to make a feature film in Singapore came from Marvin Farkas, an American stationed there during World War II. To Marvin, Singapore seemed like an old-fashioned place with seedy cafes and opium dens where an ex-patriot like Rick Blaine would be a natural for intrigue and international espionage. For the story and the script, he turned to two young foreign correspondents, Ward and Lorenz, both living in Singapore and, in their spare time, running *The Junk*, a hip night-club-bar-restaurant on a restored junk-boat.

"I had wanted to make a 1969 version of *Casablanca*," Lorenz explained as he wrote the story treatment with Ward. Their final screenplay reads like an extended episode of *Magnum P.I.* (1981), a show several years away from development at Universal by Glen Larson and Donald Belisario.

Set in Singapore 1969, the story introduced audience members to Dave Dearborn (Tom Keena), a former Marine who served in Vietnam and is now a disillusioned American journalist running a groovy nightclub on a boat called *The Junk*, moored near Clifford Pier. Through a "voice-over narrative," he reveals that he is depressed and at his "wit's end": "Look what I ended up with, a lot of bad memories and this lousy bar." Even a blow-job from a local working girl (a real prostitute from Singapore) cannot seem to rouse him from his funk. Pretty quickly, Dearborn becomes an unwitting pawn in a scenario involving the CIA, a local gangster, Chinese and Russian spies, and a defecting Chinese scientist with a formula for anti-matter. He also has a complicated love life, quickly moving from the local girl servicing him to an adoring young American innocent abroad (Janet Wood) to a buxom American stripper working a bar (Angelique Pettyjohn) and the big love of his life, Mai Lee (Vicky Racimo), who has become the mistress of Lim, a local gangster, much to Dave's chagrin.

Dearborn takes the assignment, mostly out of revenge to stick it to Mr. Lim, who may have his claws in the defector. In the course of searching for the missing scientist, Dave becomes entangled with several willing females and the body count goes up as the result of a string of shootings. We also learn Dave was once a cocaine addict, murderer for hire, and undercover homosexual! Aboard a houseboat, Bonnie tries to protect his identity, but she is shot twice in the stomach in a shootout with a corrupt government. Sadly, she dies in his arms. Ultimately, he rescues Mai Lee from a life of servitude to the gangster, shoots and kills scores of bad guys, and helps the CIA take the defecting Chinese scientist into custody.

G.I. Executioner (1975) was the last movie Angelique Pettyjohn made before turning to the adult-film market. After scoring such high marks with her excellent performance in Otto Preminger's *Tell Me That You Love Me, Junie Moon* (1970) and *Childish Things*, Pettyjohn's career seemed to take a downward spiral with each subsequent film she did, demanding more and more nudity and softcore porn. She thought of herself as a serious actress, but the parts she got could have been done by any woman who was willing to show her boobs and perform simulated sex on screen. She became discouraged and disillusioned, and started drinking much more heavily than she had before.

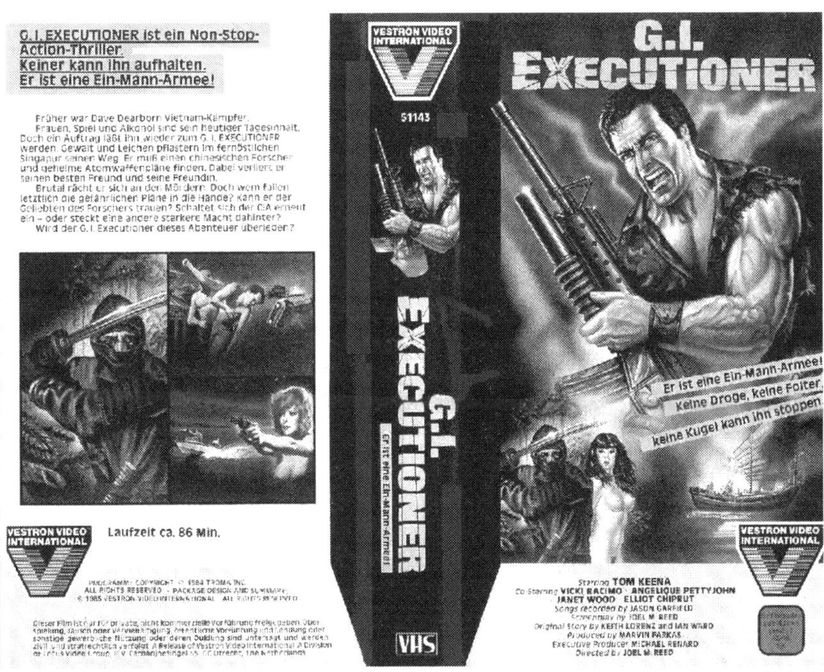

Figure 119. *The G.I. Executioner* (1975) .

In Singapore, Director Joel M. Reed introduced her to ecstasy and other drugs not readily available in the States, while seducing her with promises that her role in the film would become larger and more pivotal. Pettyjohn had every reason to believe him. He was a well-known cult director with a proven record of success. With an investment of less than $10,000, Reed had made the much-talked-about *Career Bed* (1969), with future adult-film luminaries, Jennifer Welles and Georgina Spelvin, and one year later, the top-rated *Sex by Advertisement* (1970), also with Welles and Spelvin. *Bloodsucking Freaks* later defined his career to horror-film aficionados. Angelique wanted to trust him, but then ultimately shot her big scene, where her character Bonnie is gunned down by bad guys, totally in the nude.

Production of *G.I. Executioner* was finished in 1971, but the film was not released until 1975. When the movie was finally released under the title *Dragon Lady* by Troma, her scene was tagged as "the wildest nude shootout in film history." As far as Angelique Pettyjohn was concerned, if she was going to continue showing her body and doing simulated sex scenes, she might as well do it for real in adult films and make a great deal more money doing it. She later regretted that decision as not one of her smartest moves, but between the booze and the drugs, Pettyjohn was not thinking very clearly.

Figure 120. Flashback scene from *Tell Me...Junie Moon* (1970).

8
Return to Vegas

T&A, T&A, that's all they ever want. The casting agents never saw me as anything other than a sex symbol. And I thought, if they just wanted T&A, I might as well be a nightclub performer and make more steady money. And that's exactly what I did. I was so tired of being typecast as a sex symbol that I packed up my bags and went back to Las Vegas to find work.

During the Summer of 1970, Angelique packed up her dilapidated VW bug, now covered with psychedelic paintings of her astrological sign Pisces, and headed back to Las Vegas to resume her career as a showgirl. She had last worked there in 1965 as a dancer in the *Ziegfeld's Follies* at the Thunderbird Hotel and Casino, so that's where she began looking. Angelique had to come to terms with her age: She was no longer the twenty-two-year-old, wide-eyed ingénue Dorothy "Harmonie," but the twenty-seven-year-old seasoned dancer Angelique Pettyjohn. She drank, often to excess, and had just started getting high smoking pot with the other girls. She knew that she was going to end up dead or permanently disabled if she didn't pull her life back together. Regrettably, the only work she could find was as a stripper at clubs located off the Las Vegas Strip in the industrial section of town.

Angelique first worked, but didn't work very hard, at the Cheetah Club, one of the countless seedy strip joints dotting the side streets of Las Vegas Boulevard. Crazy Horse Too, one of the oldest striptease establishments in Las Vegas, had a much better reputation and reported a better clientele, while the Topless Girls of Glitter Gulch was located in the middle of Fremont Street, a tourist destination. As an entertainer (and she hated that word to describe her stripping), she'd have to pay a fee to the club in order to work every night. Most of her customers didn't know, but would still stiff her for private lap-dances or make her work twice as hard to earn a living wage. Since she was still collecting residuals from a few of the movies and television shows made prior to leaving Hollywood, she was not about to give away her remaining self-respect to guys who saw her as nothing more than a piece of meat. The moment a male customer got too physical with her or too verbally abusive, Pettyjohn would call the bouncer. If he failed to do his job properly, she'd quit and take the next job down the street. The strippers in Las Vegas routinely changed clubs. Angelique was no exception. She'd work for couple of weeks at one strip joint, then quit and start again at another strip joint, where the male customers were all new to her. At two or three o'clock in the morning, she'd go home to a little shit-hole and drink herself to sleep.

The Wonderful World of Burlesque

On August 7, 1970, Angelique Pettyjohn was featured on the cover of *Vegas Visitor* magazine, a free tabloid distributed to tourists new to Las Vegas so they could get the most out of their trip. Robert Scott Hooper shot the photograph, his first of several featuring the lovely Pettyjohn. Within a few weeks, Angelique was recruited by Barry Ashton to work on *The Wonderful World of Burlesque '70* on the stage of the Gaiety Theatre of the popular Silver Slipper Gambling Hall and Saloon. As young Dorothy "Harmony," she had dreamt of becoming one of the "girls," but was told, rather bluntly, she wasn't ready yet. Now at age twenty-eight, Angelique was one of the famous Barry Ashton Girls. A fan of burlesque comedy, she easily traded barbs with the older, more established comedians and played the very typical dumb blonde in short skits that often brought the house down, assuring her a place in the show as long as Pettyjohn wanted to do it. Ashton and Harold Minsky created a show that combined risqué burlesque humor with titillating dance numbers, and established a show that critics labeled as "must-see" in Las Vegas. Her fellow performers were Tommy Moe Raft, Lou Ascole, Miss Disneyland, Janet Boyd, Gordon Cornish, Martin Gavin, Marina Maubert, and the Tommy Hodges Orchestra. *The Wonderful World of Burlesque '70* was subsequently followed by *The Wonderful World of Burlesque '71* and *The Wonderful World of Burlesque '72*, with legendary performer Ben Blue coming out of retirement to appear in the show.

Angelique performed as one of the Barry Ashton Girls in *The Wonderful World of Burlesque* for three years, and then left

Figure 121. ***The Wonderful World of Burlesque*** **(1970).**

the show on a high note, with audiences wanting more. Triumphantly, she returned to the show five years later in September 1978, and did another year of dancing and comedy for Barry Ashton. Photographer Robert Scott Hooper was there to document her return to the Silver Slipper Gambling Hall and Saloon.

After nearly a year of appearing in Barry Ashton's Burlesque Show, Angelique ran into an old acquaintance of hers, Valerie Perrine, and learned that Donn Arden was looking for a qualified dancer to replace her. Perrine had just been cast as Montana Wildhack, the soft-core pornography actress, in the multi-million-dollar adaptation of Kurt Vonnegut's *Slaughterhouse Five* (1972). As a dancer, Pettyjohn knew the name Donn Arden well. Arden (1916-1994) was a world-renowned American choreographer and producer who was credited with developing the image of a Las Vegas showgirl — a statuesque dancer in sequins and feathers, wearing a tall headpiece. He had a long legacy in Las Vegas that dated back to 1950 when his troupe of dancers opened the Desert Inn. His *Lido de Paris* had run at the Stardust since 1958, and his *Jubilee!* show continued its long-run at Bally's, just down the street. Arden was looking for a dancer with experience who could step into Perrine's shoes without much rehearsal. Pettyjohn was confident that she could do that job, and instructed her agent to set up the appointment with Arden. She auditioned and won him over with her energy and enthusiasm. But as she was contractually bound to Barry Ashton and the Burlesque Show at the Silver Slipper, Angelique had to acquiesce to the demands of her contract and give up the role that she had just won. Another showgirl was hired instead to take over Perrine's part in *Jubilee!* Pettyjohn continued to dream of getting to work with the famous Arden one day, who remained active up to two weeks before his death in October of 1994.

Diamonds Are Forever (1971)

Diamonds Are Forever, the seventh film in the James Bond series produced by Eon Productions and the final Eon film to star Sean Connery, was the biggest thing ever to hit Las Vegas in the 70s.

Figure 122. Poster for *Diamonds Are Forever* (1971).

Based on the 1956 novel by Ian Fleming, the story was centered around Bond's investigation of the Spangled Mob and their diamond-smuggling operation in Sierra Leone and Las Vegas; screenwriters Richard Maibaum and Tom Mankiewicz jazzed the script up with Goldfinger's brother, first, and then Ernst Stavro Blofeld of SPECTRE. Producers "Cubby" Broccoli and Harry Saltzman had decided to make their new film largely in the United States, and sought out local talent to fill out their roster of characters. Casting agents met with many of the showgirls and dancers who worked the Strip, including Angelique Pettyjohn. She and several of her girlfriends met with Weston Drury and his people at the Hotel Tropicana on the corner of Las Vegas Boulevard and Tropicana. Pettyjohn thought they were auditioning for several of the lead roles, including Tiffany Case (which ultimately went to Jill St. John) and Plenty O'Toole (which went to her friend Lana Wood). But the fact of the matter is they were merely trying out for one role as a showgirl and several background roles as Las Vegas performers. The role was a very small one, but the opportunity was rare indeed.

Historically, most Bond girls went on to do much larger parts in movies, and nearly all would agree there was a certain cache to having been a "Bond girl." The competition was fierce, with most applicants being quickly dismissed by Drury. The production had a very specific look in mind. Angelique had the benefit of having been a showgirl and dancer on her resume, but alas, she was not selected; neither were her girlfriends. Pettyjohn returned home to her room in Northeast Las Vegas, feeling dejected and depressed. A cold, hard reminder that, while diamonds may last forever, showgirls do not.

Figure 123. Sean Connery & Pat Gill, behind the scenes.

Figure 124. Shady Tree & His Acorns from *Diamonds*… (1971).

A few days later, Weston Drury hired one of Pettyjohn's friends, twenty-seven-year-old Valerie Perrine who had begun her career as a Las Vegas showgirl. Perrine had already been hired to play the role of porn-star Montana Wildhack in the big screen adaptation of *Slaughterhouse Five* (1972), so she had only a limited amount of time to shoot her big scene *in Diamonds Are Forever*. But when Director George Roy Hill's shooting schedule was changed to accommodate filming all the winter scenes in *Slaughterhouse Five* in Prague, Valerie Perrine's scenes were moved up to Labor Day. She had to gracefully back out of the role in *Diamonds*. Like Angelique, Perrine's opportunity to become a Bond girl also slipped right through her fingers. [Imdb.com still credits Perrine for work on *Diamonds Are Forever*, which has led many 007 fans to conclude that she was in the picture, but in reality, Valerie was on the other side of the world filming her scenes in *Slaughterhouse Five* when the cameras started rolling on the seventh James Bond adventure. I have met both Pat Gill, who eventually got the role, and Valerie Perrine, and they do share a passing resemblance.]

With very little press and fanfare, Drury's search for the next Bond girl was re-opened clandestinely, and the producers, along with *Diamonds* Director Guy Hamilton, reviewed dozens of other showgirls, including Cassandra Peterson (1951-) who would later be known as Elvira, Mistress of the Dark. She actually appears in the movie as one of the numerous background dancers. Angelique got a second chance to audition when Harry Saltzman and his wife Adriana took in *The Wonderful World of Burlesque '71*, but once again did not make the cut, although several of the other, younger girls in the Barry Ashton show were selected as background dancers. Pettyjohn was happy for her friends who were selected, but angry the role in the Bond film had somehow eluded her again. Angelique did, however, get one more bite of the lucrative 007 apple.

Figure 125. Elvis & Pat Gill, a renowned Las Vegas dancer.

Figures 126 & 127. Valerie Perrine & Cassandra Peterson.

As luck would have it, Tom Mankiewicz, who would later contribute to the screenplay for *Superman: The Movie* (1978), was hired to re-write certain elements of Richard Maibaum's screenplay for *Diamonds Are Forever*. The producers brought Mankiewicz aboard the production because he was American, and since so much of the film was set in Las Vegas, they wanted someone with American sensibilities. Ultimately, he contributed more than half of the film's final running time, sharing credit with Maibaum. Mankiewicz rewrote several key sequences in the film, one being the oil-rig finale. (For his finale, Maibaum had scripted an elaborate boat chase on Lake Meade, which he later re-tasked for *Live and Let Die* (1973). Mankiewicz also added another showgirl to the picture, and expanded the scene with Shady Tree. The producers now had two showgirls to cast.

One night, Albert R. "Cubby" Broccoli and his wife Dana attended *Vive Les Girls* at the Dunes hotel and spotted Pat Gill, the lead dancer, among the showgirls and other performers in the production. Gill was a South African performer who had come over from Paris in the late sixties, and was rumored to be one of Elvis Presley's favorite dancers and girlfriends. The press repeatedly photographed Pat Gill with Elvis in Las Vegas. Cubby and Dana approached Pat after the show and offered her the role of "Acorn #1." Dana said, "You look so much like Diane Cilento (Sean Connery's wife) that you must come to work for us on *Diamonds Are Forever*. We start shooting at the Dunes next week." Gill was flattered by her compliment, and accepted. The twenty-five-year-old Pat Gill (1946-), an actual dancer who knew both Angelique Pettyjohn and Valerie Perrine, turned out to be the big winner, as was fellow showgirl Jennifer Castle, who was originally from Great Britain.

Figure 128. Sean Connery & Lana Wood.

They also interviewed several other showgirls from *Vive Les Girls* and spoke with dozens of other Las Vegas performers, including Angelique Pettyjohn. In fact, Dana Broccoli liked Angelique. But when they were making their final selection, Production Designer Ken Adam introduced an English girl named Jennifer Castle to the Broccolis. Castle stood out over all of the other girls and was given the part of "Acorn #2." Pettyjohn was bitterly disappointed; her dream of being cast as a Bond girl so close she could hardly grasp it, but was offered to a rival showgirl. Later, when she sat watching *Diamonds Are Forever* at the local bijou, the scene featuring the two acorns (Gill and Castle), opposite comedian Leonard Barr (Shady Tree), Dean Martin's uncle, ran about a minute-and-a-half. Neither Pat Gill nor Jennifer Castle was "discovered," and other than receiving a small residual from the film every year, their lives were not significantly changed by their appearance in the picture. Pettyjohn left the movie theater content with the knowledge that she had not missed out on anything.

The Vegas Vampire

Shortly after *The Night Stalker*, an ABC-movie of the week about an abrasive Las Vegas newspaperman who investigates a series of murders committed by a vampire, debuted on network television on January 11, 1972, Angelique Pettyjohn met and started dating a vampire. Of course, James W. Parker (1934-2016) was not a real vampire, nor was he the seventy-year-old Romanian millionaire featured in the titular role of the made-for-TV horror movie. Jim, as he was known to his friends, was a Wisconsin-native who worked at the NBC affiliate in Las Vegas. He got his start in broadcasting locally at KORK TV-3 as a news director and then worked as a disc jockey, stock car racing promoter, and news reporter. In 1960s, soon after Universal Pictures leased a package of classic horror films and forgotten B-movies to television stations across the country, Jim pitched the idea of playing a mad scientist or vampire to emcee these movies on NBC, but the station was not interested, nor were the other network affiliate stations. Two years later, after almost every

Figure 129. James W. Parker—The Vegas Vampire.

major American city had their own TV horror host, he sold his idea to the local Channel 5 KHBV-KVVU in Henderson, Nevada. He chose the name "Vegas Vampire" because he liked the alliteration. Soon he was headlining the late-night *Shock Theater*, yucking it up with goofy skits broadcast to the greater Las Vegas area, from the late 1960s through the 1970s.

Like many other horror hosts of the day — Vampira from LAs' KABC, Zacherle from New York, Count Gore De Vol in Washington, D.C., Svengoolie from Chicago, and others — the character of Jim Parker's vampire appeared at the start of each show and during the commercial breaks, and he would critique and ridicule the classic horror movie being aired. One of his early trademark routines was to stick pins into voodoo dolls of politicians, civic leaders, and celebrities while lampooning them. The show ran on and off for nine years. Parker claims that one cancellation was, in fact, due to President Richard Nixon. After he did a routine in which he stuck pins in a Nixon voodoo doll and cut off the doll's head on a miniature guillotine, his vampire was placed on Nixon's enemies list. Of course, his show returned the next season, like a vampire returning from the dead. The character was so colorfully eccentric and popular with his young viewers that well-known celebrities would occasionally drop by his show while performing in Vegas — Red Buttons, Sammy Davis, Jr., comedienne Fay McKay, and Frank Sinatra, Jr. Angelique also appeared on his show several times, reading viewer letters on air, then burning them. The chemistry between Parker and Pettyjohn was undeniable, and soon they started dating, devoting themselves exclusively to one another.

Figure 130. Angelique on Jim Parker's show.

Because Jim Parker's "Vegas Vampire" had become such a popular, local celebrity, he spent a great deal of his personal time attending charitable events throughout Las Vegas. For two and a half years (1972-73), Angelique was often seen at his side, traveling the streets of Las Vegas and Henderson in his trademark Hearse and appearing at many local business openings. He hosted the local segments of the *Jerry Lewis MDA Telethon* and participated in local events, like the St. Jude's *Night of Stars* show and the Clark County Talent Guild's *Stars of Tomorrow* show. Universally loved and adored by his fans for his off-beat vampire persona, Jim Parker was eventually appointed director of publicity and public relations for TV-5. Fun was important to Jim because, at the time, the Las Vegas economy was in a rough spot, which gave Parker a simple goal: "Make people laugh. Put the spirit of fun into it. Even if they did have a hard way to go in life." Pettyjohn agreed with him, and enjoyed her new-found celebrity status opposite Parker, but only for a short while.

In 1974, Jim invited Paula Jane Bell Graham (1949-) to appear on his show for the first time as "Satana," the daughter of Satan, and sparks flew. Graham was beautiful, smart, sexy, and just dangerous enough to attract his attention. They began a torrid affair, which displaced Pettyjohn. Angelique added Paula Graham's name to her growing list of enemies: the late Sharon Tate, Jennifer Gan, and Linda Harrison. If Jim Parker's voodoo doll pins had actually worked, Pettyjohn might well have used one to take Paula Graham out. But alas, it was not to be. Jim and Paula were married in a civil ceremony at the Clark County courthouse on July 28, 1974. Paula, who soon took the name of P.J. Parker, became a regular fixture on Jim's show. When the show was finally canceled by Channel 5 KHBV-KVVU, P.J. left Jim and married another man, Daniel Housman.

For years, Jim Parker worked very hard to revive the show, and *Variety* and syndicated columnist Forrest Duke even reported in 1977 that there were plans to do a road show version, but that never came together. The "Vegas Vampire" made his final appearance at the opening of Circus, Circus Casino's Grand Slam Canyon (late renamed Adventuredome). For that one night, the ride complex was transformed into the Dome of Doom. In the early 80s, SCTV did a popular parody of scary movie hosts and paid tribute to Jim Parker (among others). SCTV cast member Joe Flaherty, dressed in full vampire regalia, howled, "Count Floyd, here, reminding you to watch this Saturday night on *Monster Chiller Horror Theater*."

Jim Parker passed away in June 2016.

Figure 131. Showgirls Working out a Routine.

Creating Goddesses, the Hardest Work on the Planet

In 1973, after a three-year stint of working for Barry Ashton on *The Wonderful World of Burlesque*, Angelique went to work as a dancer and comedienne for Paul Perry at the Cabaret Burlesque Palace, an old-school style burlesque show. Never raunchy, the Palace was highly regarded by its rivals on the Strip, delivering a classy and talented group of performers in a top-notch show. Angelique and the other girls were tasked with turning their traditional showgirls into Greek Goddesses for the show, and damned near succeeded, discovering yet another level of performance. She headlined the show with her elegant and stylish dances, and perfect comedic timing. The band, the other acts, and dancers were all very impressive. Suddenly, as a result of its popularity, every other show on the Strip wanted its own beautiful goddesses.

Steve Miller (1944-), a former Las Vegas city councilman for Ward 1, which included the downtown area, and columnist for *AmericanMafia.com*, an online magazine, met Angelique several times when she worked at the Cabaret Burlesque Palace, and had only good things to say about her. Born in California and raised in Las Vegas, Steve founded the *Teenbeat Club* with partner Keith Austin and is credited with inventing the casino dice clock for his father Hal's Las Vegas-based souvenir manufacturing business. A modest man, he was also a certified

Figure 132. Angelique on the cover of *Fabulous Las Vegas*.

flight instructor, pilot, Goodwill ambassador, champion of people with intellectual disabilities, and one of Las Vegas' most noted citizens and spokespersons.

"I had the pleasure of meeting Angelique on one or two occasions," Steve said recently in email correspondence with the author. "I remember that she was an intelligent and gracious woman who had the respect of all her fellow dancers and the owner of the club where she worked."

Similarly, Michael Christ (1943-), a photography professional who had worked for *Life*, *Look*, and *Playboy* magazines, among many others, had enormous respect for her as well. He shot numerous photographs of Pettyjohn between 1973 and 1992, and considered her a close personal friend. He graduated from Washington University in St. Louis in 1962 and subsequently went to work at the Dune's hotel in Las Vegas. In addition to taking photographs, he worked as a pilot, handled air transportation at McCarren Airport, and did location scouting and production for *Route 66* (CBS, 1960), where he met and befriended Elvis. With his camera in hand, Mike went in search of a beautiful goddess to shoot, and found Pettyjohn.

"The first time I took pictures of Angelique Pettyjohn was for her portfolio," he recalled in an hour-long conversation with the author. "Back in those days, the girls would bring their portfolios to auditions with them in order to show off their range as exotic dancers. Angelique didn't have a lot of money at the time, and so offered to trade sex in exchange for my time and talent. I considered her offer for about two seconds. I mean, here she was, absolutely stunning! One of the most beautiful women that I have ever had the privilege to photograph! So, I thought about it, and then just gave them to her. We became good friends, and over the years, we often laughed about that first time we worked together. She never lost the sense of humor and fun she had. A very kind soul, and just about as good as they come."

In 1974, Angelique went to work at the old Marina Hotel (which was absorbed into the MGM Grand Hotel in 1989) and did a stand-up burlesque show with Bob Mitchell and Cork Proctor. Angelique played the straight role, opposite the two very funny comedians. She got great reviews, and nearly everyone on the Strip was talking about her. Mike Christ photographed her for the cover of *Now* magazine, like *Vegas Visitor*, an entertainment weekly sponsored by the Las Vegas department of tourism. Angelique shares the cover with Mitchell and Proctor. The publicity and acclaim generated by that one *Now* cover, photographed by Christ, led to many additional jobs and offers for Pettyjohn.

In 1975, Angelique Pettyjohn was featured as the lead showgirl in the *Vive Paris Vive* show at the Aladdin hotel, and she played several parts, including the role of the comic magician's assistant to the lead magician. With each production lasting roughly an hour and a half, she worked very hard in each show, appearing three times a night (at 8pm, 11pm, 1:30am) six days a week. While most of us think Las Vegas showgirls live a glamorous lifestyle rubbing elbows with world-famous celebrities, like Elvis and Frank Sinatra, every night, we tend to forget the amount of work they put into every show. Angelique's success as a showgirl did not happen overnight; it took a lot of time and painstaking perseverance, years of training, and a lot of

Figure 133. Angelique in *Vive Paris Vive* at the Aladdin (1975).

Figure 134. A showgirl fixes her make-up between routines.

grit, determination, and stamina to perform on that stage. She was always reinventing herself in order to stay fresh and vital. For one production, Pettyjohn transformed herself into Greek goddess, and in another, she played the comic fool and brunt of a comedian's jokes.

A show like *Vive Paris Vive*, with its heavily-embellished costumes, required extensive choreography, and Angelique and the other girls in the show were expected to dance flawlessly through their various routines for the entire ninety minutes of their performance. Night after night, the showgirls make it look easy, but that was only after they had already completed years of dance training elsewhere and drilled four-to-five weeks on each routine with a choreographer. Their stamina and ability to maintain a smile for the entire length of the show was put to the test at every rehearsal — no prizes for second place, no excuses, and no second chances — and they were required to be picture-perfect every time, or they were simply out. Like the others, Pettyjohn was expected to pick up the routines quickly and remember all of the steps. If she once showed signs of not being ready — or tired during a single rehearsal — she would have been thrown out of the world-famous show.

Depending on the production, Angelique could be expected to change costumes between six and eight times per show, and those costume changes were not as simple as slipping on a new skirt and blouse. Often, she'd have to don a complicated rhinestone-studded bustier, a bejeweled pair of panties, a large, unwieldy headdress with rare, exotic feathers, and three-inch high-heeled shoes, which proved to be treacherous when she'd have to climb stairs to the stage.

Between numbers, she'd come running off the stage, covered in sweat from head to toe, and start throwing parts of her costume at the dressers who helped each showgirl get dressed and kept track of the costume parts. She'd have less than five minutes to lean over her dressing table, wipe away the sweat, and touch-up her make-up in the mirror — fix her long, luscious eyelashes, eye-brows, rosy cheeks, and lipstick. And while she was touching up her make-up with her right hand, the dressers were helping her slide her left arm into the right costume for the next number. A wrong turn or bump, would smear her mascara ruining her

Figure 135. A showgirl in *Jubilee* at Bally's.

make-up. She couldn't afford to make any mistakes. She'd have to struggle to do the best with her make-up with the precious few seconds she had before being rushed back out on the stage for the next number.

One of Angelique's fans, Inventor Natalia Franklin had seen how hard it was for Pettyjohn and her fellow showgirls to maintain that frantic pace and still keep their eye make-up fresh and beautiful. She created Butterfly Eyelash Guard to help showgirls, as well as women in general, do perfect eyelashes every time. Her beauty tool also helped prevent premature aging of the delicate skin around the eyes which proved to be a real lifesaver to women who abused their skin day and night with make-up. Unfortunately, Angelique Pettyjohn never had the chance to use her fan's invention. Lots of other women, including Las Vegas showgirls and dancers like Pat Gill, have benefited, however. In tribute to Pettyjohn, Franklin issued a limited edition of Butterfly Eyelash Guard branded the "Angelique."

Figure 136. Backstage, woman uses Butterfly Eyelash Guard®.

In her later years, as a seasoned professional, Angelique Pettyjohn frequently entertained fans she'd met backstage. They brought gifts and flowers, cards, hand-made mementoes, and photographs from their first meeting with the star. She treated each and every one of them like royalty. Pettyjohn also invited me backstage several times when I visited her in Las Vegas. I especially remember her showing me a Barbie doll one fan had made to look like Shahna, and photographs of twins from Minneapolis, one dressed in a Halloween costume as Shahna and the other dressed as Charlie Watkins. She treasured those gifts more than riches, displaying each one proudly at her dressing table. I also got to meet her fellow showgirls and to witness first-hand the ordeal they went through nightly. In fact, I gained a real appreciation and respect for all the hard work and stress that went into each production. If more people had the opportunity to look behind the curtain, they would have developed the same new-found respect I had for the women who worked one of the hardest jobs in the world.

Following her stint at the Aladdin hotel, Pettyjohn moved down the street to the Maxim Hotel and Casino where she appeared nightly in a burlesque show in the main showroom with her favorite comedian Bob Mitchell. Angelique played the straight woman, much like Gracie Allen to Mitchell's George Burns. Critics loved it, showering her with positive reviews. Like every one of her shows, she loved being on stage, whether she was the star of the production or not, and always won the respect of her peers as well as the audience.

Robert Scott Hooper and *The Women of Las Vegas*

For over five decades, Robert Scott Hooper, an artist/photographer based in Las Vegas, took photographs of beautiful women. His work has been seen on the pages of newspapers and magazines worldwide, from *Life* to the cover of *Playboy*. They have also been featured on billboards, posters, postcards, phone cards, and video game machines, and have been exhibited in galleries and private collections. He has won numerous awards for his creations in graphic arts, commercial television production, advertising, print work, and even photographing a centerfold for *Playboy*.

Born in Iowa, Bob grew up as a typical midwestern boy racing soap box derby cars and building model airplanes. After entering college to study architecture, he found that he'd rather be drawing cars and girls than buildings. An opportunity in the National Guard to learn photography quickly focused his talent, and soon he was photographing Iowa girls, while dreaming of being a *Playboy* photographer someday.

In 1966, he moved to Las Vegas and went to work for the Chamber of Commerce, photographing hotels, events, shows, stars, glamour, and hard news, as well as a motion picture film about flying. With his glamour photos, he attracted the attention of the local weekly publication, the *Vegas Visitor*, which hired him to exclusively photograph the "cover girls" that would adorn the front page of every edition. For more than sixteen years, from 1968 to 1984, a gorgeous Hooper Cover Girl decorated the front page of each of some 832 editions of the *Vegas Visitor*. Angelique was featured on three covers.

Figure 137. Angelique on three covers of *Vegas Visitor*.

During Hooper's inevitable rise to fame, he began shooting pictorials for *Playboy*. In 1976, he discovered Debra Jo Fondren, a beautiful blonde with fifty-two-inch tresses, having lunch at a local casino, and photographed her for *Playboy's* Miss September (1977). She became the longest running centerfold and most popular Playmate to date. Debra Jo also went on to become Playmate of the Year.

When Angelique Pettyjohn returned to Las Vegas in 1970, Robert Scott Hooper took her photograph for the August 7, 1970 cover of *Vegas Visitor*, then a few months later for the October 2, 1970 edition. Hooper remembered, saying, "This photo was taken at the ruins of the old burned down El Rancho Vegas Hotel, at the corner of the LV strip and Sahara Avenue, directly across from the famous Sahara Hotel. We had only met briefly before, when she was still driving her old VW bug. We only had a short time to get the shot required for the *Visitor* cover, so we jumped out of our respective cars in the heat, and she quickly revealed much more than needed for the sexy cover photo. Her charm, professionalism and graceful enthusiasm led to a long and fruitful relationship of mutual respect, both as friends and collaborators. Over the years we did many shootings together, from *Playboy* magazine layouts to a set of *Star Trek* posters. She will always be remembered and cherished."

Like Miller and Christ, Robert Scott Hooper became a loyal and trusted friend to Angelique, and photographed her many times during her time in Las Vegas. In fact, his photo spread for the "Women of Las Vegas" in the February 1979 issue of *Playboy* magazine, featuring Pettyjohn for the first time in a men's magazine, garnered her the attention of legendary George Burns. She had grown up wanting to be a great entertainer like Burns; had even patterned herself after the daffy character Gracie Allen had played opposite George Burns in vaudeville and television. In a highly intelligent move, Angelique charmed Burns with stories she had heard about George and Gracie in their days playing vaudeville. Burns was totally seduced by her charm, grace, and wit, and arranged to have her do a cameo walk-on role in his 1979 movie *Going in Style*. She was credited in the picture as "the Girl at the Crap Table."

In between the photo shoots with other glamour girls, Hooper was able to squeeze out yet another cover for Angelique for *Vegas Visitor* (September 22, 1978). The headline read: "TANTALIZING ANGELIQUE PETTYJOHN is the glamorous coquette who creates exquisite excitement on stage in the Gaiety Theatre of the popular Silver Slipper Gambling Hall and Saloon." Featured in Barry Ashton's fun new show, *The Wonderful World of Burlesque*, Pettyjohn used her seductive powers and displayed her versatility to delight audiences three times nightly at 10:00 p.m., 12:30 and 2:24 a.m.

Later in the year, Robert Scott Hooper also shot her as she teamed with burlesque "top banana" Bob Mitchell and Miss Nude Universe in *True Olde Tyme Burlesque* at the Joker Club in North Las Vegas.

Four years later, Hooper collaborated with Pettyjohn on a pair of posters she planned to sell at the *Star Trek* conventions. One poster featured her as "Shahna-the Girl in the Silver Bikini," the other poster, using the exact pose, featured her completely nude. The posters were hugely successful; very nearly sold out during her appearances at the conventions. She often spoke to me about what an incredible friend Hooper had become over the years. "I had a photographer of mine from Las Vegas, who's also a *Playboy* photographer, take new

Figure 138. Angelique & Bob Mitchell.

photographs of me as the *Star Trek* character Shahna to publish as posters," she boasted, with a big smile, full of pride. (Many photographs of Angelique Pettyjohn as well as other famous beauties Robert Scott Hooper shot over the years are available through his website www.rscotthooper.com or Hooper Productions in Las Vegas, Nevada. His selection of showgirls is the best in the world.)

Marriage # 2 — James W. Siebert

James Wallace Siebert asked Angelique Pettyjohn out for a drink one night after one of her shows, then proposed marriage to her about a week later. She was one of the most beautiful women he had ever met, and he was shopping for a wife.

James W. Siebert had been born in Los Angeles, California, May 17, 1941, to James Siebert and Mary Brown. German by nationality, his parents moved to California in the twenties, and settled in Los Angeles County. James grew up in Santa Barbara, a prosperous community located half-way between Los Angeles and San Francisco. He studied Urban Planning in college, then opened a small consulting firm concerned with urban, municipal, and town planning, land development, and a broad range of land use management activities. His consulting services were available to public and private sector clients and nonprofit, quasi-public agencies. He was in Las Vegas on business, consulting with city planners, when he first saw Angelique performing as one of the Barry Ashton Girls in *The Wonderful World of Burlesque.*

Pettyjohn was thrilled and excited, and accepted his proposal of marriage after evaluating all that he had to offer her. Siebert had money, owned his own business, and enjoyed a stable and secure homelife. She figured that by marrying him she'd never have to do another lap dance in her life.

Dorothy Lee Angelique married James W. Siebert on September 2, 1976, in a civil service at the Clark County Courthouse in Las Vegas. (Marriage Certificate # B056877). After a week of honeymooning in Vegas, Siebert brought her home to meet his family and friends.

Figure 139. Angelique Pettyjohn appeared nightly in a show in the Bagdad Theatre at the Aladdin.

After I got married again, I gave up acting for a while and stopped dancing. I even gave up my stage name and just became plain ol' Dorothy Lee again. I didn't want anything to get in the way of my being a full-time housewife. I devoted myself to building a good life for my husband and me. I stopped drinking booze and became a workaholic instead. I had so much nervous energy that I was always on the go, doing something that would make him happy. I took up jogging and tennis, and so became obsessed with becoming healthy and trim. What I didn't realize was that I had simply traded one addiction for another. I practically killed myself trying to be "the" woman that was acceptable to my in-laws, but then I realized that no matter what I did, I would never quite measure up.

Siebert's parents never fully accepted Angelique; they did not approve of her lifestyle or the way she had been earning her income, equating stripping and burlesque dancing with sex and prostitution. They certainly did not approve of her addiction to alcohol and drugs, even though she was working to eliminate those permanently from her life. They had all wanted Siebert to marry a modest Christian woman who was well-connected in their cookie-cutter community of Santa Barbara, not a divorcee with a past. Santa Barbara in those days was a very, close-knit community with very little tolerance for outsiders. Even the predominantly Christian community saw Angelique as a stranger.

Angelique tried her best to settle into domestic life as Dorothy Lee Siebert, but she was never really accepted by his family or friends, and so she returned to Las Vegas in February 1978, signing the final divorce decree on March 31, 1978 (File # D931). Broken-hearted, she went back to work in Las Vegas doing what she knew how to do.

Marriage # 3 — Carl Anthony Grohn

Angelique Pettyjohn became smitten with Carl Anthony Grohn one night when she and a couple of her girlfriends were out having a drink at the Maxim Hotel and Casino. They thought he was very handsome, charming, and debonair, but when he offered to buy them all another round, Angelique laid claim to him first.

Figure 140. AP as a pin-up girl.

Grohn wore an expensive, black Armani suit and liked to flash money around, ultimately buying them several rounds. He later lied to them, claiming to be one of the group of ten Nevada businessmen who had built the Maxim Hotel for twenty-five million in 1977. Grohn was not only a liar but also "a paranoid schizophrenic with an extensive knowledge of martial arts. "A very dangerous combination, particularly when drugs are added to the mix," according to his third wife, Sara Cooper, out of five, total.

With mounting debts and a costly addiction to alcohol and drugs, Pettyjohn married Carl Anthony Grohn on February 17, 1979 in a civil ceremony at the Clark County Courthouse in Las Vegas. (Marriage Certificate # B189439). She didn't really love him, but she thought he was nice and full of potential as a husband. She also felt that his money might help bail her out of her current situation. But when she learned the truth about him, Angelique was already too far gone. The six weeks that she was married to Groh turned out to be a real nightmare.

Carl Anthony Grohn was born on February 19, 1943, in Bexar, Texas, to Anthony Charles Grohn and Addie Izola Shaw. His father was Polish, the son of Russian immigrants, and his mother was English/Scottish. They lived in San Antonio, Texas, and raised their son Carl Anthony in a loving, middle-class household. Carl applied for a Social Security Number in 1957, then went to work as early as age fourteen, delivering newspapers from his bike. Several inches shorter than most boys his own age, he was often picked on by the other school children. With no real friends at school, he devoted himself to learning martial arts. Eventually, Carl Anthony Grohn earned a black belt in East Asian martial arts, denoting a high level of competence in the field, and all before his twentieth birthday. Other than martial arts, he also had a keen interest in drag racing — building and racing AA-fueled dragsters in his youth — and was very successful. He also taught himself electronics and became an outstanding electrician. With no formal training, he worked as an electrician for several different companies and finally opened his own shop, living in North Hollywood and then Las Vegas. Family members used to always talk about what an accomplished pianist he was as well.

One of Carl Anthony Grohn's *many* ex-wives, who chose not to be identified, said, "I can say I'm happy to have survived him. When in his right mind, he was a wonderful man. Unfortunately, he was seldom in his right mind. When his chemistry was off, he was violent and verbally and physically abusive. I wish I could recover the jewelry of mine that he kept, but I'm certain he wore it himself, or gave it to another wife. Oh, and the firearms I paid for during our marriage, including an AR15, M1 Garand, and a Browning Hi-Power rifle. I guess that's a cheap price to pay for escaping though."

Angelique quickly learned the hidden side of Carl Anthony Grohn. "I had been married to him only two days, when he asked to borrow money from me," she later recalled, sharing the whole embarrassing ordeal with me. "I didn't have much in the bank, only the last of my residuals from when I worked in Hollywood. He took it all. He took some of my jewelry, too. When I asked him later where the money went, he got very angry, confrontational, almost violent. Grohn finally explained that he was working on a big deal that was going to make us rich, and that if I ever asked him again about money, he was going to leave me."

Pettyjohn wasn't satisfied with his answer, so she privately inquired about his ownership claims of the Maxim Hotel and Casino with a few of the people she knew, which turned out to be a lie. When she confronted him with the truth, Grohn claimed that he had been cheated by two of his partners and the case was being reviewed by his own personal attorneys. Another lie. But the harder she sought a truthful answer, the more difficult things became between them. He accused her of sneaking around behind his back, then forced her into sex acts with strangers to show her loyalty to him. His demands kept getting stranger and stranger, and drove her deeper and deeper into her addictions for alcohol and drugs.

Most weekends and sometimes a night or two during the week, when Angelique wasn't dancing at strip joints to earn them money to live on, Carl would take her out to one of the local nightclubs. They'd drink a lot and dance. Then, after she was drunk or high, or both, he'd insist she dance and flirt with one of the single guys at the club. He told her that if she really loved him, she'd do whatever he asked. He'd then steer them to a hotel room nearby, where other guys were waiting. Most of them were also drunk or high on pills or hard drugs. Then the orgy would get started. She'd be forced to take three or four at a time as part of a gang bang, or give each guy a blow job while she knelt in the center of a circle of guys. Other times, she'd find herself fucking one guy and blowing yet another one. After several hours of doing the most dirty, degrading, and disgusting acts imaginable, Pettyjohn would pass out. Groh would collect money from each of the guys, then take her home and dump her in bed to sleep it off. Most times, she'd wake up the next morning, and not remember a thing, or find bruises on her body she couldn't

Figure 141. Angelique worked briefly with the legendary magician Johnny Thompson (1934-2019).

account for, and when she'd ask him, take responsibility for them herself. Other times, he'd take Angelique, after she had been drinking, to the local adult theatre, and force her to go down on the guy, sitting next to them. He'd then get a hotel room, and together with the stranger, they'd fuck her all night until she couldn't stand on her own two feet. Groh knew exactly what he was doing, but would always pretend that it was always her idea because she was a sex addict, and then beat her senseless for betraying his trust. He'd later kiss and make-up, and tell her how lucky she was to be married to him.

"Most of the time, I had no idea what was going on," Pettyjohn confessed. "He had me so twisted around in the head. I really didn't know why I was doing what I was doing. It's not like I was enjoying myself, fucking all these guys. Sexual addicts do it because they can't help themselves, just like alcoholics. It takes on a life of its own. It runs you and you have no defense."

Broke and steps away from living on the street, like a homeless person, Angelique borrowed a couple of dollars from one of her fellow dancers, and filed for divorce from Carl Anthony Grohn. The divorce was finalized on March 30, 1979. She never saw him again, and gave up all hope he would ever pay her back all the money he had taken from her. After his divorce from Pettyjohn, he married four other women: Pamela, Sara Cooper, * Joni, and Suzanne, and divorced all but the last one. Grohn died on July 6, 2009 in San Antonio, Texas.

With her divorce from Grohn final, Angelique realized she had nearly hit rock bottom. Her addiction to alcohol and drugs and her low self-esteem lead her to make some very poor decisions about her career path. With the urging of Marilyn Chambers, a long-time friend and rival, Angelique thought about it long and hard, and in the end, set her sights on the adult film industry, ultimately deciding to shoot several porn films under a pseudonym.

---

*In 1995, while researching this book, Sara Cooper contacted me by email. She had known Angelique Pettyjohn in Las Vegas during the 70s and 80s when Sara lived there. They became good friends, and maintained a lifelong friendship up until Angelique's death in 1992. Over Angelique's objections, Sara met and married Carl Anthony Grohn in 1982, and soon after divorced him. The two women comforted each other as "sister" wives, and Sara later corroborated Pettyjohn's account of her marriage to Grohn. She had lived a very similar kind of nightmare.

The Adult Film Industry

Today, the Adult Film Industry is one of the largest business enterprises in the United States, with a total market value of thirteen-billion dollars a year; 25% of all Internet requests are porn-related. Every day, new and aspiring models travel to Los Angeles or Miami with dreams of becoming adult film stars, but then earn less than $53,000 a year, the salary of a high school teacher. In 1978, during the golden age of pornography, the average adult film cost $125,000 to make and was expected to gross more than $10-12 million ($65 million in today's dollars). Adult films sold for fifty bucks on Beta or VHS tape, and tickets to theatres showing adult movies cost ten dollars. New and aspiring models traveled to Southern California, where 85% of the world's adult films were made. All of the top female talent agencies were located in or within greater Los Angeles county. The adult film industry was valued at a billion dollars a year. Successful performers, like Annette Haven, Marilyn Chambers, or Vanessa del Rio, could earn as much as a hundred thousand a year from adult films, but few female actresses during that time actually made such money, so many still had to supplement their income by stripping at local clubs.

Most adult films from the eighties were shot in a single day, and the majority of the time, shot in pairs — two movies in two days — to cut down on the costs of equipment rentals and location fees. Women were paid $300 to $700 a day, while men were paid considerably less, between $250 and $400 a day. If the women were asked to do any variations, such as anal sex or sex with two men or sex with other women, they could earn considerably more in the individual scenes. More scenes also meant more money, but contract girls who only worked a fraction of the time of freelancers could make far more money by being flexible with what they'd be willing to do on camera. Women who were willing to work with animals or do gang-rape fantasies with lots of men or BDSM freak-out scenes earned the most money of all of those shooting.

Contract girls who only worked a fraction of the time of freelancers could make far more money by being flexible with what they'd be willing to do on camera.

As her ability to get legitimate roles declined, Pettyjohn was forced to act in adult films — *Titillation* (1982), *Stalag 69* (1982), and *Body Talk* (1984), among others — to earn the money to support a thousand dollar-a-month drug habit. Pettyjohn admits, "The drugs we binged on were ecstasy, cocaine, marijuana, Xanax, Valium, and alcohol. If I had to guess, I would say the majority of girls smoked pot or snorted cocaine, while the directors, crews, and agents stuck mainly to popping pills and snorting lines. You got so little choice. You're viewed as an object, not as a human being with a soul. Adult performers do drugs or drink alcohol because they can't deal with the inhumane ways they're being treated by the industry. You feel like you're absolutely worthless, so all you want to do is stop the pain."

In an effort to protect her identity, Pettyjohn agreed fully to the terms of an adult-film contract as long as she could act under a variety of stage names — Angelique, Ashley St. John (also spelled Ashley St. Jon), Heaven St. John, and Angelique St. Heaven — but she really wasn't fooling anyone. The producers of adult films all knew Angelique Pettyjohn. By hiring her, they were buying Charlie Watkins from *Get Smart!* or Cora Sue from *The Girl from U.N.C.L.E.* or the "Girl in the Silver Bikini" from *Star Trek* for every man who had ever fantasized about taking her to bed and making love to her. Adult films were all about fulfilling the fantasies of a certain kind of man. Pretend as much as she liked to be Ashley St. John or Angelique St. Heaven, Pettyjohn knew full well what she was doing, and magazines like *Celebrity Sleuth* or *Celebrity Skin* were there to keep her honest.

Titillation (1982)

Performing under the name Heaven St. John in her first adult film, *Titillation* (1982), Pettyjohn played Brenda Weeks, the manager of a swinging singles apartment building. Her boss Felix (Roy Simpson), an eccentric, rich old man, who looks like Colonel Sanders, is obsessed with finding the "most perfect breasts," and has offered a $50,000 prize to the woman who fits a bra built in the desired size. Weeks means to get that $50,000 prize. She hires two bumbling private detectives, Spado Zappo (Eric Edwards) and Pigeon Johnson (Randy West) to find "Miss Perfect." The two spend most of the eighty-minute movie chasing down false leads, and being chased by dogs and women who think they're perfect. Meanwhile, Weeks takes dictation from Felix, plying her own charms to be noticed by the boss for her bustline, and interviewing a young, busty woman who wants to move into building. Angelique's three-some with Mike Horner and the busty blonde is very hot and steamy and well worth the price of admission. Eventually, the two private dicks track down the so-called "Miss Perfect," Candy (Kitten Natividad). Felix is happy and takes her with him on a round-the-world trip.

From VCX Productions, *Titillation* (1982) was an above-average comedy about women with large breasts and the men who worship them, and is mostly remembered today for featuring lovely Angelique Pettyjohn in her first adult film. She does two hard-core scenes — one with Eric Edwards, and the other, aforementioned threesome — and is masterful in both, suggesting that she much longer period of ti who grew up fantasizing about the "Girl in the Silver Bikini" from *Star Trek* are thrilled to see her comedic side, exchanging barbs with Roy Simpson, as well as her erotically-charged scenes with a man and a woman. Pettyjohn's friend and rival Kitten Natividad plays a small role in the movie. A

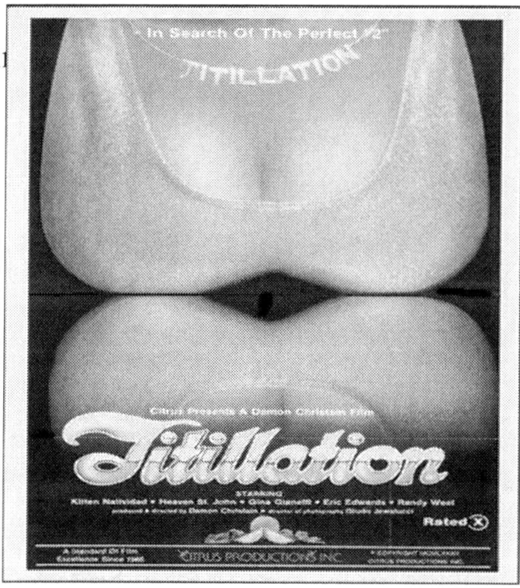

Figure 142. *Titillation* (1982).

popular redhead in Russ Meyer's movies, the forty-four-inch busty Natividad does not do any hard-core scenes, like Angelique, but is featured in several soft-core scenes of simulated sex with men, even though years later she would turn strictly to hardcore.

"Once you're in the [adult film] business, you're making $10,000 a month and working maybe five hours a day, ten to fifteen days a month. I don't know of any other business where you can make that kind of money, fast," Angelique revealed the ugly truth of the business to me. "The problem is you're not always in front of the cameras. So, you agree to work as a stripper at one of the clubs, where you can pull in lots of money on tips, but then you have to deal with all the degradation and physical and verbal abuse. Though the customers are not supposed to touch a stripper, they routinely grab our tits or ass right in front of the bouncers and other audience members. No one gets punished, so then, they get even more emboldened. Maybe next time, it's a pinch on the ass or they pull your hair. Eventually, you reach a point of no-return where you just don't care anymore. You've already lost whatever pride you once had and you start turning tricks with rich pricks for a thousand a pop to support your habit. You fall into this downward spiral. You know exactly where you're headed. You're headed to rock bottom. All you care about is your next drink or fix. You don't seem to care that they've already ripped your soul away."

Stalag 69 (1982) and _Body Talk_ (1984)

After turning in a solid performance in *Titillation* (1982), Pettyjohn did not have to wait long for her next movie. *Stalag 69* (1982) was an X-rated send-up of the infamous Ilsa series — *Ilsa, She Wolf of the SS* (1975), *Ilsa, Harem Keeper of the Oil Sheiks* (1976), *Ilsa, the Wicked Warden* (1977), and *Ilsa, the Tigress of Siberia* (1977) — of grindhouse movies that celebrated Nazi exploitation in the 1970s. As directed by Selrahc Detrevrep (Charles Perverted), *Stalag 69* is an ambitious, rarely disappointing, and sometimes unintentionally funny adult comedy.

Billed as Angelique, Pettyjohn dons a brunette wig, and steps into the role of a sadistic, Ilsa-like SS interrogator at a German POW camp located in North Africa. When three agents

Figure 143. ***Stalag 69*** **(1982).**

into the desert land right in the middle of the really low-budget Nazi installation, they are taken prisoner and tortured by the interrogator. The prisoners must fight to the death in order to escape. But after treating the GIs to humiliating and degrading torture, the interrogator gets her deserved comeuppance. Angelique is the best thing in the movie. Her German accent, while wickedly atrocious, helps Angelique chew up the scenery with every syllable she speaks, playing the larger-than-life character for satirical humor. You almost forget that Dyanne Thorne played Ilsa in a handful of grindhouse movies.

Nearly every actress in the business wants to play *Camille* (1936), the doomed socialite who ascends to the high society of

Paris only to die tragically in the arms of her suitor. Greta Garbo played Camille magnificently in the 1936 classic film, based on the novel by Alexander Dumas, so it's hard to imagine anyone besides her in the part. But, when Angelique Pettyjohn was hired as Angelique to play "Cassie" in *Body Talk* (1984), she had no idea that she was going to be playing such a classic character. Some research not only helped inform her of Camille's legacy but also led her to one of the best performances of her career, in or out of her clothes.

T.J. (Randy West) and his older yet very flexible girlfriend Laura (Kay Parker) invite his friend Mark (Steven Tyler) and her friend Cassie (Angelique) for a tennis match. Even though she is an older woman, Mark likes Cassie, and they eventually fall in love with each other. Mark's wealthy parents

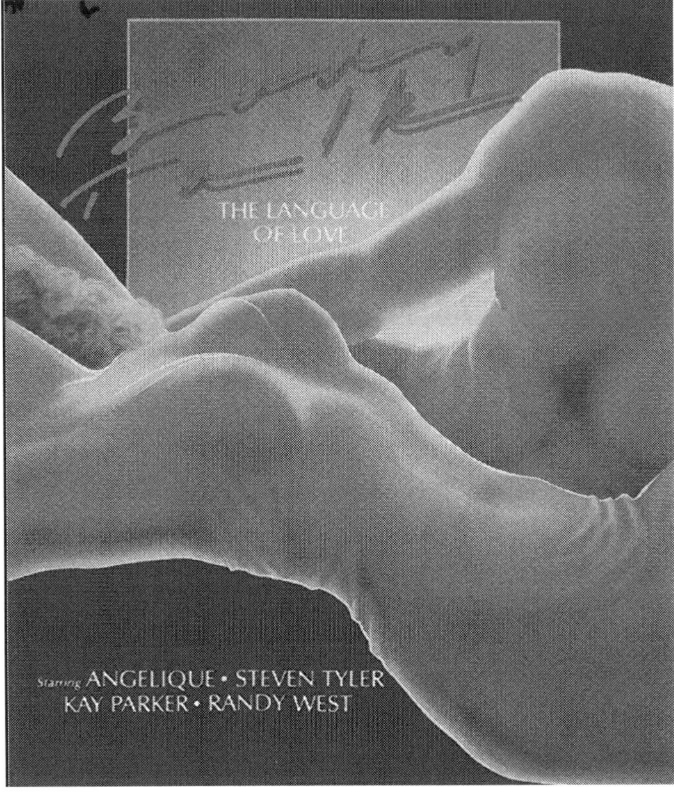

Figure 144. Poster for *Body Talk* (1984).

(Michael Devon and Ruth Morrell), who want their son to marry a healthy woman and set about to break them up. When Cassie discovers that she has bone cancer, she decides leaving Mark is for the best. Elated, Mark's parents send him to Europe to study sculpting and to forget Cassie. Later, when Mark's parents find out the real reason Cassie let Mark go, they regret what they have done, and bring the two lovers back together even though Cassie is very sick and dying. Cassie and Mark know nothing, not even death, can stop their love, and they end the film together, facing whatever is to come.

Body Talk is, at times, dreary and depressing, but also inspiring and hopeful as the two lovers, from the original story by Dumas, attempt to overcome tragedy to find a degree of happiness. Most of the sex scenes are not as inspiring, as VCX productions tries to satisfy female viewers with plenty of scenes of copulation between younger men and the older women played by Angelique Pettyjohn and Kay Parker. Overall, the eighty-one-minute movie was competently shot, and paved the way for future films with a female-centric focus. As mentioned, Angelique is excellent, playing a woman her own age who is dying from bone cancer. She should have been nominated for an Adult Film Award, but alas, that did not happen. Sadly, life would imitate art as Pettyjohn faced her own battle with cancer in 1992, and died soon after.

***Takin' It Off* (1985)**

"What's a girl to do when she's got too much of a good thing? Start…" *Takin' It Off* (1985) was the last Adult Film that Pettyjohn made. At the time when she read the original script and started rehearsal on the movie, she was suffering with extremely low self-esteem; in fact, she no longer valued her life beyond where she could get her next fix. Her days and nights just seem to race by in a drug-addled haze. Most of the time she didn't remember the names of people or even the places where she slept. Her life was completely out of control. The soft-core porn feature was actually a vehicle for her co-star, Kitten Natividad, but Pettyjohn does her best as "Anita Little," a character inspired by Annie Sprinkle, the former porn-actress-turned-sexologist.

Figure 145. Poster for *Takin' It Off* (1985).

Credited as "Angelique Pettyjohn," Anita Little is owner/manager of the Little Playhouse, a school for strippers where they go to learn their trade. The perfect role since Angelique had plenty of experience as a stripper and performer in burlesque shows, and acted in an uncredited role as an expert/researcher when she wasn't stoned out of her mind. The "B" story finds Natividad as "Betty Bigwuns," who is longing for an open spot on a TV series but whose measurements are not going to fit comfortably onto a TV screen. In desperation, Betty tries fad diets, exercise, hypnotherapy, and even a fat farm, but just cannot seem to "take it off."

The plot for the ultra-low-budget comedy serves as an excuse to showcase various good-looking women naked. While not a porn flick, numerous actresses familiar to the adult film market populate the cast, such as the mega-chested Kitten Natividad, who appears in various stages of undress, including totally nude. Critics claim the film is worth a look for all the gratuitous nudity, referring to it as a "T&A extravaganza." Otherwise, *Takin' It Off* is pretty much a rehash of any one of a dozen similar sex comedies of the 1980s.

X-Rated Compilations

In addition to the Adult Films that Pettyjohn made in the early 80s, she was also featured in two X-rated compilation videos, *Famous Ta Tas* and *Sex Game* (1986). X-rated compilation videos were usually a collection of nude and/or topless scenes from various films featuring actresses who were either famous at the time or became famous later on. *Famous Ta Tas* featured big-titted actresses, like Christy Canyon, Kitten Natividad, Rachel Ashley, Colleen Brennan, Honey Wilder, Mindy Rae, Holly McCall, and Angelique Pettyjohn. Released by Essex Video Classics in 1986, the video likely generated lots of rentals back in the day. When viewed today, by today's audience, most of the women on the video are probably unknown. Perhaps Kitten Natividad or Pettyjohn would be stand-outs, but only from a nostalgic point of view. Google search has largely rendered videos like this one a thing of the past.

Sex Game was different. Still essentially a compilation of scenes from other X-rated movies, this seventy-minute film from Electric Hollywood connects an introductory scene, specifically written for the video, with the various, preselected scenes. Bob (Buddy Love) and Carol (Elle Rio), Ted (Jesse Easton) and Alice (Gail Force) are married and madly in love with their respective spouses, but they are also interested in swinging with their best friends. So, they set up a date to play a sex game, which will ultimately lead to a foursome, and spend most of the date watching archival footage of some of the biggest names in the adult film industry. Those names include Taija Rae, Tish Ambrose, Annette Haven, Barbara Dare, Hyapatia Lee, Angelique Pettyjohn, Kitten Natividad, Kay Parker, Seka, and many others. A real turn-on in its day, now mostly nostalgia.

After her death in 1992, Pettyjohn appeared by way of archival footage (as Heaven St. John) in two X-rated compilation videos titled *Chubby Chicks Need Cock, Too* (2013) and *Classic Tits Galore* (2013).

Hitting Rock Bottom

Shortly after completing a set at the Aladdin Hotel and Casino, Angelique Pettyjohn collapsed and was admitted to the hospital with shortness of breath, blackouts, memory loss, hallucinations, dehydration, and a profound sense of anxiety and fear; bold fear running cold through her bloodstream, like the iceberg that struck the *Titanic*. When the emergency-room doctor examined her, he found her liver was enlarged and distended. He also discovered that a hole had somehow developed in her esophagus, presumably from the gin she had been drinking to excess. The gin had eaten away the flesh inside her throat. Tests also revealed a high blood alcohol level of 0.3%, the point at which the brain begins to shut down. She felt that her whole body seemed to be shutting down.

"If you don't stop drinking," the doctor told her, "and I mean stop *right now*, you are going to die, and there won't be a thing we can do to save you."

Pettyjohn had hit rock bottom, had come to the end of the line, and the hospital staff could only assure her a fifty-fifty chance of waking up the next day. She had reached the absolute lowest point in her life. And as she stared into the great abyss, the emptiness stared back at her. Pettyjohn was terrified beyond all measure. She started crying uncontrollably; tried to reach out and grab hold of something, anything, any kind of lifeline beyond herself, so that she could live just one more day.

Angelique did wake up the next day… in a different room. Sometime during the night, after she had finally passed out, they moved her to their intensive care unit where she could get special care. For the next few days, she had an IV-drip feeding her body much-needed nutrients, then she moved up to solid foods. She was given an AIDS test to rule out an immune deficiency or weakness in her body's ability to fight disease. Thankfully, she didn't have AIDS, but did freely admit a serious dependency on alcohol and drugs. She didn't dare tell them about her sex addiction, or they'd lock her away in the psych ward for sure. In time, she was released from the hospital and found a twelve-step meeting not far from home, where she could meet with others who needed help to get and stay clean.

Every one of her friends she reached out to for help, turned away, or refused to return her call. Even her agent Sol Goodman didn't call her back. Only Robert Scott Hooper returned her call, but he was really in no position to help her. She had to face sobriety and an uncertain future on her own.

Alone.

Figure 146. "I put away *childish things*." 1 Corinthians 11.

9

The Star Trek Conventions

> *I've been to several conventions. The one in New York about three or four years ago was huge! There were about eight thousand people there, and I really enjoyed it. I felt like a Rock Star. I needed several security guards because there were just so many people. I did a guest appearance consisting of a ten-minute jazz dance number with music and slides and all kinds of things to create a mood. Then afterwards I did questions and answers with the audience.*

Ten years before I met Angelique Pettyjohn, I attended my first *Star Trek* convention. *Star Trek Lives!,* the first "official" convention, was held on January 21-23, 1972 at the Statler Hilton hotel (later renamed the Hotel Pennsylvania, then the Penta Hotel) in New York City. Even though it's a commonly held belief that the first *Star Trek* convention took place in 1972 at the Hilton, die-hard *Trek* historians claim the first one was actually held on March 1969 at the Newark Public Library in New Jersey. Organized by librarian Sherna Comerford Burley, the small, celebrity-free event featured a slide show of aliens, skits, and a fan panel to discuss the *Star Trek* phenomenon. Science fiction conventions had been around since the thirties, but this was the first time a convention had been organized around a single theme, like *Star Trek*. A fan of the original show, I traveled across the country by bus and spent every last dime I had to meet others like me who truly believed that Gene Roddenberry's optimistic vision of the future was one that we all shared.

The sixties had been a such a dark and turbulent time for the United States, with the Vietnam War, social injustice and unrest, the assassinations of the Kennedy brothers and Martin Luther King, riots in the streets against what was perceived to be a police state, the counterculture movement, the peace movement, and nationwide marches of equality for blacks and women. *Star Trek* represented a kind of hope where all the disparate groups could put aside their differences and band together for a brighter future. That was the kind of future I wanted to live in, not the dark, dystopian vision that so many science fiction books, movies, and television shows had given us.

So, I dressed up in a hand-made *Star Trek* uniform, which I had created myself to show my solidarity; black pants and blue tunic with the proper Starfleet insignia for the "Sciences," which I had purchased by mail order and affixed over my heart. I didn't look like Mr. Spock or Dr. McCoy from the *Enterprise's* Sciences department, but the handful of fans I shared a room with and those I met at the convention got the idea. George Lawrence, who would become a lifelong friend, approached me in the ballroom to compliment me on my uniform, and we started talking about our favorite episodes. We hung out for a while, then with a couple of my roommates from the Hilton, we walked over to the display area to look at the items NASA had supplied, such as the Lunar Module, a full-scale mock-up of the ship that had taken man to moon, as well as some moon rocks and an actual NASA space suit. I felt like I had died and gone to heaven. Well, maybe not heaven, but certainly to the stars.

The gathering had been organized by a group of *Star Trek* fans, known as The Committee, who believed the way that I believed. They had pooled their money together and rented the Statler Hilton's ballroom to provide a meeting space for a few hundred of their fellow *Trek* fans. Members of the Committee had expected about 500 fans to attend the convention, but four hours before the doors were officially due to open, Chairman Al Schuster looked out at the mob scene on the 18th floor [of the hotel] and said, "It's wild. We're going to have at least 3,000 people here. They're coming in from all over — Arizona, California, Canada. There's a whole busload from Toronto."

STAR TREK LIVES!

A STAR TREK Convention

January 21 - 23, 1972

At The Statler Hilton

33rd St. & 7th Ave., New York City

EVERYBODY WELCOME

For Information:

STAR TREK CON

P.O. Box 95 Old Chelsea Station

New York, N. Y. 10011

LATE FLASH:

Gene Roddenberry will speak early Saturday afternoon.

Figure 147. The Original Convention Flier.

Instead of a few hundred "Trekkies," as they would later be called, roughly 3,500 of us showed up to see guests, like the series creator Gene Roddenberry his wife Majel Barrett (Nurse Christine Chapel), science fiction authors Isaac Asimov and Hal Clement, and original series writer D.C. Fontana

(“Amok Time”). Reporters from *TV Guide* and the local ABC affiliate showed up on Saturday, and began doing live news feeds from the convention. The CBS affiliate soon joined them. By Sunday afternoon, the Committee had run out of convention badges and were simply letting fans into the event for free. Ironically, word had failed to get around to all the helpers and volunteers, and so when a young volunteer demanded to see Gene Roddenberry and his wife’s badges in order to enter the exhibit hall, Gene replied, “Young man, I AM *Star Trek*,” and marched right by him, with Majel in hand. Roddenberry was good-natured about it; actually, quite stunned that so many people had turned out for the event. He was overheard by several people throughout the day, saying, “I can’t believe it! I just can’t believe it, all of these great people coming here to honor *Star Trek*.”

Figure 148. Gene Roddenberry and his wife Majel Barrett at their first *Star Trek* convention.

In addition to a keynote speech from Roddenberry, in a room which had a capacity of 500 but was attended by 1500 fans, and another one by Asimov, the program of events kept fans like me very busy. They included a dealer's room with rare props and scripts (provided by Roddenberry's own Lincoln Enterprises); an art show with drawings from some of the fan attendees; a costume contest; an exhibit hall, which included the aforementioned, gigantic, four-hundred-pound Lunar Module and other items from NASA; a mock-up of the *Enterprise* bridge; and a hospitality suite. Gene Roddenberry and Majel screened several episodes from 16mm prints, including the original pilot, "The Cage," and the never-before-seen blooper reel. A number of the *Trek*-related guests spoke for more than an hour each about *Star Trek*, others discussed the importance of science fiction ideas and themes from the show on numerous fan panels. One of the most surprising guest speakers had been Oscar Katz, a former Desilu executive, who recounted the day when Roddenberry pitched *Star Trek* to him and his colleague, Herb Solow, and their subsequent efforts to sell the series to the networks. That was Katz's one and only appearance at a *Star Trek* convention. The only thing missing from that first convention were the actors and actresses who had made the show what it was. That oversight was soon rectified as planning began for the next *Star Trek* convention.

Star Trek Lives!

When the dust had finally settled from the very first *Star Trek* convention, each Committee member — Joan Winston, Allan Asherman, Eileen Becket, Elyse Pines-Rosenstein, Steve Rosenstein, Devra Langsam, and Al Schuster — realized they had captured lightning in a bottle. Not only had they earned back $92.36 each from their initial investment, but more importantly, they had celebrated the phenomenon that was *Star Trek* with others who shared their sentiments.

Prior to 1972 and the success of that first convention, *Star Trek* fans were part of an underground fan movement of loosely-connected groups all around the world. Some of those fans had been mobilized for the letter-writing campaigns which forced

Figure 149. *Star Trek Lives!* (1975).

NBC to renew the show. *Star Trek* fandom might well have died right there had it not been for its wildly successful first convention and the dawning attention of mainstream media, like *TV Guide*, which covered the subsequent fan-run conventions that followed with keen interest.

Members of the Committee agreed to put on a second *Star Trek* convention and added a handful of new members — Stuart Hellinger, David Simmons, and Ben Yalow — in order to plan for another, larger convention in 1973. Renamed "The

International *Star Trek* Convention," the second official *Star Trek* convention was held February 16-19, 1973 at the much larger Commodore Hotel in New York City. Committee Chair Al Schuster had instructed his members to write personal letters inviting actors who had appeared on *Star Trek* during its initial run to attend the convention, and James Doohan (Scotty) and George Takei (Sulu) responded enthusiastically to their invitations. Mr. Spock (Leonard Nimoy) made a surprise appearance at the show as he happened to be in town, and was nearly mobbed by fans in attendance.

With the bigger venue, they expanded the art show, dealer's room, and exhibit hall. They also offered many more choices for programming, expanding from one track to multiple tracks. Rich Kolker, another life-long friend I met for the first time at the convention, summed up a fan's experience nicely: "I arrived at the Commodore hotel with $10 and a return LIRR train ticket in my pocket. Membership at the door was $5. I bought the original *Star Trek Concordance* from Bjo [Trimble] for $3.50, and spent the rest on food for the weekend. I remember seeing Mike McMasters' full-scale bridge [of the *Enterprise*] and was disappointed I didn't have enough money to get my picture taken sitting in the captain's chair."

The 1973 convention drew 10,000 people, and in 1974, at the third *Star Trek* convention, 15,000 people attended and an additional 6,000 more were turned away at the door due to concerns of overcrowding by the Fire Marshall at the Americana Hotel. The guest roster grew to include DeForest Kelley (McCoy), Nichelle Nichols (Uhura), and Walter Koenig (Chekov), along with returning visitors D.C. Fontana, David Gerrold, and George Takei. Makeup artist Fred Phillips rounded out the guest list, turning Chairman Al Schuster into a Klingon on stage with his make-up skills. Mariette Hartley, who had been on the flight with the others from Los Angeles, dropped into the 1974 convention, and did an impromptu speech about her episode, "All Our Yesterdays." [The amazingly funny and insightful book *Star Trek Lives!* (1975) by Sondra Marshak, Jacqueline Lichtenberg, and Joan Winston details those early

Figure 150 *Star Trek's* Federation Trading Post.

days of *Star Trek* fandom when they were working on the first conventions.]

The Schism

Following the 1974 convention, disagreements over leadership and infighting among the Committee members led to a schism in 1975. Devra Langsam assumed the role of Con Chairman with $0 in the bank, and Al Schuster left to put on his own "Star Trek" convention, taking the name "The International *Star Trek* Convention" and $6000 in profits with him. He also scooped his former committee members by signing William Shatner to make his first convention appearance, even though the star had agreed to appear at the other convention as well. Everyone feared a blood bath as members took sides, but in the end, both conventions fared well. Schuster's "The International *Star Trek* Convention" ran January 10-12, 1975, at the Statler Hilton, while The Committee's "*Star Trek* Convention" followed on February 14-17, 1975, once more at the Commodore. The biggest news came out of Chair Langsam's convention, with Gene Roddenberry telling fans that a feature film of *Star Trek* was on

Paramount's schedule, and he was optimistic this would indeed happen.

In 1976, however, the Committee assembled one last time to put on its final convention, working under the banner of "Tellurian Enterprises, Inc." Devra Langsam and her members had been forced to incorporate as a business to prevent Al Schuster or other promoters from cashing in on their successful conventions. When the "*Star Trek* Convention" opened on February 12-16, 1976, at the Commodore Hotel in New York City, it had been the third *Star Trek* convention to open in a row in Manhattan since the beginning of the year. Two others, one by promoter Lisa Boynton of Chicago and the other from Al Schuster, had garnered 20,000 fans and 4,000 fans respectively, and featured cast members from the show. New York was simply not a large enough venue to support three *Star Trek* conventions, and with many other *Star Trek* conventions appearing throughout the country and in Europe, the market was becoming saturated.

So, as a final farewell to the fans, the "*Star Trek* Convention" pulled out all of the stops to deliver an excellent convention. It featured Isaac Asimov, Majel Barrett, Hal Clement, James Doohan, David Gerrold, DeForest Kelley, Nichelle Nichols, George Takei, Gene Roddenberry, and William Ware Theiss. The five-day convention promised speeches from some of the show's principal actors, and discussions with science fiction writers and scientists about the science in/behind *Star Trek*. Exhibits, a dealer's room, a costume contest, a hospitality suite, and other programming were delivered to the 6,000 attendees at the con.

Joan Winston, then a manager of the contracts department at the American Broadcasting Company in New York, delivered the convention's eulogy, by proclaiming herself a "Trekkie" and saying, "Kirk's mission was up to us." To her, the conventions had all been a means of propagating Gene's optimistic message of *Star Trek,* one of a future when life on earth will be peaceful and multinational crews will travel through space in search of other forms of life.

Not so surprisingly, after years of searching for a community of like-minded people which I could call my own, I had found a home in *Star Trek* fandom. I had met people of widely varied ages, occupations, beliefs, and backgrounds, who were kind and remarkably gentle human beings; each sharing an affection for this universe in general and for life in particular. They were also incredibly smart with very high IQs and talents beyond measure. What most of them lacked in social skills, they more than made up for it with their fan writing and art, "filk" songs, costumes, props, and networking in building a fan community. *Star Trek* was the hope that bound us all together, with a singular vision for the future, wherein each of our unique skills would combine with others to lead us all to greatness and in the years that followed, I got to know some of the committee members and other *Star Trek* fans very well. Joan Winston, Jackie Lichtenberg, Allan Asherman and I all became professional writers, authoring science fiction books and penning articles about early fandom for Kerry O'Quinn's *Starlog* magazine. Al Schuster published some of my first articles in magazines like *Enterprise* (1984) and *Sci-Fi Movieland* (1984), and then published *Future Threads* (1985), my first book about creating costumes from *Star Trek* and science fiction films. I competed against Angelique Tuefeld and many other talented costumers at various *Star Trek* conventions, and together with Marty Gear, we formed the Costumer's Guild. George Lawrence and I built a life-size version of Robbie the Robot from *Forbidden Planet* and won Best-in-Class at the Worldcon in Atlanta (1986). Rich Kolker started August Party, an annual gathering of *Star Trek* fans at the University of Maryland, and invited me to a special party where I met and spoke with Gene Roddenberry. Over the years, I also befriended Elyse, Steve, Devra, and Stu at conventions I attended, and invariably counted them among my fan friends.

The Schuster-Townsley Conventions

The Schuster *Star Trek* Conventions continued to run under a variety of different banners and in many different cities — Philadelphia, Atlanta, and Washington D.C. — until the eighties

Figure 151. William Shatner standing on a home-made section of the Bridge at one of the early conventions.

These conventions were chaired by Al Schuster or his heir apparent, John Townsley, and featured paid guests from the roster of actors and actresses who had made Star Trek so successful. Occasionally, Harlan Ellison who had distanced himself from Gene Roddenberry over a dispute regarding his teleplay for "City on the Edge of Forever," appeared at these conventions, and told loyal *Star Trek* fans his side of the story.

Conventions during the Schuster era were noteworthy for the large numbers of fans who had never attended another *Star Trek* convention and showed up looking for the kind of convention the Committee had once put on. But that kind of convention no longer existed outside of the small, fan-run ventures.

Al Schuster had a much larger vision in mind for his conventions. He was a promoter, an entrepreneur who actually profited from his "shows," while the smaller, fan-run conventions were a labor of love, all profit aside. In order to streamline costs, programming was kept to a minimum with nothing past 5 p.m. Guests spoke for roughly an hour, and when they were finished, there were no panels, no use of famish talent, no hospitality suite, and no real exhibit hall. The products in the vendor area were all produced and sold exclusively by Al Schuster and his dealers. The costume contest was about the only hold-over from the fan-run conventions, and those were judged by the *Star Trek* guests who had very little to no experience judging costumes. Almost inevitably, the girl wearing the least amount of clothes or the costumer with the funniest presentation won. His conventions were run very efficiently, like a factory, but lacked the soul of the original ones. Fans quickly discovered what I had learned on my own. The Schuster-Townsley conventions were nothing more than money-makers for their promoters and offered very little that *Star Trek* fans actually hungered for.

Creation Entertainment

Creation Entertainment was founded in 1971 by Gary Berman and Adam Malin, two teenaged fans from Queens, New York. With money they had saved from their paper routes, the two fourteen-year-old boys held their first comic book convention, Creation Con, November 26-28, 1971 at the New Yorker Hotel, in New York City. Their first guest was comic creator Jim Steranko, known for sequential art and *Nick Fury*, among many other outstanding achievements.

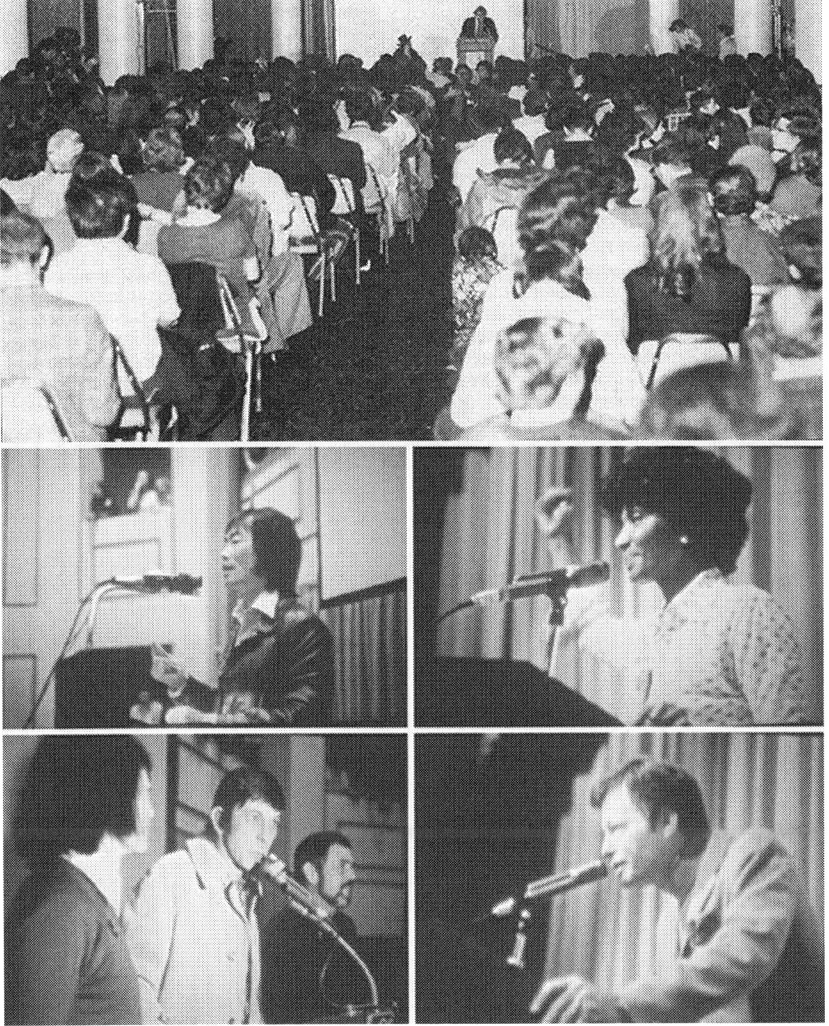

Figure 152. Leonard Nimoy, James Doohan, George Takei, Nichelle Nichols, DeForest Kelley attend an early convention.

Creation Con II took place one year later at the Statler Hilton Hotel in New York City. The guests of honor were science fiction author Philip José Farmer and fantasy illustrator Frank Kelly Freas. Other guests were chosen from the ranks of comic book writers, artists, and science fiction authors: Vaughn Bodé,

Jim Steranko, Gray Morrow, Michael Kaluta, Neal Adams, Howard Chaykin, John Severin, Frank Brunner, Isaac Asimov, Ron Goulart, Roy Krenkel, and Hans Stefan Santesson.

Both conventions were hugely popular among the attending comic book and science fiction fan groups, a popularity which prompted Gary and Adam to continue promoting their Creation Comic Cons with big-name guests every Thanksgiving weekend at the Statler Hilton Hotel through the end of the decade. Attendance at the Creation conventions averaged around 5,000 comic-book fans, with the cost of admission ideally-priced at $5.00 per day.

In 1980, Creation Entertainment expanded its conventions beyond New York City to turn out popular fan events in San Francisco and Washington, D.C. During the next four years, Creation branched out from the comics world into the very lucrative universe of *Star Trek* to produce yearly conventions for fans in Philadelphia, Rochester, San Francisco, Washington, D.C., Boston, Detroit, Denver, Chicago, New Orleans, Atlanta, Los Angeles, and St. Louis. Gary Berman and Adam Malin soon partnered with *Fangoria* magazine to produce annual horror movie conventions in Los Angeles, New Jersey, and Chicago, known as the Weekend of Horrors in 1983, and with *Starlog* magazine to create *Starlog* festivals in Los Angeles, New York, and Chicago in 1985 and 1986. Frequent guests of the Creation Entertainment Star Trek Conventions were George Takei, James Doohan, DeForest Kelley, Nichelle Nichols, Walter Koenig, and Mark Lenard (Sarek).

With the release of each new film, commencing with *Star Trek 2: The Wrath of Khan* (1982) and *Star Trek 3: The Search for Spock* (1984), the crowds of fans at the conventions seemed to double in size, attracting as many as ten to fifteen thousand people at any given event. With the debut of *Star Trek-The Next Generation* (1987), a whole new roster of guests — Patrick Stewart, Brent Spiner, Michael Dorn, and Marina Sirtis — joined the conventions, and the numbers of fan attendees again doubled in size. It was not uncommon for venues like Chicago or Boston to sell as many as fifteen-thousand tickets on a Saturday.

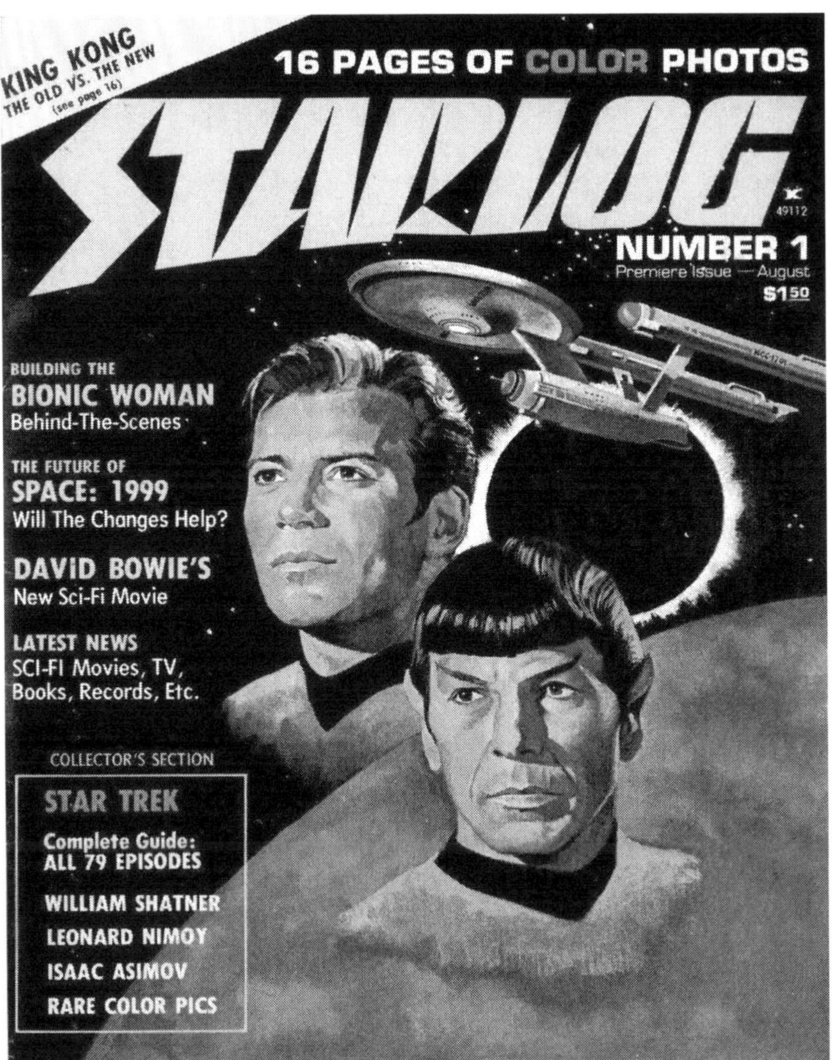

Figure 153. ***Starlog*****, the first of the serious fan magazines (8/1976).**

At the height of the series' new-found popularity in the early nineties, Creation Entertainment was juggling 110 conventions a year, sometimes as many as three distinct conventions in a single weekend. The licensing agreement Gary and Adam worked out with Paramount and Viacom Consumer

Products resulted in the sales of hundreds of millions of dollars in official *Star Trek* merchandise. In 2005, they began holding an "Official *Star Trek* Convention" annually in Las Vegas, which has netted Creation Entertainment millions more in revenue. The 50th anniversary convention was held in Las Vegas in August 2016, and ticket sales were brisk, suggesting there was no end in sight for Creation's *Star Trek* convention. Over a hundred guests attended the special gold anniversary celebration.

Angelique Pettyjohn and Star Trek Fandom

By 1982, Angelique had begun hearing rumors about the burgeoning popularity of *Star Trek* conventions, bolstered by millions of dollars in box-office receipts and sales of home videos of Paramount Pictures' *Star Trek: The Motion Picture* (1979). Early reviews of *Star Trek 2: The Wrath of Khan* (1982) suggested the new film, which was still six weeks away from release, would not only shatter all the records set by the first movie but also challenge the box office records of *Star Wars* (1977) and *The Empire Strikes Back* (1980). Angelique saw an opportunity to cash in on her earlier association with *Star Trek*, notably the character of "Shahna-the Girl in the Silver Bikini," and consulted with her close friend Sara Cooper and Cooper's mother Judith Ward. Ward, a big-name *Trek* fan in San Antonio, said Pettyjohn would do quite well selling her autographs at *Star Trek* conventions. Both were very enthusiastic about her prospects, and helped her select the handful of 8 x 10 photos she'd reproduced to sign for her fans. She also worked on recreating the famous silver bikini she had worn on the show. In the end, she simply called Adam Malin and Gary Berman at Creation Entertainment, and arranged to appear at a couple of shows as sort of trial run. Clearly, Angelique was not as well known to *Trek* fans as DeForest Kelley or George Takei, but she was new blood for the male fans who would remember her fondly.

I was one of those male fans. I met Angelique Pettyjohn for the first time in 1982 at a *Star Trek* Creation convention at the Centre Hotel in Philadelphia, Pennsylvania. She was dressed as Shahna in her silver bikini, sitting behind a huge, eight-foot table

Figure 154. Angelique Pettyjohn at an early convention.

with about a dozen black-n-white and color stills from her appearance on the *Star Trek* episode "The Gamesters of Triskelion." The blonde bombshell wore a green wig, which accented her beautiful green eyes, and thigh-high silver boots to match her costume. A hand-painted, 3-D sculpture of the planet Triskelion's three-pronged symbol was propped up on the wall right next to her silver warrior's spear. For all intents and purposes, Angelique looked like she had just stepped out of a time machine from 1967. She didn't look a day older and had still maintained her beautiful 38-24-36 physique.

At first, when I tried to talk to her, I was tongue-tied and couldn't seem to get an intelligible word out of my mouth. Here I was, a college graduate with a BA and MA in English, a professional author with dozens of writing credits, and a Ph.D. candidate, studying to become a psychologist, but Angelique was very kind and gracious, and didn't take my guttural grunts or misspoken words as anything other than my being extremely shy around beautiful women. When I finally found my voice, I apologized to her and revealed I had been in love with "Shahna-the Girl in the Silver Bikini," for years. She smiled and thanked me for my honesty.

We stood in that corridor, outside the main ballroom where DeForest Kelley was speaking, for about an hour, getting to know each other. I told her what I knew about *Star Trek* conventions and she shared some of her stories about being on the set of *Star Trek*. After about an hour, the corridor suddenly became crowded when Kelley finished speaking, and Pettyjohn went back to work selling her stills to fans who had come out of his speech. I bought a few stills from her myself and asked her to personalize them to "John." I was totally smitten with her again, like I was in 1967.

Not wanting to be labeled a "nerd" by her, I left Angelique at her table and continued to make my rounds of the convention. I listened to George Takei's speech, one I had heard before at other conventions, then dropped by the vendor room where dealers sold books and rare memorabilia. I knew several of the vendors by their first names, and spoke to them briefly about meeting Pettyjohn. Most had not had the opportunity to meet her as they were busy working their sales tables in the vendor room. I stopped by Creation Entertainment's table to say hello to Gary and Adam. I had met them years earlier, and they knew me because of my articles in *Starlog*, *Enterprise*, and *Sci-Fi Movieland*. I suppose if they ever needed a publicist to come work for them, I was always available and hungry. Towards the end of the day, I sat in the ballroom with the majority of fans waiting for Angelique Pettyjohn to speak. Then we all learned from Adam Malin that in place of a speech, she had chosen to share a dance routine she had choreographed to the music from her episode of *Star Trek*.

That afternoon, wearing her homemade replica of the original William Ware Theiss-designed silver bikini, with parts invariably made of aluminum foil, Pettyjohn climbed up on stage, and cued her music. As footage of her fifteen-year-old *Star Trek* appearance played out on the screen above the stage and the music track blared, Pettyjohn began to dance. She weaved and ducked away from imaginary opponents, waving around a metallic, duct-taped facsimile of the warrior's spear she had used as a drill thrall. At least a dozen jaws dropped; mouths remained

Figure 155. Angelique Pettyjohn answering questions for fans.

open of the men sitting near me; both in shock and awed by the caliber of her performance. She continued moving on the stage, zipping back and forth, fighting back against her unseen, Triskelion enemies. Then, with mere seconds remaining of her routine, Angelique came to a complete stop. She looked up at the crowd gathered in the ballroom and recited her final, inspiring words to Captain Kirk with all of the emotion and depth she had left in her. As the lights went out on stage, the place went wild.

Fans leapt out of their seats and started cheering and clapping their approval. Like an early Brittany Spears or a Lady Gaga rock video, Pettyjohn had succeeded in creating an exciting, nostalgic, futuristic, and incredibly erotic live performance art. Few men (and women) in that ballroom at the Philadelphia Centre Hotel would go home feeling like they hadn't gotten their money's worth.

Shortly after Angelique returned to her table, she was swamped by fans wanting her autograph. Casting directors may not have been eager to see her, but the fans certainly went wild for her! She kept busy, signing autographs, until the last hour of the show. As a courtesy, I stopped by her table around 7 p.m. and assisted her with cleaning up. Together, we packed up her stills and props, and delivered them to the loading dock. She was planning on taking a cab to her hotel room on the outskirts of Philadelphia. At the time when Gary and Adam had agreed to try her out, Pettyjohn couldn't afford to stay at the Centre, and had opted for a less expensive room in Conshohocken, on the Schuylkill River in suburban Philadelphia. I knew it well, and offered to drive her there on my way home to Baltimore. She turned me down twice, but when Angelique eventually ran out of excuses why she shouldn't accept my ride, she agreed to let me drive her. I loaded her and her stills, props, and costume into my van, and dropped her at the door to her hotel. The Bell Captain helped me to move her items into the room and I went home… but not before we exchanged numbers, and she gave me a friendly kiss on the cheek. I liked Angelique. I liked her a lot. And in the last ten years of her life, we became very close personal friends.

Trekking to the Conventions

In 1982, Angelique Pettyjohn had agreed to appear at four shows as part of a trial run for Creation Entertainment. Following the huge success of her first appearance in front of *Star Trek* fans in Philadelphia, Berman and Malin scheduled her for two two-day shows in Boston and Chicago and for their huge, three-day Thanksgiving show in New York City. She was thrilled they wanted her for three more shows, and called me at home to tell me the news. I didn't have the heart to tell her these three shows were still part of her original trial run. Instead, I congratulated Pettyjohn on her success and told her I was available to help her in whatever way I could. She thanked me, then said I was the only "real" person she knew; that my knowledge of *Star Trek* fandom would be "infinitely beneficial" to her new role as a celebrity guest at conventions. I was flattered and also quite surprised by the way she conferred with me about those three upcoming shows like a manager or agent who offered advice on his client's career choices.

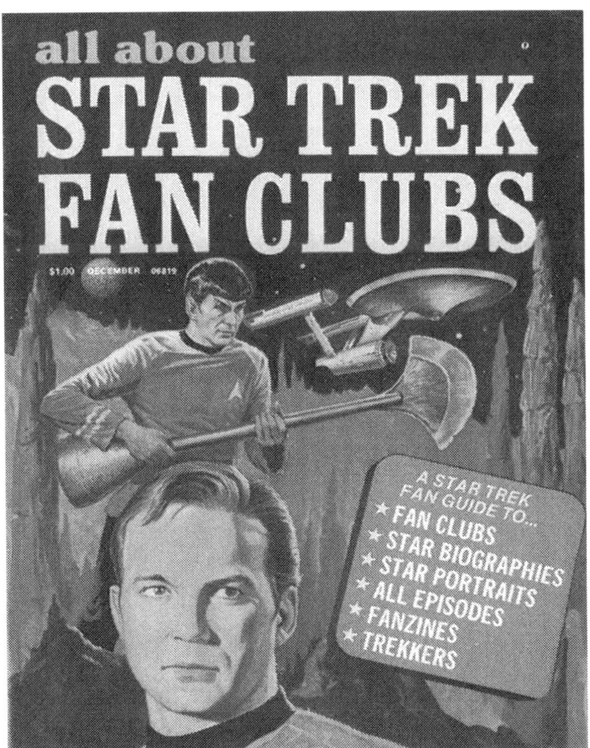

Figure 156. Fanzines proliferated during that time with the latest up-to-date information about *Star Trek* fan clubs and conventions.

We spent several hours on the phone, discussing a number of different things. I thought she should hold off wearing her costume in public until after her "live" performance. She understood my rationale and said she would seriously consider my recommendations. I also suggested we create a huge banner with her name and several pictures to hang up on the wall above her table. She talked to me about a poster idea she had discussed with Robert Scott Hooper. I honestly thought the idea was somewhat risky and risqué, but if it worked with fans, it would generate plenty of additional revenue for her. Hooper's poster idea was simple enough. He had already photographed two different shots of Angelique: one dressed as "Shahna" in her famous silver bikini, the other completely nude. Since both poses were identical, he suggested mounting one on the front of the poster and the other on the back. Eventually, after lots of discussion, we settled on two separate posters fans could purchase. They would actually double her sales by simply printing two posters. Prudes would be satisfied to buy the one of her dressed in the silver bikini, men who read *Playboy* would be happy to buy her nude, and collectors would buy both.

Later on in the conversation, we came up with more than a few workable plans to monetize her appearances at those final three shows of the year. The convention season, which typically ran from February through November, was short for her that year because she had gotten a late start, and both of us knew she needed to make a huge splash in Boston, Chicago, and New York in order to be invited back for future shows. Therefore, we left very little to chance. Together, we selected about two dozen photos of her to be available for sale and signing. One dozen offered family-friendly images from *Star Trek*; the other dozen photos was targeted at the over-twenty-one crowd, showcasing her appearing topless or otherwise semi-bare during her time in Las Vegas. She added several matchbooks, which carried her image and the name of the Vegas revue she had appeared in, and then the Robert Scott Hooper posters we had previously discussed.

Figure 157. Robert Scott Hooper shot one of two posters of Angelique Pettyjohn as Shahna. (Signed "to John.")

At the end of our call, Angelique also made me promise to attend all three shows and help her with her table. I had already planned to help, in whatever capacity I could, but I was even more thrilled she had asked me. That call was the first of many calls we would exchange over the next decade. The calls started innocently enough with her asking my advice about something, like an upcoming show. Then as we became closer friends, we talked about the ups-and-downs of life, notably hers, and the phone calls took the form of therapy, maybe even relaxation or stress management. Over the years, I've been told by many women, including a couple of ex-wives, that I have a very soothing voice and peaceful demeanor. You might say those were a couple of the reasons why I had decided to study psychology and take classes to become a clinical psychologist. I had always had a high degree of empathy — a capacity to understand or feel what another person was experiencing — and I thought I would make a good therapist for people who needed help. Without a second thought, I agreed to help Pettyjohn with her next three conventions.

I met her plane from LAX for the next three shows, and escorted Angelique and her merchandise to the hotel in my late-model van. In Boston, it was the Marriott Copley Place; in Chicago, it was the Continental Hotel; and in Manhattan, it was the Omni Park Central Hotel. With help from the hotel concierge, we brought in several boxes from my van and quickly set the merchandise up at her table. For that first convention, Angelique took my advice and did not put on her costume until it was time in the afternoon to do her dance routine. Fans were both shocked and surprised to see her dressed as "Shahna- the Girl in the Silver Bikini," and followed her back to her table for personalized photos with their favorite *Star Trek* guest. She looked up and nodded at me, mouthing the words "you were right" about the costume. Yes, she looked stunning in her silver bikini-like costume, but by holding the costume back until later in the show, we created a kind of allure for those fans who hungered to see her as "Shahna." She repeated my idea in Chicago, but not in Manhattan. For the Big Apple's grand three-day extravaganza, Pettyjohn wore her costume on all three days.

The schedule of events at all three shows were nearly identical to each other, which is really not at all surprising. Creation Entertainment, unlike the fan-run conventions, followed

Figure 158. Pettyjohn enjoyed Q&A with the fans.

a very familiar formula for all its shows. Pre-registration for all attendees started at 9:30 a.m. on each day, and ran through 11:00 a.m. During this time, fans who had paid for their tickets in advance could swap receipts for wristbands, but the rest who had not could buy their tickets at the ticket counters and then swap receipts for wristbands. At 11:00 a.m., attendees were welcomed into the vendor area where they could purchase rare *Star Trek* memorabilia, 8 x 10 stills of the day's guests, movie posters and lobby cards, toys, books and comic books, patches, and other related merchandise. The first guest was introduced on stage at 12:15 p.m. and spoke for an hour. Then he signed stills and posters and took photographs with the attendees for the remaining forty-five minutes to an hour. At 2:00 p.m., Gary Berman or Adam Malin teased guests with trivia questions for thirty minutes and/or auctioned off rare items from previous shows. The second guest was introduced on stage at 2:30 p.m. and spoke for an hour. Then he signed stills and posters and took photographs with the attendees for the remaining forty-five minutes to an hour. At 4:30 p.m., Gary or Adam recognized fans in their costumes, awarding them with prizes, usually pre-selected from among leftover items or out-of-date merchandise. At 5:00 p.m., Angelique Pettyjohn was introduced on the main stage where she performed her dance routine. The remaining hour and a half of the show was given to her to sign autographs and take photographs with the attendees. The show closed at exactly 7:00 p.m. The schedule never changed, and those volunteer fans who had agreed to help out (usually in exchange for a day-pass to the show) kept the events moving along and on time. Creation Conventions ran smoothly and predictably, like the large, industrialized factories of Victoria's England.

During the day, I covered for her at the table when she was on stage or needed to take a restroom break. I brought her lunch at noon and supplied her with cold soft-drinks throughout the afternoon. If we ran short of singles or change, I'd exchange larger bills with the hotel cashier. At night, I helped pack up her table and secure it for the next day, or drive her to the airport for her flight home. The work was never boring, and we'd always find a way to make things fun. I thoroughly enjoyed her company and honestly loved every moment of the time we had together.

In those ten weeks before the end of 1982, I got to know her very well, better than she knew herself, and I had begun to learn the different players in her life. She was actually a very smart woman, despite the persona she often adopted on film, and had boundless amounts of creative energy she channeled into her various convention appearances. We spoke nearly every day of the week on the phone, then on the weekends, when Angelique was not working or otherwise engaged in some kind of production, we'd share secrets or exchange personal stories about our lives. She took great pleasure in not only learning I was a regular guy but also discovering my faults and idiosyncrasies.

Figure 159. Angelique made and wore her own Shahna costume.

Once Pettyjohn had satisfied the terms of her trial period for Creation Entertainment, the promoters signed her for an additional dozen shows over the next two years. She made return visits to Philadelphia, Boston, and Chicago, and also went to Detroit, Denver, Washington D.C., Rochester, Atlanta, San Francisco, Seattle, and Los Angeles. Her year always culminated with an appearance at Gary and Adam's big Thanksgiving show in New York City. All throughout 1983 and 1984, she continued working the convention circuit, signing autographs, distributing posters, and often performing her dance routine, dressed as Shahna in her famous silver bikini, as part of the main show. I'd pick her up at the airport, return her, and helped her out as much as I could during that weekend.

Eventually, Pettyjohn's fame grew and she began headlining these shows as the main guest of honor. *Star Trek* fans had gotten their fill of George Takei and Walter Koenig, DeForest Kelley, Mark Lenard, and Nichelle Nichols, but Angelique Pettyjohn was a fresh face to most attendees. The convention route proved to be a very good one for Pettyjohn who, in conjunction with these appearances, experienced a decided renaissance in the eighties. Her appearance on the convention circuit raised her profile in the movie industry. Independent film directors, like Jim Wynorski, Alex Cox, and Mike Jittlov, who grew up seeing her earlier work on *Star Trek*, began hiring her for bit parts or extended cameos in their films. She even had the casting director of *Hill Street Blues*, one of the top-rated shows on television, call about a character that was perfect for her. While most actresses in their forties were finding it hard to land new roles, Angelique had to hire an assistant to keep track of all of the guest appearances and roles she was taking on.

Tackling the Fan-Run Conventions

For more than two years, I had been talking to Angelique about the differences that existed between Creation Entertainment's commercial shows and those smaller, fan-run conventions. I thought she'd do a bang-up job and endear herself with the people who really mattered. She agreed, but each time I suggested a specific fan-run convention, she balked, fearing she would endanger her working relationship with Gary Berman and Adam Malin. I understood her reasons completely. She was a very smart businesswoman who had tapped into a market with a seemingly unlimited potential for the future.

But then in the summer of 1984, the bottom of that market fell out. First in Boston and then in Detroit, we started to notice sales were way off from what they had been a year earlier, during that same period. Ironically, *Star Trek III: The Search for Spock* (1984) dominated other films at the box office, and conventional wisdom held that *Star Trek* fans wanted more *Star Trek* events. True, but what they really wanted were more of the family-friendly, fan-run conventions. The market was already saturated with the kind of cookie-cutter *Star Trek* shows like Gary and Adam had routinely promoted through their multi-million-dollar business. They had also seen the writing on the wall and quickly shifted their focus to another fan favorite. One year earlier, Creation Entertainment had begun promoting its *Doctor Who* shows and simply added more of those shows to replace *Star Trek*, which left many Creation fans and loyalists, such as Angelique scrambling to schedule other local and regional appearances.

Figure 160. With her own Mego doll, Pettyjohn had "made it!"

I had known, through my many contacts in *Star Trek* fandom, a number of the key players involved in running fan-run conventions. Rich Kolker ran a small show at the University of Maryland, August Party, and Marion McChesney and Geraldine Sylvester were founding members of S.T.A.T.-the *Star Trek* Association of Towson, which ran Shore Leave. I had gone to August Party and Shore Leave as a fan, and competed in their masquerade competitions. I had also spoken on panels at both conventions and knew many of the regulars, like Gus Liberto, John Olsen, Kathy Roark, and Robin and Bev Volker. With both of their conventions only a few weeks away, I was much too late to recommend guests to the committee. However, the committee for Shore Leave 7, scheduled for July 1985, did take my recommendation. I was also able to include her in plans for other conventions:

PhoenixCon was held August 23-25, 1984 at the Hampton Inn in Easton, Maryland, and featured Judson Scott, Richard Lynch, and Angelique Pettyjohn as guests of the small, fan-run convention. With less than 200 fans in attendance, PhoenixCon celebrated the 1982 ABC television series *The Phoenix*. Its plot revolved around an ancient extraterrestrial, Bennu of the Golden Light (Judson Scott), who is discovered in a sarcophagus in Peru and awakened to the 20th Century. Government agent Justin Preminger (Richard Lynch) is obsessed with capturing Bennu, who, despite what his superiors say, believes him to be nothing more than some sort of a New-Age con man. Because I served with several other *Star Trek* fans on the convention committee, I arranged to have Angelique invited to the convention as a special guest at the last minute.

She proved to be very special, indeed.

In addition to signing autographs and doing her *Star Trek* stage routine for the fans gathered at the convention, Angelique surprised all of us by not only befriending a severely-handicapped little boy named Jason (and his mom Rita), but also auctioning off several of her prized movie props to raise funds to send him to Johns-Hopkins hospital in Baltimore City for treatment.

Figures 161, 162 & 163. Cosplayers Genevra Croft, Desert Rose, and Marissa Regrann dress as Shahna at conventions.

As a courtesy and pleasure, I picked Pettyjohn up at the Baltimore-Washington Airport on Friday morning, and drove her sixty-three miles to Easton for the convention. On the return trip Sunday evening, I couldn't stop talking about the generosity she had showed the little boy. She just looked at me and smiled, saying, "It was the right thing to do."

Years later, she confessed to having had an incredible crush on Judson Scott, of *Star Trek 2: The Wrath of Khan* (1982). When he made a pass at her over dinner, she gave him her room number at the Hampton Inn and he paid her a discrete visit on Saturday night. She didn't need to say anything more, and I didn't ask her for details.

Regrettably, during the late-night hours of the convention, a long-time rival of Pettyjohn took over the convention's video conferencing system in order to play a terrible prank on her. Instead of showing a repeat of the binge-worthy *Phoenix* episodes, featuring Judson Scott and Richard Lynch, the woman cued up *Titillation* (1982) and *Body Talk* (1984), two of the pornographic films Angelique had made during a difficult time in her life. The movies were telecast throughout the Hampton Inn on televisions in guest rooms and video monitors in the movie room. Pettyjohn was mortified to learn these films were shown to the attendees, but she maintained her dignity regardless.

LACon II - The 42nd World Science Fiction Convention was held August 30-September 3, 1984 at the Anaheim Hilton and the Anaheim Convention Center located in Anaheim, California. The guests of honor were Gordon R. Dickson (professional writer) and Dick Eney (fan writer). Robert Bloch, author of *Psycho,* was the toastmaster for the Hugo Ceremony and Author Jerry Pournelle was the master of ceremonies. Angelique Pettyjohn was welcomed as a special guest of the convention and given her own table to sell her merchandise. The total attendance was 8,365 fans, a record and the largest Worldcon to date.

Less than a week after the small, fan-run convention in Easton, Maryland, I flew to the West Coast to participate in the convention. The World Science Fiction Convention or Worldcon had been produced by fans since 1939, and this latest convention was the 42nd of its kind in the history of science fiction fandom. Not only was I speaking on several panels as a professional author — newly-confirmed as a member of the Science Fiction Writers of America — but I also had an entry for the LACon II masquerade competition. "A Victorian Fantasy" was my tribute to the works of Jules Verne and H.G. Wells, and featured costumes designed by me and a magic box cobbled together by George Lawrence and me. I won a special "workmanship" award from the panel of judges, which included Angelique Pettyjohn, and bested nearly 176 fellow entries in the eight-and-a-half-hour competition, the longest masquerade in the recorded history of the Worldcon conventions. I didn't win Best in my Class, as I had expected I might, but I treasured the special "workmanship" trophy, the only one awarded for that competition. My fellow competitors did not fare as well.

Figure 164. Angelique sits at her LACon II table.

On the next day, I introduced Angelique to my mother, Norma Jean, and my stepfather, James Hazelgrove, who were living in Porterville, California at the time. My parents had driven down for the day to visit me and I was really anxious to introduce them to my very special friend. They all seemed to hit it off well. My mother and Angelique shared the same birthday, March 11th, both Pisces. My stepfather also confessed to having seen Pettyjohn perform in a live show in Las Vegas back in her glory days. She thanked him for not making any more of it.

A week later, she called me on my 30th birthday and told me how lucky I was to have had such loving parents who had taken a genuine interest in my life. That was something she had never experienced, and regretted more and more as the days of her life began to dwindle down. During the ten years we knew each other, we spoke a great deal about life, in particular her incredible life in and out of the spotlight, but she never again spoke to me about regrets she had about her family. I felt sorry for her, and just wanted to take her in my arms, like a baby, to wish away the hurt, but we were separated by three thousand miles and a phone cable from AT&T.

RovaCon 9 was held October 26-28, 1984 at the Roanoke Valley Civic Center located in Roanoke, Virginia. The guests of honor were author Jo Clayton and actors George Takei, Angelique Pettyjohn, and Ann Jillian. The art guest of honor was Frank Kelly Freas, and the science guest of honor was Fred Dihnzaio.

The 1200-person, fan-run convention was the brainchild of Dr. Fred Eichelman, a public-school teacher whose career at Northside High School spanned four decades. Fred, a graduate of Bridgewater College, with a Master of Education degree from the University of Virginia and a Ph.D. of Social Studies Education degree awarded by Virginia Polytechnic Institute and State University, conceived of running a science fiction convention in which all the profits went right back into the school. An educator myself, I had attended a number of Fred's shows (before RovaCon 9) and witnessed first-hand the spirit of volunteerism, the cornerstone of his convention. I offered my skills as a writer and costumer, and worked hard each subsequent year to make the convention a success.

Since I knew Fred didn't have a lot of money to pay expensive guests, I spoke with Angelique about RovaCon and convinced her to wave her usual fee. She agreed, very graciously, and also promised to leave her nude posters and photos at home, believing Roanoke was probably not the right venue. In exchange for cutting her fee, Fred Eichelman scheduled Pettyjohn for every conceivable event possible. For example, on Friday morning, Fred had scheduled Angelique for a one-hour teaching seminar at a local health spa, an appearance at a bank opening, and an appearance at the Crossroads Mall. Hollywood had come to small town Roanoke! Throughout the rest of the weekend, Pettyjohn did a make-up demonstration, screen-test judging at Hotel Roanoke, a media workshop, an awards banquet, judging for the costume contest, a worker's brunch, and a presentation in the auditorium. Dr. Eichelman literally kept her running every moment.

In the evening, when it was time to retire and get some rest, Fred had arranged lodging for us as well. We were given cabins not far from the venue for pennies on the dollar, and I drove Angelique each day to and from the Civic Center.

On Saturday night, after a particularly busy day, Pettyjohn asked me why, in the two years we had known each other, I had never made a pass at her. We stood outside her cabin on that cool October evening for what seemed like an eternity, as I thought long and hard about my answer. I did love her, like a friend, and I cared about what happened to her. I also enjoyed being her escort and confidant and partner at the conventions, but my heart was already promised to a woman I had been seeing in Maryland. Sure, I could have easily lied to Angelique about my situation, said the right words to get me into her bed, but I wouldn't have been able to live with myself afterwards if it had been some sordid game. I opted to tell her the truth about my life in Baltimore.

She later kissed me on the cheek and thanked me for being so honest. I knew I had won a much greater prize, her undying love and friendship. We never spoke about the issue again, and grew even closer as the years passed by.

Shore Leave 7 was held July 12-14, 1985 at The Marriott Hunt Valley Inn located in Hunt Valley, Maryland. Although Angelique Pettyjohn had missed out of attending the previous year's convention, she was accepted by the committee as one of the guests of honor along with DeForest Kelley and Robert Fletcher, the costume designer for the *Star Trek* films, for the 1985 convention.

I helped Angelique with her table and cheered her on during her dance routine. The *Star Trek* fans at Shore Leave 7 responded to her with a great deal of enthusiasm. Even though the money she earned at the convention was far less than what she made at the Creation shows, she enjoyed herself, and made a number of life-long friends there.

With Angelique's support and urging, I shared my portfolio of costumes and costume designs with Robert Fletcher. He was very impressed with my work and said I could come work for him any time at Western Costume. He was just starting work on the miniseries *North and South* and said I could join him on the set, starting out as a cutter or sewer. I thanked him for the offer and told him I would consider it. Pettyjohn said it was quite an impressive offer. I considered it for about five minutes, then declined, saying my course was already set.

Los Angeles Starlog Festival was held July 12-13, 1986 at The Ambassador Hotel located in suburban Los Angeles. The guests were George Takei, Walter Koenig, Mark Lenard, James Doohan, DeForest Kelley, and Angelique Pettyjohn. The special guests were *Starlog* publisher Kerry O'Quinn and editor David McDonnell. I knew both of them very well from writing articles for the magazine over the years. The *Starlog* name was well-known to fans throughout the world for bringing exceptional coverage to science fiction and fantasy films. Creation Entertainment had licensed the name "Starlog" for special events, and while the magazine's creative staff often made suggestions about guests and programming, Adam and Gary actually ran the show and made all of the decisions.

Angelique was invited to the show, along with a half-dozen other *Star Trek* guests. She lived in a suburb of Los Angeles, like so many of the others, so expenses were limited. The historic but deteriorated Ambassador Hotel, where Robert F. Kennedy had been assassinated in 1968, was rented to provide a large enough venue for the show. Once a vibrant part of the city's social scene, the building had been left to rot and decay. The Ambassador Hotel wasn't exactly the kind of venue the two of us had expected. Other LA *Starlog* events had been scheduled in the LAX Marriott or the fabled Disneyland Hotel in Anaheim.

During the day, Pettyjohn signed autographs and took photographs with the fans at her table, and she also agreed to do her dance routine on Saturday night. Both of us were tired from the long convention schedule, and she was fighting a stomach flu that had left her feeling weak and debilitated. Like a trooper though, Angelique did her best to entertain the *Star Trek* fans gathered at the show. Regrettably, her dance routine was the worst of her career. Her timing was off, skipping several key transition steps, and narrowly missed striking a volunteer with her silver Triskelion spear. For a woman who had spent most of her career dancing, she couldn't seem to do anything right. The musical number went on and on, long after the audience had tired of it. I just felt bad for her. When Angelique came off the stage, I could see she was crying. I took her into my arms and held her tight, reassuring her the fans had loved her dance. What more could I do or say?

Sometime later, David McDonnell wrote a scathing review about Pettyjohn's dance number for *Starlog* magazine. He called it "misconceived," "a bad idea," and "an embarrassment." "It was a train wreck, one of the saddest things I have ever experienced at an SF convention." Even though as a freelance writer I technically worked for McDonnell when my articles appeared in *Starlog* Magazine, I despised him for trashing Angelique the way he did. He could have just as easily written a review of the horrible venue in which we found ourselves, or not said anything at all. David McDonnell further compounded

Angelique's shame by adding that she had attempted to "buy" Kerry O'Quinn off by giving him a handful of her "nude" and "semi-nude" stills from her table. According to McDonnell, O'Quinn was gay and would not have had any interest in seeing Pettyjohn in the nude. She took his criticism pretty hard and not only stopped doing the dance routine but also ended her association with Creation Entertainment. I was sad to see her leave the convention scene, but she had accomplished everything she had originally set out to do. We went home to our respective homes in Los Angeles and Baltimore to pick up the pieces of our lives.

Even though we left the conventions behind us, Angelique and I blazed a new trail as we continued to develop our friendship. We spoke nearly every day on the phone. I used to look forward to her calls at 10:30 at night. You might say her calls were what kept me going, as I soon recognized the huge empty hole that had developed in my own life.

Figure 165. Angelique's final appearance as Shahna.

During the next few years, we'd meet for dinner after a show in Las Vegas, or I'd surprise her on the set of her next film, or I'd arrange to pick her up at the airport and we'd drive to some tourist spot neither of us had ever seen and spend the weekend. God only knows how many frequent flier miles she amassed! In those final few years of her life, we'd often talk about the conventions with great fondness; sometimes we just couldn't stop laughing as we reminisced. She had an incredible sense of humor and optimism about the future.

10
Tragedy and Triumph

When I was twenty-eight, all the casting agents saw was my body. They never noticed my mind. My talent. But now that I'm forty, I've had a lot of people give me some recognition for my mind, my intelligence, and my talent. I've gotten so much recognition lately, my ego is satisfied, and now I'm glad that they still think of me as a sex symbol. So, you see, life goes on.

F. Scott Fitzgerald once wrote, "There are no second acts in American lives." But Fitzgerald had never met Angelique Pettyjohn. Not only had she experienced a successful life as a dancer and showgirl in Las Vegas, but she also had a journeyman's profession as a television actress and a star-studded career in motion pictures. At a time when most women in their forties were considered old and had stopped performing altogether, Angelique was enjoying a renewed career in the movies. Many of the directors and producers, young boys when they first saw Pettyjohn on *Star Trek* in that memorable silver bikini, were now adults in key roles in Hollywood. Her appearances at the *Star Trek* conventions not only reminded them of their first love but also prompted them to hire her for their movies. She suddenly had more work than she could manage, as she celebrated a sort of renaissance in motion pictures. Clearly, Fitzgerald had never encountered a woman of Angelique's caliber, but if he had, she would have been a flapper from the twenties, like Zelda or Daisy, who took a man's breathe away and left him wanting for more. A lot more.

Good-bye, Cruel World (1983)

Good-bye, Cruel World was a 1983 independently-made, American anthology, comedy film, produced by Louis Sardonis, Leopold Zahn, and Stephen L. Newman, and directed by David Irving. Dick Shawn and Nicholas Niciphor wrote the screenplay. Among the numerous star cameos were Dick Shawn, Cynthia Sikes, Pierre Jalbert, LaWanda Page, Priscilla Pointer, Chuck Mitchell, Darrell Larson, John Alderman, Buckley Norris, Barbara Pilavin, Brad Harris, Dan Frischman, and Angelique Pettyjohn. The film contained largely unconnected sketches to parody the various gimmicks used to get audiences into the theatres, and was sold with images of a man flushing himself down the toilet.

The dominant sketch involved newscaster Rodney Pointsetter (Shawn) who is so depressed with his life, job, and family he plans to commit suicide on air during an upcoming story about his life. The sketch is interrupted by an emcee (Allan Stephan) who offers the audience a choice: Maybe, they would prefer to watch a sketch about a nun (played by Angelique Pettyjohn) who is a professional stripper? Or a sketch with Dan Frischman hosting *Things Your Parents Used to Say*, while Rodney's gay brother, Ainsley (also Shawn), plans to stage an opera at his house? Conventional wisdom held that audiences didn't like movies composed of sketches, but the box-office success of *The Groove Tube* (1974) and *Kentucky Fried Movie* (1977) shattered those myths, and unleashed a whole sub-genre of anthology films.

The real inspiration for David Irving's *Good-bye, Cruel World* was to parody Sidney Lumet's Oscar-nominated *Network* (1976). In the latter film, Howard Beale, the longtime anchor of the Union Broadcasting System's UBS Evening News, learns he is going to be fired, so he announces on camera he will commit suicide on next Tuesday's broadcast. Beale doesn't go through with his planned suicide, but does inspire the titular network to pump up Nielsen ratings by trying all sorts of new and unconventional programming, one being an hour-long drama series featuring Patty Hearst and her terrorist friends with the

Symbionese Liberation Army, and a news program titled *The Mao Tse-Tung Hour*. It's all pretty silly, but then no more so than Irving's sketches about a "stripping" nun or an opera at a gay man's home. By the way, the inspiration for Paddy Chayefsky's *Network* screenplay came from the real on-air suicide of television news reporter Christine Chubbuck in Sarasota, Florida, two years earlier.

Figure 166. *Goodbye, Cruel World* (1983)

The non-PC humor, raunchy jokes, and sexy Angelique Pettyjohn as a "stripping" nun were highly amusing and decidedly refreshing, but they failed to raise this low-budget motion picture above its competition. *Good-bye, Cruel World* failed miserably at the box office, and is rarely shown on movie channels, like Turner Classic Movies (TCM) or American Movie Classics (AMC).

Repo Man (1984)

With her very next outing, Angelique Pettyjohn scored far better with Alex Cox's *Repo Man* (1984), a science-fiction comedy with a truly fresh idea. Frustrated punk rocker Otto Maddox (Estevez) quits his dead-end supermarket job after slugging a co-worker, then is later dumped by his girlfriend at a party. Angry and alone, he wanders the streets, looking for a clue to his next job. He witnesses the repossession of a car by Bud (Stanton), a repo agent, who gives him $25 for helping out. Bud also offers him a job, but Otto has other plans. When he finds out his parents have donated his college fund to a televangelist, Otto tracks Bud down and agrees to work as an apprentice "repo man" for the

Helping Hand Acceptance Corporation. He quickly learns, during his training, that repo drivers are both mercenary and paranoid. In no time, Otto gets caught up in a series of off-the-wall adventures involving government agents, UFO cultists, hired thugs, rival repo men, sex-starved repo wives, a lobotomized nuclear scientist, and an incredibly valuable '64 Chevy Malibu containing top secret cargo in the trunk that could change the course of civilization. Which way to Area 51?

Repo Man (1984) was an explosive action-packed film that instantly became a cult classic overnight. Initially, in the days following his stint at UCLA, Alex Cox had been hired by Adrian Lyne to write a serious movie about nuclear war, which turned out to be *The Happy Hour*. Lyne read it and did *Flashdance* instead. Cox then met a real repo man, Mark Lewis, and decided he would write a comedy that combined the seedy world of car repossession with the quirky realm of science fiction. While writing the screenplay for *Repo Man*, he met Angelique at a *Star Trek*

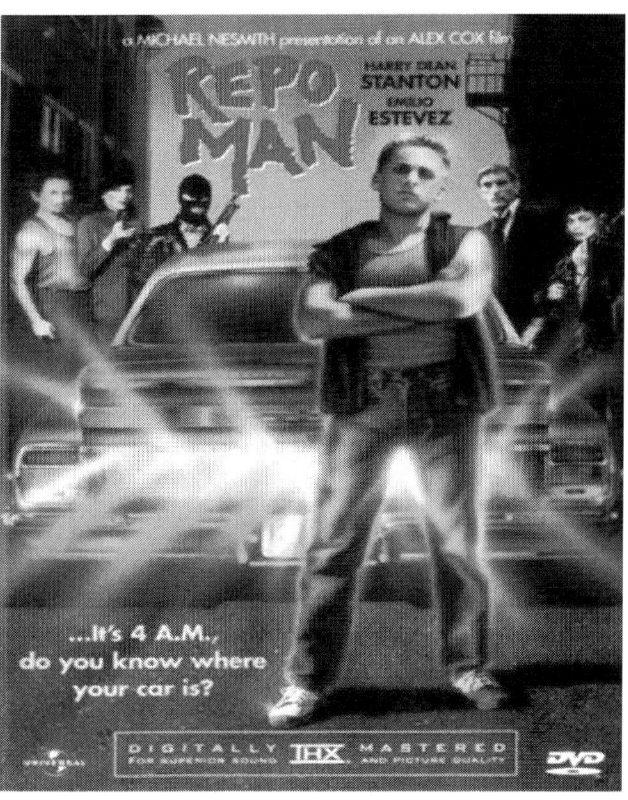

Figure 167. Poster from *Repo Mam* (1984).

convention and was totally charmed by the forty-year-old actress. He wrote a part specifically for her (as Repo Wife #2) and made her promise she would play the role when he got the "green light" from Universal. As good as her word, Pettyjohn reported to duty on the Universal lot and Cox shot her scene in one afternoon. The role was not a big one, but she was perfectly cast as Repo Wife #2. At the bar, while she is being watched by her husband, sexy, sultry, and hot Angelique in a red dress puts the moves on Otto, the new star in auto repossession. He is flattered by her attention, but then another Repo Wife enters the scene, and Otto has two hot babes vying for his attention. I can't think of too many men who would have turned down her advances, but alas, Otto Maddox does. At age forty, she was truly the hottest woman in the film! Whenever I watch that scene, I am wondering what is going on in Maddox's head. Take the hot blonde, Otto!

One of the ten best films of 1984, *Repo Man* received widespread acclaim, and broke all sorts of box office records. Rotten Tomatoes gave the film a 98% rating, and suggested it "is many things: an alien-invasion film, a punk-rock musical, a send-up on consumerism. One thing it isn't is boring."

Figure 168. Angelique competes for Otto's attention in *Repo Man*.

Figure 169. Angelique Pettyjohn tries her hand again at wedded bliss in the suburbs of Los Angeles.

Marriage # 4 — Ronald Bernard Flynn

Angelique Pettyjohn met Ronald Bernard Flynn (no relation to the author) at an Alcoholics Anonymous meeting in Los Angeles and were married on Valentine's Day 1984 in a religious ceremony at the Clark County Courthouse in Las Vegas, Nevada, (Marriage Certificate #B486686). To Flynn, she was one of the most beautiful women he had ever met. For Pettyjohn, he was kind, hardworking, and more importantly, he offered her a stable and secure homelife in the suburbs. After all that she had been through with men in her life, "kind" and "hardworking" were two adjectives she embraced whole-heartedly.

Ronald Bernard Flynn was the proverbial nice guy. Born on December 21, 1942, in Los Angeles, California, to Peter Bernard Flynn (1900-1983) and Lydia Fulscher (1906-1944), Ronald grew up in a large, middle-class Catholic family with lots of brothers and sisters. His grandfather, Bernard McNiff Flynn, had been born in Ireland in 1867, then immigrated to Portland, Oregon, where Ronald's father was one of eight children Bernard and his wife Catherine Ann Burke had. His mother came from Canada, and was a naturalized citizen.

They celebrated all Catholic and Irish festivals with great gusto and plenty of Irish whiskey. Ronald knew the value of a hard day's work and worked hard most of his adult life to build a home for himself and his teenaged son, Ronnie.

Angelique Pettyjohn, adapting to the name Dorothy Lee Flynn, moved into his home in Los Angeles County, and settled into a very quiet, happy, domestic life. Ten-to-twelve weekends a year, she worked the *Star Trek* conventions. During the week, she answered letters from adoring fans on a manual typewriter and acted in the occasional movie. She had more work in film than most other women her age. Life was sweet, at least for a while.

Angelique Tuefeld*

During the Summer of 1984, Angelique Pettyjohn received a special request from another Angelique, a young, beautiful, red-headed fan from the *Star Trek* conventions who idolized her. Angelique Tuefeld (1951-) (* Angelique's last name was changed to "Tuefeld" to protect her family name and out of respect for her privacy as a retired senior citizen) studied fashion art, design, and construction in college, and created some of the most beautiful and elaborate costumes I had ever seen at the fan-run conventions. [Full disclosure: Angelique "Angie" Tuefeld was also my friend. When she ran into some financial troubles in the eighties, I put her up in my guest room and saw her through some very desperate times.] She cosplayed a variety of characters, most of them drawn from comic books and popular movies. She even made her own version of the Shahna silver bikini from "The Gamesters of Triskelion." She was a very talented costumer who should have been working professionally in Hollywood. When her partner dissolved their New York-based business, she called on Pettyjohn to put her up for a couple of months in Los Angeles, so she could cold-call some of the studios and seek work as a costume designer at one of the studios. Angie had an excellent portfolio, with lots of beautiful costume designs. She also refused to take "no" for an answer. So, at the end of August 1984, Angelique welcomed Angie. Regrettably, that was not one of her better decisions.

Initially, Pettyjohn was thrilled and excited to help someone like Angie break into show-business, but then, after about a week, she began to regret her decision. As a former addict, Angelique had worked very hard to break her addiction to drugs and clean up her life. The last thing she wanted, or was willing to tolerate in her home, was marijuana. Tuefeld claimed the pot was Ronnie's, and as a young, teenaged boy, Ronnie told his father a completely different story. Then instead of cold-calling the studios for work, like she had planned, Tuefeld had littered Pettyjohn's small, suburban house with fabric, patterns, sewing millinery, and trim, and started making a costume, based on designs for a princess costume from a popular, sci-fi movie for the 1984 Worldcon masquerade competition, just a week away.

Finally, Pettyjohn came home one day, somewhat unexpectantly, and discovered Tuefeld shacked up with Ronnie, smoking pot after they had presumably had sex. That was the last straw. Pettyjohn threw Angie Tuefeld out of her house, and slammed the door behind her.

That same night, Angelique Tuefeld moved into a hotel in Anaheim, near the convention center hosting the 1984 Worldcon and worked around-the-clock to finish her costume. She competed in the LACon II masquerade against me and 175 fellow costumers in the now infamous eight-and-a-half-hour competition. I won a special workmanship award from the judges for "A Victorian Fantasy," while my friend Angie walked away as one of the night's big losers. During her stay in Los Angeles, she never called on a single studio, and she never shared her beautiful portfolio with a single professional costume designer. On Monday, September 3, 1984, Tuefeld climbed aboard an airplane heading east, back home to New York.

Three days later, Angelique called me on my 30th birthday to share the nightmarish, darkly-comic tale of Angie Tuefeld's visit. Her narrative, which sounded more like an anecdote from *The Twilight Zone* than a spot on the local nightly news, ran on for more than an hour, and had equal parts of humor and sorrow. When she finished telling me her story, I decided not to debate the accuracy of her account nor get into a "he said/she said" argument. I'm sure my friend Angie had a completely different take on events, even though we never discussed it. I confessed I had known Tuefeld for many years through the *Star Trek* conventions and thought she was not only a truly talented costumer but also a nice person. Pettyjohn agreed with me, then dropped the whole issue. She turned to other subjects, in particular remorse that her parents had never shown her the kind of love and interest mine did. I closed our call by wishing her and Ronald, as newlyweds, long life and happiness.

***Biohazard* (1985)**

Biohazard (1985) was an American science-fiction horror film, written and directed by Fred Olen Ray, that was loosely inspired by the writings of H.P. Lovecraft and the movie *Alien* (1979), which starred Aldo Ray, Angelique Pettyjohn, William Fair, David O'Hara, Art Payton, and Carroll Borland. Florida schlockmeister Ray had already built a reputation as a low-budget auteur with *The Brain Leeches* (1978), *Alien Dead* (1980), and *Scalps* (1983), but demonstrated he was ready for the big time with this clever story about a busty psychic researcher who uses a trans-dimensional machine to teleport an alien creature with ravenous desires to earth.

Fred Olen Ray was born September 10, 1954, a few days after me, and was, in fact, a contemporary of mine. Like Ray, we both grew up, reading Forry Ackerman's *Famous Monsters of Filmland* magazine and being fans of horror and science fiction films such as *Abbott and Costello Meet Frankenstein* (1948) and the AIP movies of the fifties and sixties. He was born in Ohio, but grew up in Sarasota, Florida. I was born and raised in Chicago, but spent several of my formative years in St. Petersburg, Florida. He started making his own movies when he was fourteen. I started writing my first science fiction stories and making my sci-fi costumes when I was fourteen. We might as well have been brothers. I was actually surprised we had never met. I enjoyed most of his movies very much, and I can only hope, over the years, he had enjoyed one or more of my science fiction or mystery novels.

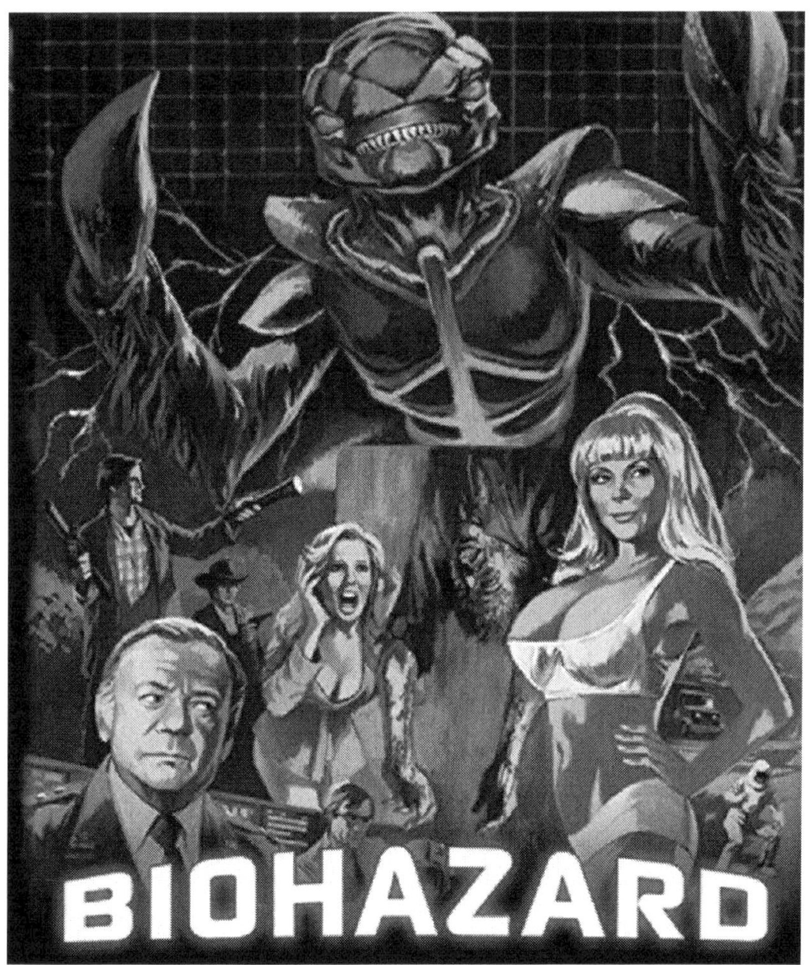

Figure 170. Angelique played a psychic in *Biohazard* (1985).

On the night Angelique met Fred Olen Ray, she was so excited to meet someone who reminded her of me, she couldn't wait to call me. She had been out at a comedy show in North Hollywood, when a nice young man about thirty came up and asked her, "Are you the same Angelique Pettyjohn who starred in *The Mad Doctor of Blood Island*, the movie on Elvira's show last night?" She told him "yes," and then Fred spent twenty minutes pitching the premise of *Biohazard* to her. He wanted her to play Lisa Martyn, one of the lead roles. Pettyjohn agreed without seeing a contract or even a completed script; said she simply trusted him. Then during our call, she wouldn't stop talking about him. Angelique said he was just like me — thoughtful, well-spoken, and incredibly creative. She felt like she had just met my twin brother. Naturally, I was very flattered by her comparison and looked forward to the opportunity of meeting Mr. Ray, following each step of the production of his magnum opus. I was mostly happy for Pettyjohn. She was not only excited about Fred's new film, but also thrilled by the prospect of working. First and foremost, she saw herself as an entertainer. The only way she was ever going to be truly happy was performing before an audience. Here was also another director who had grown up loving her work and was willing to put her in his picture.

At a remote, secret Government research facility in the California desert, a U.S. Army truck arrives with a single occupant aboard. Her name is Lisa Martyn (Angelique Pettyjohn), a psychic with unusual abilities. A general (Aldo Ray) and a couple of senators have been waiting for her covert arrival. Martyn's unusual ability to see things beyond her scope of eyesight allows governmental scientists to transfer and reassemble matter from an unknown dimension.

Figure 171. Lisa Martyn (Angelique Pettyjohn) attempts to communicate using her psychic powers.

After fitting Lisa with a device designed to amplify her brainwaves, Dr. Williams (Arthur Payton) initiates a top-secret experiment that allows her to teleport a massive, metal trapezoid into the laboratory. At about the same time, a field assistant sent to repair a damaged conduit fails to complete his mission in time, and his body is burnt to a crisp.

With interests in developing the ultimate bio-weapon, General Randolph decides to pull rank and demands the materialized item be sent directly to his base for a thorough analysis and review. Williams and Martyn disagree, arguing they should keep the metal cannister there at the secret research facility for further study. All agree the cannister bears an interdimensional being. Of course, the bio-monster, a four-foot, child-like humanoid (actually, the director's son in a rubber suit) with pincers and an insectoid face, breaks free and goes on a rampage killing spree. Predictably, the story follows a narrative similar to *Alien* (1979), *The Thing* (1982), and *From Beyond* (1985) as three unlikely heroes (William Fair as Carter, Frank McDonald as Hodgson, and David Pearson as Reiger, the mercenary with bloodlust and bad attitude) must put aside their petty differences in order to try to stop the creature from destroying everyone they know. In several key shots, Fred Olen Ray references *Alien* as the inspiration for his film, but it's really unfair to make such a comparison as a lot of contemporary filmmakers were copying the 1979 masterpiece as well. In the end, they destroy the monster, but room for a sequel remained.

Many fans of horror and science fiction films enjoyed *Biohazard* when it was released in August 1985, but the critics at large did not. They called it a "hysterically" bad film with no redeeming qualities. A critic writing for Imdb.com claimed it had everything a terrible movie needs: "a screenplay featuring jaw-dropping dialogue and baffling detours in plot," "wacky science involving psychics and other dimensions," "continuity that seems to travel through wormholes," "gratuitous nudity," and a "five-foot monster played by a kid." Personally, I enjoyed Fred Olen Ray's loving pastiche of *Alien*.

As far as Pettyjohn was concerned, she thought Ray had created a very impressive production and was thrilled by the way Ray connected with his actors, providing them with the kind of motivation only a skilled writer-director would invoke.

Lost and Phantom Empires

During the final days of shooting, Ray told Angelique about his next project, *The Phantom Empire* (1986). Pettyjohn expressed some interest, particularly with the chance of working with Sybil Danning and Michelle Bauer, two actresses who really owed their career to her.

Angelique had played soft-porn T&A movies and B-grade horror and science fiction films for a large part of her career; when she returned to Las Vegas in the seventies, she left a vacuum to fill for women with an impressive bustline and some talent as an actress. Sybil Danning was born in 1952 in Austria. After her impressive debut in Roger Corman's *Battle Beyond the Stars* (1980) as the sexy, Valkyrie-like Saint-Exmin, she played in numerous B-grade movies, *Chained Heat* (1983) and *Hercules* (1983) to name a couple, relying largely on her healthy bust-line and image as a sex symbol. Similarly, Michelle Bauer, born in 1958, established herself as a porn star first under the name Pia Snow, then later worked with Fred Olen Ray on *The Tomb* (1986). Ray had already hired Danning and Bauer for *The Phantom Empire* and seemed ready to hire Pettyjohn, but alas, Angelique had already agreed to make Jim Wynorski's *The Lost Empire* (1984). Two film projects with similar subjects being made at the same time was not unusual, except they may have featured the same actress.

Twin films are two different productions, sharing the same or a very similar plot, released at the same time by competing studios. The phenomenon is not a unique one. In 1938, after Bette Davis failed to win the highly-coveted role of Scarlett O'Hara in *Gone With the Wind* (1939), she decided to make *Jezebel* with Director William Wyler. In 1964, while trying to make a movie about an accidental nuclear war, Stanley Kubrick learned a rival production was being made of *Fail Safe* (1964), so he changed the somber tone of *Dr. Strangelove* to be a dark comedy. Many attribute twin films to industrial espionage, the movement of staff between studios, or the fact that two similar screenplays make the rounds of several film studios before being accepted. In 1998, *Deep Impact* was released a few months before *Armageddon*, two disaster films centered around an impending impact event that threatens to destroy all life on Earth. And in 2013, both *Olympus Has Fallen* and *White House Down* depicted terrorist attacks on the White House.

Figure 172. Poster for *The Lost Empire* (1984).

Jim Wynorski's *The Lost Empire* (1984), shot in a record amount of production time, beat Fred Olen Ray's *The Phantom Empire* (1988) by three years to the box office, even though both were shot basically at the same time and boasted a similar premise. *The Lost Empire* took audiences on a journey to the mysterious island fortress of Golgotha, where women-in-prison are forced by sexy Angelique Pettyjohn into kung-fu-like gladiatorial contests. *The Phantom Empire* dug down deep into a subterranean world where man-eating cave creatures guard uncut diamonds and a sexy, alien queen, Sybil Danning (with Robby the Robot at her side), rules over a prehistoric land where dinosaurs still roam. Sounds like Jim and Fred should have pooled their resources and shot one movie with Pettyjohn, Danning, and Bauer. Two studios have been known to pool resources to shoot one movie. In 1974, *The Towering Inferno* was made by 20th Century-Fox and Warner Brothers, adapted from a pair of novels about a burning skyscraper. But alas, Jim and Fred did not get the memorandum, and produced two separate films. Jim Wynorski's *The Lost Empire* was significantly better, featuring Pettyjohn in one of her favorite roles.

The Lost Empire was a fantasy-adventure comedy directed by first-timer Jim Wynorski. Born August 14, 1950, in Glen Cove, New York, he grew up watching science fiction and horror films as a child, and daydreamed of making his own one day, much like the younger Fred Olen Ray. In 1972, after flunking out of film school, he went to work at Double Day publishing in the fiction department. Jim read the stories of many would-be authors, and worked editorially on a few that went on to be best sellers, but didn't see himself doing it for the rest of his life. He really wanted to make movies, and so quit his job and moved to Los Angeles. There, he went to work for Roger Corman in the publicity department. His first produced screenplay was *Forbidden World* (1982), a cheapie *Alien* rip-off Corman made with Director Allan Holzman (on sets designed by future Oscar-winner James Cameron). Encouraged by the success of his first screenplay, Wynorski wrote the story treatment for with the thought of producing and directing it himself.

Figure 173. Angelique shows off her villainous side.

His 1984 film opens at a jewelry shop in Chinatown, the camera focused squarely on a rare statue with one glowing red eye. Three masked figures break into the shop, kill the shopkeeper, and attempt to steal the "Eye," but police arrive in time. A pitched gun battle ensues, and all of the intruders and all but one of the police are killed; the lone survivor (Bill Thornbury) is seriously wounded. Angel Wolfe (Melanie Vincz), a decorated L.A.P.D. inspector, gets a call from the hospital revealing her brother's condition and that he was the lone survivor. So, she and Federal Agent boyfriend Rick Stanton (Paul Coufos) rush to his side. He is feverish and keeps talking about "the devil" and how the Eye knows where he exists. Rick remembers a story about Lee Chuck (Angus Scrimm), a kung-fu master who gained immortality at the price of giving the devil a new soul every day.

Angel goes to the crime scene to investigate. While there, the Eye drops conveniently into her purse, then a mysterious Chinese man shows up, explaining that the Eyes of Avatar represent the most powerful force on earth. The Dragon God has placed enough power into the pair of Eyes to rule the world. Lee Chuck is real, has one eye already, and is searching, with Dr. Sin Do (Angus Scrimm, in the second of two roles), for the other eye to rule.

Figure 174. Sweet Angelique plays a bad ass Whiplash.

Figure 175. As Whiplash, Pettyjohn kicks serious ass.

When Angel's brother dies from his injuries, she decides to get her revenge against Lee Chuck and Dr. Sin Do. Together with Whitestar (Raven De La Croix), a native woman, and Heather McClure (Angela Aames), a criminal recently paroled, she travels to the mysterious island fortress of Golgotha. There, Angel finds a land time forgot, where women are held captive in chains to take part in gladiatorial games, and a male genius plots diabolically to take over the world. Angelique Pettyjohn, decked out in sexy attire as a dominatrix, plays Whiplash, the keeper of the captive women. She does battle with Angel and her two friends in the arena, and while she temporarily succeeds, is eventually defeated. The three outsiders then go after Lee Chuck and Dr. Sin, to capture the Eyes of Avatar and bring down their reign of terror.

Thoroughly engaging, with plenty of beautiful naked babes, an evil Chinese warlord, the devil, the threat of world destruction/domination, and girls who just want to have fun, *The*

Lost Empire was a fun little film that regrettably never found its niche audience. It did, however, anticipate John Carpenter's *Big Trouble in Little China* (1986), which was still two years away from production, and provided Pettyjohn with one of her best vehicles yet to chew up scenery. Like her Interrogator from *Stalag 69* (1982) she was perfectly cast as the villainous Whiplash. When she cracks her whip on all those buxom babes in chains, wearing her dominatrix attire, Pettyjohn takes full command of the narrative. Audience members never doubt for a second who is actually in charge. Her presence is so much larger than life! Handily defeated by the three outsiders, most of the rest of us secretly yearn for her to keep striking that whip of hers. She is deliciously scary. And under Wynorski's direction, she turns in one of her best performances.

Later, with his new friend Fred Olen Ray, Jim directed *Scream Queen Hot Tub Party* (1991), which was shot in one day. Both of them would have liked to use Angelique Pettyjohn as an aging scream queen, but she was already suffering with the cancer that would eventually take her life. The two friends did collaborate on *Dinosaur Island* (1994), and made both *Dark Universe* (1993) and the sequel to *Biohazard, The Alien Force* (1994) together. Just imagine, if they had combined their efforts, what kind of an epic movie they might have made together?

> *I've been very active doing films. I've done four in the last six months, and the best of them, I feel, is a horror-fantasy directed by Jim Wynorski, which also features Kenneth Tobey, Tom Rettig, Angus Scrim and others.*

Angelique Pettyjohn, Your Life is Calling

Released May 2, 1986, *Jo Jo Dancer, Your Life is Calling* (1986) was a film that not only closely paralleled Richard Pryor's own life story, but also served as a kind of wake-up call to others in the entertainment industry who may have screwed up by following their own pathway to self-destruction. When Angelique first read the script, she broke down and started crying. She could easily identify with Pryor's struggle with those vile voices in his head. She had struggled with them for most of her life. In fact, Pettyjohn had barely survived her own battle with substance abuse (and sexual addiction). She was still in a twelve-step program, trying to maintain sobriety. She thought long and hard about the script. Ultimately, her decision to make the movie was a difficult one, but in the end, she realized it was important for entertainers to talk to the public about their addictions.

Richard Pryor's story is told through flashbacks. Jo Jo Dancer, a popular stand-up comedian, has severely burned himself while freebasing cocaine. (The motion picture came out not long after Pryor had set himself on fire during a drug

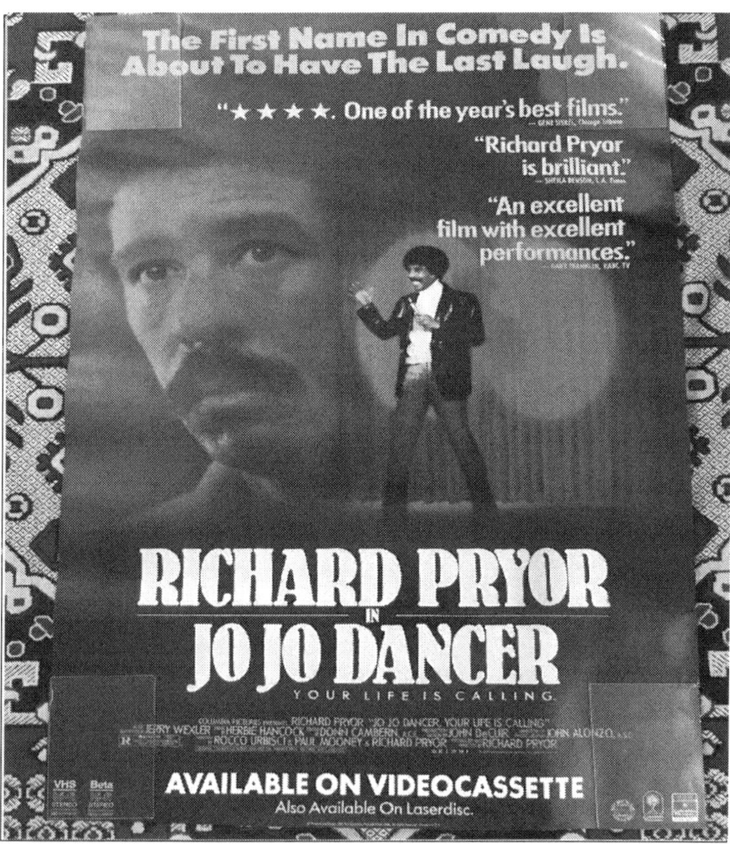

Figure 176. Poster art for *Jo, Jo Dancer* (1986).

incident.) As he lies unconscious in a hospital, his spiritual alter ego climbs out of the hospital bed and begins a journey of his own. He revisits his life, growing up in a brothel as a child and struggling to become a top-rated comedian. However, his success brings new problems as he develops a tragic pattern of substance abuse. First, with all the womanizing he did, then more drug use, and finally, he relives the incident when he set himself ablaze.

Throughout the movie, Jo Jo's spirit watches these events and attempts to convince his past self to turn away from his path of self-destruction. As the writer, director, producer, and star, Pryor created an excellent film that was at times entertaining, funny, thought-provoking, bitterly heartbreaking, personally revealing, and raw. *Jo Jo Dancer, Your Life is Calling* was considered a bomb when it came out in 1986, but has continued to show improvement over the years.

In the film, Pettyjohn played a showgirl, Roxanne Rolle, whose fellow showgirls were Angela Mitchell and Geraldine Mason. When she saw the final cut of the movie, she was in tears. The early scenes with E'Lon Cox as young Jo Jo took her back to her own childhood, those days just after her mom Maia and she arrived in Salt Lake City. She thought of Otho Pettyjohn and how poorly she'd treated him, while she had sex with every hot male actor on Hollywood Boulevard. She recalled all the drinking and the drugs, and the lies she told herself to get through the day. Jo Jo turned out to be very cathartic for Pettyjohn. She remembered details in her own life that had been buried for years. She cried about them with me, and achieved a sense of relief and cleansing.

Filing for Divorce, Again

Angelique Pettyjohn never found long life or happiness. Attempting to slip into a kind of domestic bliss as Dorothy Lee Flynn, she found it difficult to balance her career obligations with those of a stepmom and wife. Struggling to stay clean and sober, she also had to be honest with herself. Ronald B. Flynn was a nice, hard-working man who treated her well, but she was not in love with him or his ideas about wedded bliss.

After five years of marriage, Pettyjohn just couldn't keep pretending anymore, and filed for a divorce on the grounds of irreconcilable differences. She was granted a divorce on April 28, 1989. (File #D116650).

She returned to Las Vegas to star at the Cabaret, now known as the Pussycat, in what was considered one of the classiest strip shows in the city. Angelique had a sexy-comic mind-reading act for the nightclub and showroom circuits she had been working on, and hoped to use it fairly soon.

In the five years she had been away, Las Vegas had changed. It was now more family-oriented, with each of the major casinos along the Strip building what amounted to theme parks in order to attract families with children as its new customers. The old burlesque shows were gone, and the low-class strip joints were moved far off Las Vegas Boulevard, so far off patrons had to engage special mini-vans in order to find them.

Angelique felt privileged to have been able to see both sides of Las Vegas in her lifetime.

***The Wizard of Speed and Time* (1988)**

Based on a 16mm short, *The Wizard of Speed and Time* (1988) was the low-budget feature film version, written, directed, and starring animator Mike Jittlov. For ten long years, Jittlov made the rounds of the science-fiction and *Star Trek* conventions with a 16mm short, showcasing his work as an animator and special effects wizard at Disney Studios. The short film told the story of a young man in a green wizard costume who runs through America at turbo speed, much like DC's superhero "The Flash." Along the way, he picks up a pretty girl and carries her between cities. Suddenly, every woman wants a ride. He then slips on a banana peel and comes comically crashing down on a film stage where he brings other items to life. The short version of *The Wizard of Speed and Time* was impressive. Nearly everyone who saw his work was convinced Jittlov would go far. He just needed someone willing to put up the money for him to make the feature film version.

In 1983, shortly after showcasing his work at Constellation, the World Science Fiction Convention in Baltimore, Jittlov began filming his magnum opus with only a couple thousand dollars in the bank. He would shoot segments of the movie until he ran out of money, close the production down, and then shoot more when he had more money. Pettyjohn, who provided her own costumes, played Dora Belair, an assistant with a dual personality who worked with a competing show's producer. Pettyjohn shot her segment in 1984. Jittlov finally completed all principal photography, then went to work on the special effects and editing. A total perfectionist, he worked another five years on the project, then *The Wizard of Speed and Time* was finally released to a handful of theaters in 1989 (even though it was never widely distributed by a studio). It was later released on VHS and Laserdisc, but never on Blu-Ray or DVD.

Figure 177. ***The Wizard of Speed & Time*** **(1988).**

The screen story is significantly different from the short. *The Wizard of Speed and Time* was a satire about an aspiring special effects creator, Mike Jittlov (Jittlov) who desires to work in Hollywood on a show called *Doctor Magic*. Although Jittlov is extremely talented and creative, a top-notch special effects wizard, he has no name recognition and he is not a union member of any of the Hollywood guilds. When an open-minded director, Lucky Striker (Broadie), who works for a rival studio, sees Jittlov's work on a pirated videotape, he shows his penny-pinching producer Harvey Bookman (Kaye) what Jittlov can do. Bookman is skeptical, and the two make a $25,000 bet on whether Jittlov can produce an effects sequence for their upcoming TV special *Hollywood's Greatest Effects*. Of course, Bookman is willing to do anything to sabotage Jittlov and win the bet. Jittlov contacts his friends, Brian Lucas (Conrad) and Steve Shostakovich (Massari), and together they design a sensational effects showcase of stop-motion, speed-motion, animation, rotoscoping, and every other form of special effect, in Jittlov's garage.

Meanwhile, a romance develops between Jittlov and an aspiring actress (Moore), and two thugs (Schwartz and LaLoggia), disguised as police officers, try to stop Jittlov from completing his project. In the end, following a Keystone Kops-like chase, Mike Jittlov delivers his reel of special effects imagery and is proclaimed a genius.

When Angelique Pettyjohn finally saw *The Wizard of Speed and Time* in 1989, she was very nearly a completely different woman. Now divorced from Ronald Bernard Flynn, she had worked through her substance abuse problems and was looking good and fit. She had no way of knowing cancer was spreading through her breasts and would soon require a double mastectomy.

***Sorority Girls and the Creature from Hell* (1990)**

Credited as Ashley St. Jon, Angelique Pettyjohn made one final movie in her career, opposite Uncle Leo (Len Lesser) from *Seinfeld* and scream queen Deborah Dutch in *Sorority Girls and the Creature from Hell* (1990). Pettyjohn did not want her name associated with this cheapo, low-budget slasher film, so used one of the pseudonyms from her days making adult films. Smart move. Critics have often referred to this motion picture as one of the worst films ever made. Rent it on home video, if you can find it, and see for yourself.

Figure 178. Angelique Pettyjohn's last movie.

A group of approximately thirty twenty-something sorority sisters from the Kappa Meno Pausea, their boyfriends, hitchhikers, and many others decide to take a break from college and rent a creepy cabin in the woods from a creepy uncle (Koth) of one of the girls. The sorority sisters haven't brought much luggage with them because they spend most of the movie naked in a hot tub or drying off after a shower in front of a window or running around screaming. The boys seem to like this and spend the majority of their time creeping after the naked girls. Then in a secret cavern nearby, an archeologist has unearthed an ancient Indian spirit, which looks surprisingly like the floating head from *Zardoz* (1974). The spirit, in turn, changes the archeologist into the titular "creature from hell," with orders to bring fresh bodies to his new master. Apparently, he needs blood to grow strong. At the same time, a serial killer has escaped from the police and is also running around killing people. In a tavern close to the cabin in the woods, sexy, desirable Pettyjohn sits at the bar, alone, counting down the minutes until this awful film is over, and she can go home.

Sorority Girls and the Creature from Hell was sort of entertaining in the worst of all possible ways. You want to cheer for the monster and the serial killer to reduce the number of brainless idiots in the gene pool.

Double Mastectomy

Late in her life, Angelique Pettyjohn was diagnosed with Stage II breast cancer, and was told she would have to undergo a double mastectomy. She didn't know how to tell me, her other friends, and all her fans, and she'd kept it hidden for a long time. Months would go by, not a word. But the longer she hid her illness, the sicker she got. Eventually she could no longer keep it a secret. When I finally heard the news, I was absolutely heartbroken for her. I hung up the phone and just sat there alone in the darkness, crying my eyes out. My dear, sweet friend had relied so heavily on her breasts for dancing and other aspects of her career, I just didn't know how she would survive. Neither did she. Pettyjohn was so terrified of losing her breasts that she briefly thought about canceling the procedure and living out whatever time she had left. Perhaps another two to five years, maybe less. Angelique was anxious, trembling, and nearly on the edge of a panic attack, convinced her fans wouldn't love her anymore. But I told her that was ridiculous. Loyal fans — and one thing about *Star Trek* fans, they were extremely loyal — would want to see her healthy and happy once again.

Science had made such strides in medicine that breast cancer was no longer considered a death sentence for women. Similarly, breast reconstructive surgery had promised great results with all of the new options and procedures. Pettyjohn had opted to have reconstructive surgery performed at the same time as her mastectomy. Her doctor agreed with her decision and just reminded her that the recovery time was long, approximately three to four weeks.

At the hospital where Angelique was recovering from the double mastectomy and reconstructive surgery, the walls were covered with fan art; dozens of pen-and-ink drawings, lavish paintings, and comic book art depicting her as "Shahna-the Girl in the Silver Bikini." There was even a crude, stick-figure illustration little Jason from Maryland, now much older and healthier, had sent her, no doubt with help from his mother Rita. Pettyjohn smiled, with tears of joy in her eyes, showing off individual works, and telling me who they were from. She seemed to have remembered all of their names, even if I did not. The outpour of love and affection for this very special woman was truly heart-warming.

God bless the *Star Trek* fans for turning out in force to let her know she was still loved.

The Palomino Club and Circus Circus

When Angelique was finally released from the hospital, a job was waiting for her at the Palomino Club on North Las Vegas Boulevard. The world-famous Palomino Club was a real burlesque palace, the last of its kind in Vegas, perhaps even the United States. During its heyday in the sixties, when most strip joints in American cities were low-class dives where creeps and perverts hung out, the Palomino was decidedly upscale and classy, where women were comfortable among the mostly male clientele. Its amateur, all-nude dance contest welcomed women from all walks of life to realize their stripper fantasy. The Palomino Club was featured in *Playboy* magazine in 1979, and stayed the top Vegas club for 21 years until it was sold in 2000.

Pettyjohn's job at the Palomino Club was not on the dance stage stripping, but rather in the souvenir shop where she signed autographs, took photos with patrons, and entertained visitors with stories about the old days in Las Vegas. She was considered a genuine asset to the club, providing the right local flavor for both old and new alike. Although dancing was sorely missed, Angelique really enjoyed meeting new people every day. She was, after all, a people person, and loved entertaining.

In addition to her work at the Palomino Club, Pettyjohn was asked several times to fill-in for the Ringmaster of Ceremonies at Circus Circus, and those were pretty big shoes to fill. Clarence Hoffman, a veteran of the Chicago Opera, had been the Ringmaster there for more than thirty years, since the Casino's opening was broadcast live on the *Ed Sullivan Show* on October 18, 1968. At the opening, Hoffman set the standard for future ringmasters by shouting, with a big, booming voice, "Ladies and Gentlemen, introducing Circus Circus, the most exciting casino in the world! We proudly welcome the Flying Palacinis…" (Hoffman's larger-than-life character was played by Actor Don Messick in *Diamonds Are Forever*, 1971.)

Never one to shy away from fabulous opportunities like that, Pettyjohn stepped confidently into Hoffman's shoes and delivered an exciting rendition of her own, night after night until 2:00 a.m., when the acts finally came to a stop. She was regarded as the perfect Ring-mistress of Ceremonies on the nights when she performed there.

Angelique Pettyjohn's Death and Aftermath

On Valentine's Day, Friday, February 14, 1992, Angelique Pettyjohn (aka Dorothy Lee Perrins) died of cervical cancer. She was only forty-eight years old.

A few months earlier, while undergoing a routine follow-up with her doctor, she discovered she had terminal cancer. Cervical cancer is a type of cancer that occurs in the cells of the cervix, the lower part of the uterus that connects to the vagina. Doctors are still not clear (in 2020) what causes cervical cancer, but they all agree that certain strains of the human papillomavirus (HPV), which is a sexually transmitted infection, play a role. HPV is quite common, and most people with the virus never develop cancer. Other factors, such as the environment and lifestyle choices, may determine whether a woman will develop cervical cancer. Annual tests are recommended.

Pettyjohn told a few of her closest friends she was dying, in particular Joanne Loring (1946-), her next-door neighbor and friend. "She was the bravest woman I ever knew," Loring said, in an interview with *The Las Vegas Review-Journal*, February 17, 1992. During the last few weeks of Angelique's life, Loring gave up everything important in her own life so that she could care selflessly for her friend. "She went through hell. She really did. It was a real hard way to go."

A hastily-arranged memorial service was scheduled for March 4, 1992, at the Davis Funeral Home in Las Vegas. Several family members, a few co-workers and friends attended, including Loring, Steve Miller, Mike Christ, and Robert Scott Hooper. The service was delivered by friends.

Figure 179. Davis Funeral Home in Las Vegas.

Hooper said, “My wife [Theresa] and I were at her memorial service in 1992, and then later at her home [on Coconut Grove Court]. There were many people there that knew her very well. The hostess told everyone attending to go through her photographs and proof sheets and take some to remember her by. I looked through them, and most all of the pictures were ones I shot. I had them all in files at home, so I just left them for the others to have. She was such a big part of our life for so many years that she’ll be definitely missed.”

Loring remarked, “She was a star, but she didn’t act like it. She was as down-to-earth and wonderful as she could be, but she was a star in every way. She had the heart of a lion.”

Angelique Pettyjohn’s body was cremated, and her ashes were given to her two half-sisters, Diana Kay Bourgon of Las Vegas and Janice Marie Salazar of Salt Lake City, now both deceased as well. Angelique is survived by her nephew, Real Sean Bourgon, her niece, Kim Salazar, and her son Elvis Aaron Presley Junior.

Figure 180. Angelique's Memorial Booklet.

Turn Again to Life

If I should die and leave you
here a while,
Be not like others, sore undone,
who keep
Long vigil by the silent dust
and weep.
For my sake turn again to life
and smile,
Nerving thy heart and trembling hand
to do
That which will comfort other souls
than thine:
Complete these dear unfinished tasks
of mine.
And I, perchance, may therein
comfort you.

MARY LEE HALL

IN MEMORY OF

ANGELIQUE PETTYJOHN

MEMORIAL SERVICE
Davis Funeral Home
March 4, 1992 2:00 P.M.

Epilogue
The Legacy of Angelique Pettyjohn

I was fortunate enough to have done a variety of different things in my career. I headlined stage shows in Vegas, starred in movies opposite some of the biggest and brightest talent in Hollywood, and played on television on the highest-rated shows. I don't regret a single thing I did. It's been a hell-of-a good life. I wouldn't have changed a thing.

"The Girl in the Silver Bikini" lived her life on her own terms, with a great deal of class, dignity, respect, grace, and beauty. She wanted to be remembered as an entertainer, like the great entertainers she had loved growing up. And if one looks back over her thirty-year career on stage and screen, Pettyjohn achieved her goal, and then some. She was a woman unlike most women, not afraid to strip aside her façade to show the real beauty emanating within her. To me, she was more than just a Hollywood star, she was a cultural icon who came to represent a certain "era" that had long since passed into legend and obscurity.

Had Angelique survived her cancer, she would have turned seventy-seven on March 11, 2020. I doubt if she would have recognized much of Hollywood or Las Vegas, but she would have been pleased by the changes. Each was especially keen to her heart.

The "Me-Too" Movement

For years, Angelique Pettyjohn and other actresses her age had suffered sexual harassment and sexual assault at the hands of the studio bosses who ran Hollywood, as well as their casting agents and managers. Pettyjohn not only told me about the infamous "casting couch" nearly every executive had in his office, but she also revealed a number of incidents when she was assaulted by these men in power. I have documented a few of her stories in this book. The vulgarity they displayed towards her as a professional SAG member went far beyond anything that would have been considered "acceptable" today. The lewd comments about her 38-24-36 body, the forced kisses, the inappropriate gropes, and the abusive and often illegal behavior had taken its toll on her from an emotional and psychological point of view. She blamed herself and spent hours after each assault wrestling with a sense of guilt and shame. Had she somehow asked for it? Was she making a big deal out of nothing? Could she have done something different? She didn't dare report these incidents to the police for fear of retaliation, of being blackballed, of being fired from a job she desperately needed. So, Angelique cleaned herself up and went home, with the prayer it would never happen again. But it did. It happened throughout her career in Hollywood. She was one of the many, many victims who remained silent about the physical abuse for fear of reprisals and retribution from the studios.

In 1997, five years after Pettyjohn's death, Actress Ashley Judd was invited to a meeting with Harvey Weinstein, boss of the influential Miramax Films and The Weinstein Company, at the Peninsula Hotel in Beverly Hills. She thought they were going to discuss roles that might help launch her career, but he had a different agenda in mind. Weinstein had planned to sleep with her in exchange for consideration of certain movie parts. Offended by his clumsy attempts to coerce her into bed, Judd escaped his hotel room and went right to the lobby. But instead of remaining silent about Weinstein's inappropriate behavior, Judd started talking about it. She refused to be shamed into silence by his enormous power and prestige and began spreading the word.

On April 30, 2018, Ashley Judd sued Weinstein for allegedly making false statements about her because she rejected his sexual advances. She claimed those statements damaged her career and cost her a role in *The Lord of the Rings*.

Inspired by Judd, other women began to speak out. First, Rose McGowan brought harassment claims of her own. Then, Gwyneth Paltrow, Uma Thurman, Jennifer Lawrence, and Alyssa Milano spoke about the widespread prevalence of sexual assault and harassment in the workplace, not just Hollywood. Tarana Burke, an American social activist and community organizer, began using the phrase "Me Too" in 2006, and the phrase was adopted to encourage victims of sexual harassment to speak out about the problem.

"Empowerment through empathy" continues to inspire women today to share their stories with others, and to gain strength in numbers. Feminist author Gloria Feldt has revealed employers are now being forced to make changes in response to the "Me-too" movement. Those changes are not only transforming Hollywood and Vegas, but also the music industry, the sciences, politics, academia, financial institutions, the military, sports, and nearly every aspect of life.

Had Angelique lived beyond her 48th birthday, she would have not only supported the "Me-too" movement, but also have been a proponent of destroying the casting couch. During her lifetime, she spoke up, but her voice often fell on deaf ears. She would have felt vindicated by the actions of today's courts as they convict producers of rape and sexual assault.

In 2017, criminal investigations into complaints from at least a dozen women were launched against Harvey Weinstein in New York, Los Angeles, and London. A year later, in May 2018, Weinstein was arrested in New York, and charged with rape as well as other offenses. In February 2020, he was found guilty of rape in the third degree and a criminal sexual act, and subsequently, sentenced to 23 years of imprisonment. He now serves his time in Wende Correctional facility. Additional criminal charges were announced in 2020 by the Los Angeles County District Attorney. Weinstein is charged with one felony count of rape, and awaits his day in an LA court. To date, as this book goes to press, 95 women have spoken up and said they were sexually harassed or assaulted by Weinstein, and 15 women have accused Weinstein of rape.

Sex Addiction

Throughout her career, Angelique Pettyjohn also struggled with her addiction to alcohol, drugs, and sex. Most doctors and clinicians were quick to recognize her problems with substance abuse, offering her treatment and counseling, but dismissed her "addiction" to sex as nothing more than a compulsion to act out. They did not take her seriously. I had read Patrick Carnes' book *Out of the Shadows: Understanding Sexual Addiction* (1983) as part of my study to become a clinical psychologist. I recognized sex addiction was a growing problem mainstream literature and research had largely ignored.

Carnes characterized sexual addiction as a pattern of excessive and/or atypical sexual behavior through which certain people attempted to relieve deep-seated feelings of depression, frustration, anxiety, loneliness, or worthlessness with a sexual high. Most of those in his study claimed that their unhealthy use of sex had been a progressive process, starting with an addiction to masturbation, pornography, or casual sexual encounters, and soon lead to increasingly destructive behaviors. People who were sex addicts confessed to experiencing a sense of powerlessness, a belief that their lives were out of their control, and had profound feelings of shame, guilt, and self-loathing. While all expressed a desire to put an end to their behavior, very few had succeeded on their own, and most had failed repeatedly to break the cycle of addiction. The unmanageability of their lives had, in turn, created a whole new set of consequences for which they had to suffer; many facing divorce, separation, or the loss of relationships with their loved ones, arrest and public humiliation, or difficulty on the job. Others merely struggled with low self-esteem, feelings of hopelessness and despair, suicide, and sexually transmitted diseases (STDs); some of which became widely-known killers, like AIDS, and others that a person could never get rid of, like herpes or other serious viruses.

At the time of his study in 1983, Carnes asserted that one in twelve people in the United States was a sex addict, but the estimate in the nineties was considerably higher, in light of the growing annual rate (30%) of grass-roots organizations, treatment clinics, and counseling centers.

Seven different nationwide fellowships for sex addicts and their spouses, with such names as Sex Addicts Anonymous, Sexaholics Anonymous, Sex and Love Addicts Anonymous, and Sexual Compulsives Anonymous, held close to 2,000 meetings for sex addicts each and every week. Today, that number is even higher, with more than two hundred individual sites on the Internet providing FAQs (Frequently Asked Questions), personal confessions, discussion groups, and online referrals. Dozens of self-help books fill the shelves of bookstore chains, and scores of tests on sexual addiction and treatment programs offer professional help to the addict. In fact, the first in-patient program was started at Golden Valley Heath Center's Sexual Dependency Unit in Minneapolis in 1985. Today, referrals to local clinics and treatment centers are quite common. Sex addicts can even dial a 900-number (at the cost of $3.99 per minute) for information and referral to a counseling center.

Soon after Pettyjohn's death in 1992, and as a tribute to her legacy, I decided to write my doctoral dissertation about the problem of sexual addiction, specifically the etiology or cause of the disorder. My friend had suffered with the disorder most of her life, and yet there was so little known about the reasons why people become sex addicts. Numerous theories have been advanced to explain the causes for the disorder of sexual addiction. Some researchers have suggested that the problem of excessive or uncontrolled sexuality, as well as other sexual disorders, can be traced directly back to early childhood experiences. Others blame overly-zealous religious training, distorted cognitive sexual views, and poor sex education. Some cite reactions to moral and societal prejudices; others contend that certain individuals have a genetic predisposition to the disorder.

When my *Etiology of Sexual Addiction: The Significance of Childhood Trauma as a Primary Determinant* was published by Southern California University for Professional Studies in partial fulfillment of my Doctoral Degree in 1997, I suggested that childhood trauma was the primary determinant of sexual addiction. Childhood trauma included (but was not limited to) sexual, physical, or emotional abuse and victimization, divorce, abandonment, little affection or support (particularly in times of great need), the death of a parent or sibling, rigid and arbitrary family rules reinforced with harsh punishment, constant criticism, and conflicting or prohibitive messages about sex. I conducted a study among people who self-identified themselves as "sex addicts" and found nearly all of them had suffered from basic hostility and parental neglect, low self-esteem, and feelings of shame, guilt, and disgust. They all confessed to needing love from their parents who remained aloof and neglectful. I concluded that homes in which a child suffers from neglect or rejection, had a direct correlation between the child's feelings of shame, loneliness, and inadequacy to the lack of intimacy on the part of the parents. In all likelihood, Angelique Pettyjohn's issues with low self-esteem, drinking, and meaningless sex were all tied to never receiving love from the two people in her life who mattered the most, her mother and her father.

The Legend Lives On... Elvis Aaron Presley, Jr.

Angelique Pettyjohn's greatest legacy may well be her son, Elvis Aaron Presley, Jr. He looks a great deal like his father, Elvis, and travels around the country performing concerts with a rolling exhibit of rare and unique memorabilia, in The Private Collection of the King on Tour. With a whopping twenty-one DVDs and thirty-four CDs to his credit, he has a prolific recording career as well. I got to know him well while writing this book, and honestly, I can say I have never met a kinder, more humble, and truly gifted individual. Angelique would have been extremely proud of the man her son has become.

For several decades now, Elvis Aaron Presley Junior has been entertaining audiences all throughout the world with his incredible singing voice, naturally reminiscent of his father, The King. Most agree he has that rare capacity to establish a very special rapport with his audience. His fine sense of humor continues to thrill them as well. A gifted linguist, Junior also likes to surprise his many crowds by serenading them in their native tongue. He has appeared in 18 countries and 6 islands, sometimes performing in small, intimate clubs and then, at other times, in large concert halls. His performances have generated a prolific recording career. Copies of his CD's and DVD's are available through his website http://elvisaaronpresleyjr.com/index.html:

DVD's:

- **Live from Tokyo (**1996).
- **In Concert At the Whitby Arena** (1986).

CD's:

- **Destinations (**2010).
- **The Legend Lives On** (2010).
- **Live from Birmingham, Volume 1** (2010).
- **Pink Cadillac N' A Lot of Cash** (2010).
- **We All Nations** (2014).

Figure 181. Elvis Junior today.

DVD's and CD's are available for purchase. Albums or individual songs are available for purchase as a Mp3 download. Apparel and autographed photos are also available. Paypal accepted. Mention the name "Angelique" for special shipping.

Filmography

A complete list of her films and television shows:

Films:**

The Love Rebellion (1965). Cannon Productions, 87/71 min. Director and Writer: Joseph W. Sarno. Producer: Donald Havens. Cinematographer: Bruce G. Sparks. Film Editor: Kemper Peacock. Cast: Angelique (Pettyjohn), Melissa Ford, Alan Hoff, Barbara Johnson, Jeremy Langham, Nick Linikov, Gretchen Rudolph, Nadine Stark, Peggy Steffans, and Max Sydney.

Bad Girls Go to Hell (1965). Juri Productions/JER Pictures Inc/Sam Lake Enterprises Inc. 65/71min., B&W. Director and Producer: Doris Wishman. Writer: Doris Wishman (as Dawn Whitman). Cinematographer. C. Davis Smith. Film Editor: Ali Bendi. Cast: Gigi Darlene George La Rocque, Sam Stewart, Gertrude Cross, Alan Feinstein, Bernard L. Sackett, Darlene Bennett, Marlene Starr, Harold Key, and Angelique.

Another Day, Another Man (1966). Juri Productions/JER Pictures collaboration, 66 min, B&W. Director and Producer: Doris Wishman. Writer: Doris Wishman (as Dawn Whitman). Cinematographer: C. Davis Smith. Film Editor: Wishman. Cast: Gigi Darlene, Rita Bennett, Darlene Bennett, Tony Gregory, Barbara "Barbi" Kemp, Mary O'Hara, Bob Oran, June Roberts, Sam Stewart, and Angelique.

Clambake (1967). United Artists, 98min. Director: Arthur Nadel. Producer: Jules Levy, Arthur Gardner, and Arnold Laven. Writer: Arthur Browne, Jr. Cinematographer: William Margulies. Editor: Tom Rolf. Production Designer: Lloyd S. Papez. Cast: Elvis Presley, Shelley Fabares, Will Hutchins, Bill Bixby, Gary Merrill, James Gregory, Amanda Harley, Angelique Pettyjohn, and Suzie Kave.

Professor Lust (1967). Director: William Rose (as Werner Rose). Producer: Herbert Lannard. Cinematographer: William Rose (as Werner Rose). Cast: Janet Banzet, Angelique, Madison Arnold, Rita Bennett, Herbert Lannard, Jacqueline Michelin, and Larry Swenson.

The Touch of Her Flesh (aka *The Touch of Her Life, Way Out Love*, 1967). Rivamarch Productions, 78min. Director and Writer: Michael Findlay. Producers: Michael and Roberta Findlay. Cinematographer: Roberta Findlay (as Anna Riva). Film Editor: Michael Findlay (as Julian Marsh). Cast: Suzanne Marre, Angelique, Michael Findlay, Vivian Del Rio, Marre Lamont, Peggy Steffans, Ron Skiden, and Rit Dexter.

The Cool Ones (1967). Warner Brothers Pictures. 90 min. Director: Gene Nelson. Producer: Jimmy Lydon. Writers: Joyce Geller and Robert Kaufman. Cast: Roddy McDowall, Debbie Watson, Teri Garr, Gil Peterson, and Angelique Pettyjohn.

A Guide for the Married Man (1967). Twentieth Century-Fox, 89min. Director: Gene Kelly. Producer: Frank McCarthy. Writer: Frank Tarloff. Cinematographer: Joseph MacDonald. Film Editor: Dorothy Spencer. Cast: Walter Matthau, Inger Stevens, Sue Anne Langdon, Jackie Russell, Robert Morse, Aline Towne, Claire Kelly, Eve Brent, Majel Barrett, Linda Harrison, Darlene Tompkins, Delores Wells, and Angelique Pettyjohn. Cameos by Lucille Ball, Jack Benny, Joey Bishop, Sid Caesar, Art Carney, Wally Cox, Louis Nye, Jayne Mansfield, Terry-Thomas, Carl Reiner, and Phil Silvers.

Hotel (1967). Warner Brothers Pictures, 160 min. Director: Richard Quine. Producer and Writer: Wendell Mayes, based on the novel by Arthur Hailey. Cinematographer: Charles Lang. Editor: Sam O'Steen. Cast: Rod Taylor, Catherine Spaak, Karl Malden, Kevin McCarthy, Michael Rennie, Melvyn Douglas, and Angelique Pettyjohn.

The President's Analyst (1967). Paramount Pictures. 100 min. Director and Writer: Theodore J. Flicker. Producer: Stanley Rubin. Cinematographer; William A. Fraker. Editor: Stuart H. Pappé. Cast: James Coburn, Godfrey Cambridge, Severn Darden, Joan Delaney, and Angelique Pettyjohn.

Rough Night in Jericho (1967). Universal Pictures, 100 min. Director: Arnold Laven. Producer: Martin Rackin. Writers: Sydney Boehm and Marvin Albert, based upon his novel. Cinematographer: Russell Metty. Editor: Ted J. Kent. Cast: Dean Martin, George Peppard, Jean Simmons, John McIntire, Slim Pickens, and Angelique Pettyjohn.

Cargo of Love (1968). Director: Anton Holden. Producer: Charles Abrams. Cast: Sheila Britt, Gloria Irizarry, Tony Pascal, Sam Stewart, William Countryman, Barbara Wallace, Charles Abrams, Jean Parker, and Angelique Pettyjohn.

Hell's Belles (1969). American International Pictures, 98 min. Director: Maury Dexter. Producer: Robert George. Writers: James Gordon White and Robert McMullen. Cinematographer: Ken Peach. Editor: James Gordon White. Cast: Jeremy Slate, Adam Roarke, Jocelyn Lane, Angelique Pettyjohn, Bill Lucking, and Eddie Hice.

For Singles Only (1968). Four-Leaf Productions, 90 min. Director and Producer: Arthur Dreifuss. Writers: Hal Collins and Arthur Dreifuss. Cast: John Saxon, Mary Ann Mobley, Lana Wood, Peter Mark Richman, Ann Elder, Molly Bee, Lara Harris, and Angelique Pettyjohn.

The Odd Couple (1968). Paramount Pictures, 100 min. Director: Gene Saks. Producer: Gene Saks. Writer: Neil Simon, based upon his play. Cinematographer: Robert B. Hauser. Editor: Frank Bracht. Cast: Jack Lemmon, Walter Matthau, John Fiedler, Herb Edelman, and Angelique Pettyjohn.

Where Were You When the Lights Went Out? (1968). Metro-Goldwyn-Mayer, 89min. Director: Hy Averback. Producers: Everett Freeman and Martin Melcher. Writers: Claude Magnier, Everett Freeman, and Karl Tunberg. Cinematographer: Ellsworth Fredericks. Film Editor: Rita Roland. Cast: Doris Day, Lola Albright, Robert Morse, Terry-Thomas, Patrick O'Neal, Steve Allen, Jim Backus, Pat Paulsen, Earl Wilson, Morgan Freeman, James McEachin, and Angelique Pettyjohn.

The Mad Doctor of Blood Island (aka *Tomb of the Living Dead*, 1968). USA and Philippines, 110min. Directors: Gerardo DeLeon and Eddie Romero. Producer: Sam Sherman. Writer: Reuben Canoy. Cinematographer: Justo Paulino. Cast: Angelique Pettyjohn, Alicia Alonzo, John Ashley, Ronald Remy, and Ronaldo Valdez.

Childish Things (aka: *Confessions of Tom Harris, Tale of the Cock*, 1969). Filmworld Productions, 98min. Directors: John Derek and David Nelson. Producers: Don Murray and Jeffrey M. Sneller. Writer: Don Murray. Cinematographer: John Derek. Production Design: Jonathan Haze. Editor: Maurice Wright. Art Director: Fernando Valento. Cast: Don Murray, George Atkinson, Gypsy Boots, David Brian, Gary Clark, Linda Evans, Claire Kelly, Angelique Pettyjohn, Jack Griffin, Eric Holland, Leroy Jenkins, Don Joslyn, Rod Lauren, Gene LeBell, and Logan Ramsey.

Heaven with a Gun (1969). Metro-Goldwyn-Mayer, 90 min. Director: Lee H. Katzin. Producers: Frank King and Maurice King. Writer: Richard Carr. Cinematographer: Johnny Mandel. Editor: Herman King. Cast: Glenn Ford, Carolyn Jones, Barbara Hershey, John Anderson, David Carradine, J. D. Cannon, William Bryant, and Angelique Pettyjohn.

The Love God? (1969). Universal Pictures, 88 min. Director: Nat Hiken. Producer: Edward Montagne. Writer: Nat Hiken. Cinematographer: William Margulies. Editor: Sam E. Waxman.

Cast: Don Knotts, James Gregory, Edmond O'Brien, Anne Francis, and Angelique Pettyjohn.

Tell Me that you Love Me, Junie Moon (1970). Paramount Pictures, 98 min. Producer, Director: Otto Preminger. Writer: Marjorie Kellogg, from her novel. Cast: Liza Minnelli, Kay Thompson, Emily Yancy, Julie Bovasso, Angelique Pettyjohn, Ken Howard, Robert Moore, James Coco, and Fred Williamson.

The Seduction of a Nerd (aka: *Up Your Teddy Bear, Mother*, 1970). 90 min. Director, Producer, Writer: Don Joslyn Cinematographer: Robert Maxwell. Film Editor: John Levin. Cast: Julie Newmar, Claire Kelly, Valora Noland, Angelique Pettyjohn, Wally Cox, and Victor Buono.

The Curious Female (aka *Love, Computer Style*, 1970). Fanfare Film Productions, Inc., 87min. Director and Producer: Paul Rapp. Writer: Winston R. Paul. Cinematographer: Don Birnkrant. Film Editor: Reg Browne. Set Designer: Ray Boltz. Cast: Angelique Pettyjohn, Charlene Jones, Bunny Allister, David Westberg, Julie Conners, Michael Greer, Sebastian Brook, Ron Gans, David Pritchard, Slim Gaillard, Elaine Edwards, and Carol-Jean Thompson.

The G.I. Executioner (aka *Dragon Lady*, *Wit's End*, 1975). 21st Century Film Corporation, 83 min. Director: Joel Reed. Producer: Jason Garfield. Writer: Ian Ward, based upon a short story by Keith Lorenz. Cinematographer: Marin Farkas. Editor: Joel Reed. Cast: Vicki Racimo, Janet Wood, Angelique Pettyjohn, Brian Walden, Peter Gernert, Walter Hill, Jonathan Grant, Tom Kenna, and Anna Ling.

Bordello (1974). Cast: Angelique Pettyjohn.

Going in Style (1979). Warner Brothers, 97min. Director: Martin Brest. Producers: Tony Bill and Fred Gallo. Writers: Edward Cannon and Martin Brest. Cinematographer: Billy Williams.

Film Editors: Carroll Timothy O'Meara and Robert Swink. Cast: George Burns, Art Carney, Lee Strasberg, Charles Hallahan, Pamela Payton-Wright, Brian Neville, and Angelique Pettyjohn.

Stalag 69 (1982). VCN Productions, 87 min. Director, Producer: Selrahc Detrevrep. Cinematographer: J.B. Mallin. Film Editor: Bella Forlan. Cast: Dorothy LeMay, Angelique Pettyjohn, Madge Gande, Kathy Melodi, Gene Culot, and Stacy Evans.

Titillation (1982). Select/Essex, 80 min. Director: Damon Christian. Writer: John Finegold. Cinematographer: Giudo Jewalucci. Film Editor: Terrance O'Reilly. Cast: Kitten Natividad, Heaven St. John (aka Angelique Pettyjohn), Gina Gianetti, Sandra Miller, Shery Carter, Eric Edwards, Randy West, Mike Horner, Mike Zempter, and Roy Simpson.

Body Talk (1984). VCX Productions, 81 min. Director: Pedie Sweet. Producer: Robert Holcomb. Film Editor: Pearl Diamond. Cast: Angelique Pettyjohn, Kay Parker, Steven Tyler, Randy West, Don Hart, Amber Rae, Steven Tyler, and Billy Dee.

Takin' It Off (1985). 90 min. Director: Ed Hansen. Cast: Angelique Pettyjohn, John Alderman, Paul Hampton, Gail Harris, Becky Le Beau, Ashley St. John, Kitten Natividad, and Jean Proemba.

Good-bye Cruel World (1983). 100min. MSM Productions. Director: David Irving. Producers: Louis Sardonis and Leo Zahn. Writers: Nicholas Niciphor and Dick Shawn. Cinematographer: Jerry Hartleben. Film Editors: Marshall Harvey and Rob Smith. Cast: Dick Shawn, Cynthia Sikes, Pierre Jalbert, Pamela Brull, LaWanda Page, Marius Mazmanian, Priscilla Pointer, Chuck Mitchell, Darrell Larson, Harris Kal, Wendy Shawn, and Angelique Pettyjohn.

Repo Man (1984). Universal Pictures, 92 min. Director, Writer: Alex Cox. Producer: Peter McCarthy. Film Editor: Dennis Dolan.

Cinematographer: Robby Muller. Cast: Olivia Barash, Susan Barnes, Angelique Pettyjohn, Emilio Estevez, Harry Dean Stanton, Tracey Walter, Tom Finnegan, Eddie Velez, and Del Zamora.

Biohazard (1985). 84 min. Director, Producer: Fred Olen Ray. Writers: Fred Olen Ray, T.L. Lankford, and Miriam Preissel. Cinematographer: Paul Elliott. Editor: Jay Tucker. Cast: Aldo Ray, Angelique Pettyjohn, William Fair, Richard Hench, David O'Hara, Frank McDonald, and Carroll Borland.

Famous Ta-Tas (1986). Essex Video Classics, 84 min. Compilation Video. Cast: Christy Canyon, Kitten Natividad, Rachel Ashley, Colleen Brennan, Honey Wilder, Lee Carroll, Mindy Rae, Holly McCall, Angelique Pettyjohn, Eric Edwards, John Leslie, and Tom Byron.

The Lost Empire (1984). JGM Enterprises, 100 min. Director/Writer: Jim Wynorski. Producers: Wynorski, Bob Greenberg, and Alexander Tabrizi. Cinematographer: Jacques Haitkin. Editor: Larry Bock. Cast: Angela Aames, Raven de la Croix, Melanie Vincz, Linda Shayne, Angelique Pettyjohn, Paul Coufos, Robert Tessier, Kenneth Tobey, and Angus Scrimm.

Sex Game (1986). Essex Video Classics, 84 min. Compilation Video. Cast: Taija Rae, Tish Ambrose, Annette Haven, Barbara Dare, Elle Rio, Erica Boyer, Hyapatia Lee, and Angelique Pettyjohn.

Jo Jo Dancer, Your Life is Calling (1986). Columbia, 97min. Director and Producer: Richard Pryor. Writers: Rocco Urbisci and Paul Mooney. Cinematographer: John Alonzo. Film Editor: Donn Cambern. Production Designer: John DeCuir. Cast: Richard Pryor, Debbie Allen, Art Evans, Fay Hauser, Barbara Williams, Paula Kelly, Wings Hauser, Michael Ironside, J.J. Barry, Dennis Farina, Frederick Coffin, Ken Foree, Cheri Wells, and Angelique Pettyjohn.

The Wizard of Speed and Time (1988). Jittlov/Kay Productions, 95 min. Director: Mike Jittlov. Producers, Writers: Mike Jittlov, Richard Kaye, and Deven Chierrighino. Cinematographer: Russell Carpenter. Editor: Mike Jittlov. Cast: Paige Moore, Amertia Walker, Mike Jittlov, Angelique Pettyjohn, Deven Chierrighino, Steve Brodie, John Massari, and Richard Kay.

Sorority Girls and the Creature from Hell (1990). Director, Producer: John McBrearty. Writers: John and Lynn McBrearty. Cinematographer: Vincent Ellis. Editors: Ellis and Ellen Keneshea. Cast: Len Lesser, Deborah Dutch, Eric Clark, Carl Johnson, Douglas Koth, Gloria Hylton, Angelique Pettyjohn (as Ashley St. Jon).

Television Appearances:

Get Smart! (1967). Episode 2.22 — "Smart Fit the Battle of Jericho" (2/18/1967). Show created by Mel Brooks and Buck Henry. Director Bruce Bilson. Writer: Arne Sultan.
Cast: Don Adams, Barbara Feldon, Edward Platt, Stacy Keach, William Chapman, and Angelique Pettyjohn as Cigarette girl/Agent Charlie Watkins. Episode 2.27 — "Pussycats Galore" (4/1/1967). Show created by Mel Brooks and Buck Henry. Director Bruce Bilson. Writer: Arne Sultan.
Cast: Don Adams, Barbara Feldon, Edward Platt, Ted Knight, and Angelique Pettyjohn as Cigarette girl/Agent Charlie Watkins.

Batman (1967). Episode 2.51 - "A Piece of the Action" (3/1/1967). Director: Oscar Rudolph. Developer: Lorenzo Semple, Jr. Writer: Charles Hoffman. Cast: Adam West, Burt Wards, Dusty Cadis, Roger C. Carmel, Seymour Cassel, Bruce Lee, Van Williams, Jay Watkins, Alex Rocco, Diane McBain, and Angelique Pettyjohn.

The Green Hornet (1967). Episode 1.18 — "Corpse of the Year: Part 1" (1/13/1967). Producer: William Dozier. Cast: Van Williams, Bruce Lee, Walter Brooke, Lloyd Gough, Wende

Wagner, Nora Marlowe, Barbara Babcock, and Angelique Pettyjohn.

Felony Squad (1967). Episode 1.24 — "Target!" (2/20/1967). Director: Allen Reisner. Writer: Frank L. Moss, Tony Barrett, and Frank Moss. Cast: Howard Duff, Dennis Cole, Steve Inhat, Will Kuluva, Angelique Pettyjohn, Jason Wingreen, and Frank Maxwell.

The Girl from U.N.C.L.E. (1967). Episode 1.27 — "The Samurai Affair" (3/28/1967). Director: Alf Kjellin. Producer: Douglas Benton. Writer: Tony Barrett. Cast: Stefanie Powers, Noel Harrison, Leo G. Carroll, Randy Kirby, Signe Hasso, James McCallion, Richard Roat, Michael J. Pollard, and Angelique Pettyjohn.

Mr. Terrific (1967). Episode 1.3 — "I Can't Fly" (1/23/1967). Director, Producer: Jack Arnold. Producer, Developer: Budd Grossman. Cast: Stephen Strimpell, John McGiver, Dick Gautier, Paul Smith, and Angelique Pettyjohn.

Star Trek (1968). Episode 2.16 — "The Gamesters of Triskelion (1/5/1968). Director: Gene Nelson. Writer: Margaret Arman. Producer: Gene Roddenberry. Cast: William Shatner, Leonard Nimoy, Nichelle Nichols, Walter Koenig, DeForest Kelly, George Takei, Angelique Pettyjohn, Joseph Ruskin (Galt), Jane Ross (Tamoon), Steve Sandor (Lars), Dick Crockett (Andorian), and Mickey Morton (Kloog).

Good Morning, World (1968). Episode 1.24 — "Here Comes the Bribe" (2/27/1968). Producers: Bill Persky and Sam Denoff. Cast: Joby Baker, Ronnie Schell, Julie Parrish, Billy De Wolfe, Goldie Hawn, and Angelique Pettyjohn.

Love, American Style (1969). Episode 1.5a — "Love and the Modern Wife" (10/27/1969). Director: Alan Rafkin. Producer:

William P. D'Angelo. Writer: Allan Burns. Cast: Bob Crane, Patricia Crowley, Elena Verdugo, and Angelique Pettyjohn.

Bracken's World (1969). Episode 1.8 — "Don't You Cry for Susannah" (10/10/1969). Director: Allen Reisner. Writer: Oliver Hailey. Cast: Eleanor Parker, Dennis Cole, Peter Haskell, Elizabeth Allen, Linda Harrison, Laraine Stephens, Karen Jensen, and Angelique Pettyjohn.

Bracken's World (1969). Episode 1.12 — "Move in for a Close-Up" (12/12/1969). Director: Allen Reisner. Writer: Oliver Hailey. Cast: Eleanor Parker, Dennis Cole, Peter Haskell, Elizabeth Allen, Linda Harrison, Laraine Stephens, Karen Jensen, Madlyn Rhue, Kathleen Hughes, Peter Donat, and Angelique Pettyjohn.

Hill Street Blues (1984). Episode 5.5 — "Bangladesh Slowly (11/1/1984). Director Rick Wallace. Writers: Jeffrey Lewis, David Milch, and Roger Director. Cast: Daniel J. Travanti, Veronica Hamel, Charles Haid, Taurean Blacque, Bruce Weitz, Joe Spano, and Angelique Pettyjohn.

Hill Street Blues (1984). Episode 5.6 — "Ewe and Me, Babe" (11/8/1984). Director: Jeff Bleckner. Writers: David Stenn and Floyd Byars. Cast: Daniel J. Travanti, Veronica Hamel, Charles Haid, Taurean Blacque, Bruce Weitz, Joe Spano, and Angelique Pettyjohn.

**While thoroughly researching Angelique Pettyjohn's life over the last twenty-eight years, I found contradictions between social media websites, including Wikipedia, and established facts in her life. Two films, for example, claim she played uncredited roles. *Sabaleros (aka Put Up, Shut Up, 1959),* an Argentinean film by Armando Bo, states erotic scenes with Angelique were added. *The Phantom Planet* (1961) states Angelique played a juror. I was unable to substantiate either claim, but I welcome details for a "second" edition of this book.

Appendix 1: Angelique Pettyjohn and Her Roles

Film	Year	Character	Type
Sorority Girls and the Creature from Hell	1990	"Girl at the Bar"	Movie
The Wizard of Speed and Time	1988	Dora Belair	Movie
Jo Jo Dancer, Your Life is Calling	1986	Roxanne Rolle	Movie
Sex Game	1986	Uncredited	Movie
Biohazard	1985	Lisa Martyn	Movie
Famous Ta-Tas	1985	Uncredited	Movie
Takin' It Off	1985	Anita Little	Movie
Body Talk	1984	Cassie	Movie
Hill Street Blues	1984	Lotta Gue	TV
The Lost Empire	1984	Whiplash	Movie
Repo Man	1984	Repo Wife #2	Movie
Good-bye Cruel World	1983	Stripping Nun	Movie
Stalag 69	1982	Nazi Interrogator	Movie
Titillation	1982	Brenda Weeks	Movie
Going in Style	1979	"Girl at the Crap Table"	Movie
G.I. Executioner	1975	Bonnie	Movie
Bordello	1974	Uncredited	Movie
Seduction of the Nerd	1970	Miss Honeysuckle	Movie
Tell Me That You Love Me, Junie Moon	1970	Melissa	Movie
The Curious Female	1970	Susan Rome	Movie
The Love God?	1969	Model	Movie
Childish Things	1969	Angelique	Movie
Heaven with a Gun	1969	Emily	Movie
Bracken's World	1969	Elizabeth "Ellie" Plover	TV
Hell's Belles	1969	Cherry	Movie
Love, American Style	1969	"Girl at the Bar"	TV

Cargo of Love	1968	Prostitute	Movie
For Singles Only	1968	Apartment hunter	Movie
Good Morning World	1968	Mitzi	TV
Mad Doctor of Blood Island	1968	Sheila Willard	Movie
The Odd Couple	1968	Go-Go Dancer	Movie
Star Trek	1968	Shahna	TV
Where Were You When the Lights Went Out?	1968	"Girl on Subway Platform"	Movie
A Guide to the Married Man	1967	"Girl on Wilshire Blvd."	Movie
Batman	1967	1st Model	TV
Clambake	1967	Gloria	Movie
The Cool Ones	1967	"Girl on Tony's Staff"	Movie
Felony Squad	1967	Felicia Majeski	TV
Get Smart!	1967	Charlie Watkins	TV
The Girl from U.N.C.L.E.	1967	Cora Sue	TV
The Green Hornet	1967	Girl	TV
Hotel	1967	1st Stripper	Movie
Mister Terrific	1967	Carol	TV
The President's Analyst	1967	Uncredited	Movie
Professor Lust	1967	Uncredited	Movie
Rough Night in Jericho	1967	Prostitute	Movie
The Touch of Her Flesh	1967	Claudia	Movie
Another Day, Another Man	1966	Uncredited	Movie
Bad Girls Go to Hell	1965	Uncredited	Movie
The Love Rebellion	1965	Pam Carpenter	Movie

After her death in 1992, she appeared via archival footage in two compilation films:

Chubby Chicks Need Cock, Too	2013	Uncredited	Movie
Classic Tits Galore	2013	Uncredited	Movie

Appendix 2: Press Release* for "The Gamesters of Triskelion"

NBC-TV PROGRAM HIGHLIGHT MAY 3

STAR TREK: "The Gamesters of Triskelion." Captain Kirk and part of his crew become the prisoners of brain masses. (Color. Repeat.)

Captain Kirk (William Shatner), Lt. Uhura (Nichelle Nichols) and Ensign Chekov (Walter Koenig) are taken prisoners by highly developed masses of brains without bodies, in "The Gamesters of Triskelion" on NBC Television Network's "Star Trek" colorcast Friday, May 3 (8:30 to 9:30 p.m. NYT; repeat of Jan. 5, 1968).

During the transporting process, the three are forced down on a planet of slaves called Thralls, who exist solely for the benefit of the brain masses, called Providers. Their only diversion is to watch and gamble on combat to the death among humans. Galt (guest star John Ruskin), the master Thrall, assigns drill Thralls to train the three officers for combat. Shanna (guest star Angelique PettyJohn) is assigned to Kirk and falls in love with him. Mr. Spock (Leonard Nimoy) and Dr. McCoy (DeForest Kelley) locate the missing trio, beam down to help and are seized. Kirk then challenges the Providers to a daring wager.

-----o-----

NBC-New York, 4/17/68

***The errors belong to NBC.**

Appendix 3: Letter from John C. Harris to Elvis Aaron Presley Junior

UNITED AMERICAN PICTURES

Executive Director
JOHN C. HARRIS

Dear Elvis Jr.:

It was a pleasure working with you on the Hawaiian documentary. Elvis, I have never told you this but I think I should because I am getting a little older and your career is starting to blossom. The reason I wanted you in my pictures is because I knew you were the son of Elvis Presley Sr. and because I worked with Angelique Dolores Pettyjohn. And, Angelique told me that she was your mother and that your father was indeed the great Elvis Presley Sr.

I was going to film a film entitled, "The King of Burlesque" starring Benny Hill and Angelique Pettyjohn. During many conversations I had with Angelique, she told me about her son who was the son of Elvis Presley. And, she wanted to meet you but was terrified of Colonel Parker for some reason. I don't want to say anything bad about Colonel Parker as we were friends, yet he had many ways to silence any adverse publicity against Elvis Presley who was his main source of income. When I worked with Jayne Mansfield, I also would keep her image as a saint. I did the same with all the celebrities I worked with, and I worked with many. I don't want you to be angry at the Colonel.

The Colonel and I had discussed you on many occasions and I felt the need to talk to you to assure you that I know you are the son of Elvis Presley Sr. And, your father was a great entertainer and you are following in his footsteps.

Wishing you all the best.

Sincerely yours,

John C Harris 11. 16 99

John Harris

5460 WHITE OAK AVE. SUITE E321 ENCINO, CALIF. 91316 TEL. (818) 7620498

Appendix 4: Notary Document for the John C. Harris Letter

CALIFORNIA ALL-PURPOSE ACKNOWLEDGMENT

State of California
County of LOS ANGELES } ss.

On NOV. 16, 1999 (Date), before me, JANE M. GARCIA (Name and Title of Officer (e.g., "Jane Doe, Notary Public"))
personally appeared JOHN HARRIS (Name(s) of Signer(s))

☒ personally known to me
☐ proved to me on the basis of satisfactory evidence

to be the person(s) whose name(s) is/are subscribed to the within instrument and acknowledged to me that he/she/they executed the same in his/her/their authorized capacity(ies), and that by his/her/their signature(s) on the instrument the person(s), or the entity upon behalf of which the person(s) acted, executed the instrument.

JANE M. GARCIA
Commission # 1224972
Notary Public - California
Los Angeles County
My Comm. Expires Jun 18, 2003

Place Notary Seal Above

WITNESS my hand and official seal.

J. Garcia
Signature of Notary Public

OPTIONAL

Though the information below is not required by law, it may prove valuable to persons relying on the document and could prevent fraudulent removal and reattachment of this form to another document.

Description of Attached Document
Title or Type of Document: LETTER OF REFENCE
Document Date: NOV. 16, 1999 Number of Pages: 1
Signer(s) Other Than Named Above: NONE

Capacity(ies) Claimed by Signer
Signer's Name:
☐ Individual
☐ Corporate Officer — Title(s):
☐ Partner — ☐ Limited ☐ General
☐ Attorney in Fact
☐ Trustee
☐ Guardian or Conservator
☐ Other:

Signer Is Representing:

RIGHT THUMBPRINT OF SIGNER
Top of thumb here

Selected Bibliography

Books:

Ackerman, Forrest J., editor. *Famous Monsters of Filmland* Magazine. Philadelphia: Warren Publishing, 1958.

__________. *Monsterland* Magazine, nos. 1-6. Los Angeles, California: New Media Publishing, 1986.

Aldiss, Brian W. *Billion Year Spree: The True History of Science Fiction*. New York: Schocken Books, 1973.

Alexander, Andrew. *We Were Scotty and Bones: James Doohan and DeForest Kelley*. Amazon LLC, 2016.

__________. I Was Spock: Leonard Nimoy. Amazon LLC, 2015.

Andrews, Nigel. *Horror Films*. New York: Gallery Books, 1985.

Aylesworth, Thomas G. *Monsters from the Movies*. New York: Bantam Books, 1972.

Baxter, John. *Science Fiction in the Cinema*. New York: Paperback Library, 1970.

Burbank, Jeff. *Lost Las Vegas*. New York: Pavilion, 2014.

Butler, Ivan. *Horror in the Cinema*. New York: Paperback Library, 1971.

Carnes, Patrick J. *Out of the Shadows: Understanding Sexual Addiction*. Hazelden Publishing, 2001.

Chung, Su Kim. *Las Vegas, Then and Now*. Pavilion, 2016.

Clark, Mark and David Gerrold. *Star Trek FAQ: Everything Left to Know about the First Voyages of the Starship Enterprise*. Applause, 2012.

Clute, John and Peter Nicholls. *The Encyclopedia of Science Fiction*. New York: St. Martin's Press, 1993.

Cohen, Daniel. *Horror in the Movies*. New York: Houghton Mifflin Company, Inc, 1982.

Doohan, James, with Peter David. *Beam Me Up, Scotty*. NY: Pocket Books, 1996.

"Entertainer, Actress Dies." *The Las Vegas Review-Journal*, February 17, 1992.

Fern, Yvonne. *Gene Roddenberry: The Last Conversation*. Berkeley: University of California Press, 1994.

Flynn, John L. *75 Years of Universal Monsters*. Maryland: Galactic Books, 2006.

___________. *Dissecting Aliens*. Maryland: Galactic Books, 2006.

___________. *Etiology of Sexual Addiction: The Significance of Childhood Trauma as a Primary Determinant.* Southern California University: Doctoral Dissertation, 1997.

___________, and Bob Blackwood. *Everything I Know about Life I Learned from James Bond*. New York: Library Tales, 2015.

Forshaw, B. *Sex and Film: The Erotic in British, American and World Cinema*. Pan-Macmillan, 2015

Halliwell, Leslie. *Halliwell's Film Guide.* New York: Scribner's, 1984.

Hamilton, Carolyn V. *Coming to Las Vegas: A True Tale of Sex, Drugs & Sin City in the 70's.* Swift House Press, 2014.

Hopwood, Jon C. "Angelique Pettyjohn." *Super Strange Video*. Retrieved 2009-01-01.

Hosoda, Craig. *The Bare Facts Video Guide*. Santa Clara, CA: Bare Facts, 1998.

Huss, Roy Gerard. *Focus on the Horror Film*. NY: Prentice-Hall, 1972.

Justman, Robert H. and Herbert Solow. *Inside Star Trek: The Real Story*. New York: Pocket Books, 1996.

Koenig, Walter. *Warped Factors.* New York: Taylor Publishing, 1998.

Lichtenberg, Jacqueline, Sondra Marshak, and Joan Winston. *Star Trek Lives!* New York: Bantam Books, 1975.

Lisanti, Tom. "Angelique Pettyjohn." *Drive-in Dream Girls: A Galaxy of B-movie Starlets of the Sixties*. North Carolina: McFarland, 2003.

Maltin, Leonard. *Leonard Maltin's Movie and Video Guide*. New York: Signet Publishers, 1994.

Martinko, Jason S. *The XXX Filmography, 1968-1988*. North Carolina: McFarland, 2013.

Mondon, Karl. *Las Vegas: Then and Now*. New York: Pavilion, 2018.

Nash, Alanna. *Baby, Let's Play House: Elvis Presley and the Women Who Loved Him*. It Books, 2010.

Newcomb, Horace, ed. *Encyclopedia of Television*. NY: Routledge, 1997.

Nichols, Nichelle. *Beyond Uhura: Star Trek and Other Memories*. New York: G.P. Putnam's Sons, 1994.

Nimoy, Leonard. *I Am Spock*. New York: Hachette Books, 2014.

Pohl, Frederick. *Science Fiction Studies in Film*. NY: Ace Books, 1981.

Rioux, Terry Lee. *From Sawdust to Stardust: The Biography of DeForest Kelley, Star Trek's Dr. McCoy*. NY: Gallery Books, 2005.

Ruditis, Paul. *The Star Trek Book: Strange New Worlds Boldly Explained.* Penguin Group, 2016.

Schumacher, Geoff. Sun, *Sin & Suburbia: The History of Modern Las Vegas,* Revised. University of Nevada Press, 2015.

Settel, Irving. *A Pictorial History of Television.* New York: Frederick Ungar, 1983.

Shatner, William, and Chris Kreski. *Star Trek Memories*. NY: HarperCollins, 1993.

________________. *Leonard: My 50-year Friendship with a Remarkable Man*. NY: Thomas Dunne Books, 2016.

Simone, Sophia. *Fun and Interesting Facts about Las Vegas: A Captivating Picture Photography Coffee Table Photobook Travel Tour Guide Book with Brief History*. Independently published, 2020.

Summers, Dusty. *The Magical World of Burlesque.* Infinity Publishing, 2014.

Takei, George. *To the Stars: The Autobiography of George Takei.* Gallery Books, 2015.

Terrance, Vincent. *Complete Encyclopedia of Television Programs*. New York: A.S. Barnes, 1979.

Zoglin, Richard. *Elvis in Vegas: How the King Reinvented the Las Vegas Show*. Simon Schuster, 2019.

Websites:
www.elvisaaronpresleyjr.com (2018-11-28) "Elvis Aaron Presley, Jr.: The Legend Lives On..." Retrieved 2018-11-28
GetSmartCONTROL (2008-11-28), *Get Smart: Scenes from "Pussycats Galore."* retrieved 2017-12-27
Memory-alpha.fandom.com/wiki/StarTrek.com (2020-04-07) "Memory Alpha: Star Trek Continuum."
www.startrek.com (2020-04-07) The Official *Star Trek* website.
en.wikipedia.org/wiki/Angelique_Pettyjohn (2018-03-11) Wikipedia entry for Angelique Pettyjohn

Films:
American Grindhouse: The History of the American Exploitation Film. Narrated by Robert Forster. Director: Elijah Drenner. Gravitas Ventures, LLC, 2010.
Finding the Future: A Science Fiction Conversation. Narrated by Casey Moore. Producers: Joseph Formichella, Casey Moore, and Michael R. Pryor. Director: Casey Moore. Anomalous Entertainment, 2006.

Pictorials:

Celebrity Sleuth (USA)	1993, Vol. 6, Issue 4, pg. 26-29, by: staff, "Sequels Without Equal: Angelique Pettyjohn, Star Trek, R.I.P."
Celebrity Sleuth (USA)	1989, Vol. 3, Issue 2, pg. 8-9, by: staff, "Star Trek – Shahna"
Celebrity Sleuth (USA)	1986, Vol. 1, Issue 2, pg. 54-55, by: staff, "Star Trek's Angelique Pettyjohn"
Playboy (USA)	February 1979, Vol. 26, Issue 2, pg. 131, R.S. Hooper, "The Girls Of Las Vegas"

Puritan Issue #12 (1984)

Vegas Visitor 7 Aug. 1970: P1

Vegas Visitor 22 Sep. 1978. P1

Acknowledgments

I have spent the last twenty-eight years of my life writing this book, or should I say, this love letter to Angelique Pettyjohn, a woman whose kindness, generosity and strength of character touched my life during the last ten years of hers. We were friends, never lovers or business partners. I did love her in my own way, and that love continues even to this day as I put the final touches on this tribute to her indomitable spirit.

In 1992, a few weeks before her death, Angelique made me promise to tell her story, warts and all, and now, I feel as if I have fulfilled that promise. She was loved by millions of fans worldwide, and this book is dedicated to all those who also loved her in their own way, too.

The completion of this book would not have been possible without the participation and assistance of so many people whose names may not all be enumerated here. Their contributions are sincerely appreciated and gratefully acknowledged: Forrest J. Ackerman, Majel Barrett, Diana Bourgon, Marilyn Chambers, Michael Christ, Sara Cooper, James Doohan, Dr. Fred Eichelman, Natalia Franklin, Pat Gill, Jim Highley, Theresa Holmes, Robert Scott Hooper, Darlene Jensen, Joanne Loring, Mark Lenard, David McDonnell, Rick Melton, Steve Miller, Leonard Nimoy, Kerry O'Quinn, Janice Salazar, William Shatner, Matt Sherman, Eleanor Spencer, and of course Angelique Pettyjohn herself who spent countless hours of her last ten years telling me her story.

I wish to express my sincere gratitude to Elvis Aaron Presley, Jr., for his friendship and encouragement to tell his mother's story, and my agent, Jeanie Loiacono.

Thanks must also go to my family: my brother, Bob Flynn, my sister, Jackie Johnston, my late mother, Norma Jean, and stepfather, James Hazelgrove, both of whom met Angelique in 1984, and my grandparents Norman and Angeline Gertsen.

I am also indebted to my extended family of *Star Trek* fans in whose company I found a home in 1972. I have spent nearly the last fifty years living among the most gifted and intelligent people on the planet: Lenny Provenzano, Allan Batson, George Lawrence, Rich Kolker, Al Schuster, Joan Winston, Elyse Rosenstein, Devra Langsam, Allan Asherman, Heather Nachman, Marion McChesney, Geraldine Sylvester, Bev Volker, Jacqueline Lichtenberg, Gary Berman, Adam Malin, and of course Gene Roddenberry, the Great Bird of the Galaxy.

Above all, I must thank God, the Great Almighty, the Author of all knowledge and wisdom, for His abundant love and guiding light in my life. Without Him, I am nothing but dust on the ground.

Figure 182. Shahna (Angelique Pettyjohn) as imagined by Rick Melton, an amazing artist based in the United Kingdom.

About the Author

Figure 183. John L. Flynn.

Dr. John L. Flynn is an author, screenwriter, and three-time Hugo nominee. A member of the Science Fiction Writers of America and the Mystery Writers of America, he has been a regular contributor and columnist to dozens of science fiction magazines and is a much sought-after guest speaker. A former college dean and professor, he routinely speaks at science fiction and comic conventions about the writing process. In 1977, he received the M. Carolyn Parker award for outstanding journalism for his freelance work on several Florida daily newspapers.

Flynn sold his first book, *Future Threads*, in 1985, and has subsequently had nineteen other books published: *Cinematic Vampires*, *The Jovian Dilemma, The Films of Arnold Schwarzenegger*, *Dissecting Aliens*, *Visions in Light and Shadow*, *War of the Worlds: From Wells to Spielberg*, *75 Years of Universal Monsters*, *50 Years of Hammer Horror*, *101 Superheroes of the Silver Screen*, *2001: Beyond the Infinite*, and *Phantoms of the Opera: Behind the Mask*. With Dr. Bob Blackwood, he also penned the humorous and thoroughly amusing *Everything I Know about Life I Learned from James Bond*, along with *Future Prime: The Top 10 Science Fiction Films*. In 2014, *Intimate Bondage*, the first of his Kate Dawson thrillers, was published, followed by *Architects of Armageddon*, *Murder on Air Force One*, *Terror at G-20*, and *Merchants of Death*. In 2019, ten of his books were made into audio books, and in 2020, John wrote three screenplays based on his best-selling books which he hopes to see made into movies.

In addition to his writing, he is a Master-Class costumer, having won the requisite number of costume contests at the Worldcon level to qualify for this title. A fan of both *Star Trek* and *Star Wars*, he has made dozens of Starfleet uniforms and Jedi costumes over the years. His screen-accurate reproduction of the Darth Vader costume from *The Empire Strikes Back* earned him many prizes and entry into the 501st Legion. The costume on a mannequin looms over his home office. After winning the 1986 Worldcon Masquerade in Atlanta, with his recreation of Robby the Robot from *Forbidden Planet* (1956), he retired from costume competition. Today, John is still active, and volunteers his time with the 501st and the Rebel Legion.

In 1997, John switched gears from writing and literature to study psychology, and earned a Ph.D. as a clinical psychologist. His doctoral dissertation, titled *Etiology of Sexual Addiction: The Significance of Childhood Trauma as a Primary Determinant* (1997), has broken new ground in the diagnosis and treatment of sexual addiction.

From 2002 to 2004, Dr. Flynn was also nominated for three Hugo Awards for his science fiction writing. Today, John makes his home in Lake Worth, Florida, and writes full time daily. His biography of Angelique Pettyjohn, *The Sci-Fi Siren Who Dared to Love Elvis and Other Stars,* is his 20th book. His website is https://johnlflynn.com/

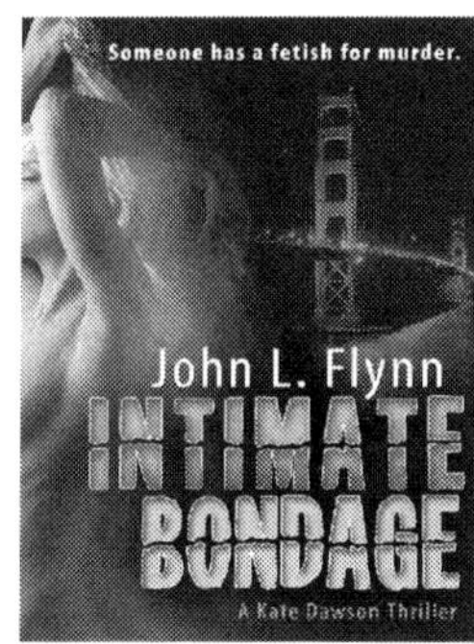

Figure 184. Three of John L. Flynn's 20 books.

Photographic and Illustrative Credits

Figure 1. EAPJ	Figure 32. JLF	Figure 63. STKN
Figure 2. AP	Figure 33. NSS	Figure 64. PIN
Figure 3. JLF	Figure 34. NSS	Figure 65. PIN
Figure 4. AP	Figure 35. NSS	Figure 66. STK
Figure 5. STK	Figure 36. NSS	Figure 67. STK
Figure 6. STK	Figure 37. NSS	Figure 68. FF
Figure 7. STK	Figure 38. NSS	Figure 69. RB
Figure 8. AAC	Figure 39. NSS	Figure 70. STK
Figure 9. STK	Figure 40. NSS	Figure 71. STK
Figure 10. STK	Figure 41. NSS	Figure 72. PP
Figure 11. WHS	Figure 42. NSS	Figure 73. STK
Figure 12. STK	Figure 43. NSS	Figure 74. STK
Figure 13.WHS	Figure 44. NSS	Figure 75. AP
Figure 14. STK	Figure 45. NSS	Figure 76. AP
Figure 15. STK	Figure 46. NSS	Figure 77. AP
Figure 16. STK	Figure 47. NSS	Figure 78. AP
Figure 17. STK	Figure 48. NSS	Figure 79. AP
Figure 18. STK	Figure 49. FOX	Figure 80. AP
Figure 19. STK	Figure 50. FOX	Figure 81. AP
Figure 20. STK	Figure 51. STK	Figure 82. AP
Figure 21. PP	Figure 52. STK	Figure 83. STK
Figure 22. PP	Figure 53. STK	Figure 84. STK
Figure 23. NSS	Figure 54. STK	Figure 85. STK
Figure 24. STK	Figure 55. STK	Figure 86. AP
Figure 25. MC	Figure 56. STK	Figure 87. STK
Figure 26. NSS	Figure 57. STK	Figure 88. PP
Figure 27. NSS	Figure 58. PP	Figure 89. STK
Figure 28. NSS	Figure 59. PP	Figure 90. STK
Figure 29. STK	Figure 60. PP	Figure 91. PP
Figure 30. JLF	Figure 61. STK	Figure 92. STK
Figure 31. STK	Figure 62. STK	Figure 93. TVG

Figure 94. NBC	Figure 127. NSS	Figure 160. STK
Figure 95. NBC	Figure 128. NSS	Figure 161. TUM
Figure 96. AP	Figure 129. JP	Figure 162. TUM
Figure 97. AP	Figure 130. JP	Figure 163. TUM
Figure 98. AP	Figure 131. STK	Figure 164. LJP
Figure 99. PP	Figure 132. STK	Figure 165. JLF
Figure 100. RA	Figure 133. AP	Figure 166. NSS
Figure 101. PP	Figure 134. STK	Figure 167. NSS
Figure 102. PP	Figure 135. STK	Figure 168. NSS
Figure 103. PP	Figure 136. JLF	Figure 169. MC
Figure 104. PP	Figure 137. RSH	Figure 170. NSS
Figure 105. NSS	Figure 138. RSH	Figure 171. NSS
Figure 106. NSS	Figure 139. MC	Figure 172. NSS
Figure 107. NSS	Figure 140. MC	Figure 173. AP
Figure 108. NSS	Figure 141. MC	Figure 174. NSS
Figure 109. NSS	Figure 142. NSS	Figure 175. NSS
Figure 110. NSS	Figure 143. NSS	Figure 176. NSS
Figure 111. NSS	Figure 144. NSS	Figure 177. NSS
Figure 112. NSS	Figure 145. NSS	Figure 178. NSS
Figure 113. NSS	Figure 146. JLF	Figure 179. FH
Figure 114. NSS	Figure 147. JLF	Figure 180. FH
Figure 115. NSS	Figure 148. JLF	Figure 181. EAPJ
Figure 116. NSS	Figure 149. JLF	Figure 182. RM
Figure 117. NSS	Figure 150. JLF	Figure 183. JLF
Figure 118. AP	Figure 151. JLF	Figure 184. JLF
Figure 119. VV	Figure 152. JLF	Figure 185. MC
Figure 120. NSS	Figure 153. STK	
Figure 121. STK	Figure 154. LJP	
Figure 122. NSS	Figure 155. JLF	
Figure 123. STK	Figure 156. LJP	
Figure 124. NSS	Figure 157. RSH	
Figure 125. PG	Figure 158. LJP	
Figure 126. STK	Figure 159. LJP	

*Photographers and Sources**

AAC – Army Air Corps	RSH -Robert Scott Hooper	PP – Publicity Photo
MC – Michael Christ	JP – Jim Parker	EAPJ – Elvis Junior
JLF – John L. Flynn	AP – Angelique Pettyjohn	LJP-Len J. Provenzano
FOX – 20th Century-Fox	NBC - Nat'l Broadcast Com	NSS-Nat'l Screen Service
FH – Funeral Home	TUM - Tumblr	RM - Rick Melton
PG – Pat Gill	PIN - Pinterest	VV - Vestron Video
STK – Stock Photo	FF – Frank Frazetta	WHS - West High School
TVG – TV Guide		RB – Ray Bradbury

*All photographs and illustrations are identified by a figure number. All figure numbers are laid out on pages 397 and 398. After the number is a 2-or-3-digit code which identifies the photographer or source from the list above. (Example: All photos taken by Robert Scott Hooper are identified by an RSH beside the figure number, while NSS identifies the National Screen Service as source.)

Photographic Sources:

1. National Screen Service - The NSS was a company that controlled the distribution of theatrical advertising materials (like photographs and posters) in the United States from approximately 1940 through the 1980s. These materials were sent free of charge to promote motion pictures, and were used commonly in newspapers, books, and magazines.

2. Publicity Photos - Publicity Photos are distributed individually or as part of a press kit by celebrities and/or studios to increase public awareness of a motion picture. These photos are widely distributed for free for reuse by the media to promote celebrities or films under the doctrine of fair use.

3. Stock Photos - Stock Photos are royalty-free, professional photographs of common places, landmarks, nature, events or people that are reused for commercial design purposes. Stock photos provide cheap content to online and professional publications and blogs.

4. Tumblr Photos - Tumblr photos are generally stock photos developed as part of a network of millions of user-generated websites to create and produce their own original content. Tumblr photos are royalty-free.

Figure 185. Angelique Pettyjohn at age 48, a few months before her death.

Made in the USA
Columbia, SC
10 July 2021

41547257R00220